A COMPLETE GUIDE TO
KNITTING

PAM DAWSON

Marshall Cavendish London & New York

CONTENTS

Photographers

Stuart Brown; John Carter; Roger Charity; Monty Coles; Richard Dunkley; Alan Duns; David Finch; Jeany; Chris Lewis; Sandra Lousada; Tony Page; Peter Pugh-Cook; John Ryan; John Swannell; Jean Claude Volpeliere.
Photographs on p. 3 courtesy the Victoria & Albert Museum.

Acknowledgements

Knitted apron (page 3) and Egyptian sock (page 3), courtesy of the Victoria and Albert Museum, London.

Knitting abbreviations

alt	alternate(ly)	**P**	purl
approx	approximate(ly)	**P up**	pick up and purl
beg	begin(ning)	**P-wise**	purlwise
cm	centimetre(s)	**rem**	remain(ing)
cont	continu(e)(ing)	**rep**	repeat
dec	decrease	**RS**	right side
foll	follow(ing)	**sl**	slip
g st	garter stitch,	**sl st**	slip stitch
	every row knit	**sp**	space(s)
grm	gramme(s)	**st(s)**	stitches
gr(s)	group(s)	**st st**	stocking stitch,
in	inch(es)		1 row knit, 1 row purl
inc	increase	**tbl**	through back of loop
K	knit	**tog**	together
K up	pick up and knit	**WS**	wrong side
k-wise	knitwise	**yd(s)**	yard(s)
No.	number	**ybk**	yarn back
psso	pass slipped	**yfwd**	yarn forward
	stitch over	**yon**	yarn over needle
patt	pattern	**yrn**	yarn round needle

Symbols

An asterisk, *, shown in a pattern row denotes that the stitches shown after this sign must be repeated from that point. Square brackets, [ ], denote instructions for larger sizes in the pattern. Round brackets, ( ), denote that this section of the pattern is to be worked for all sizes.

To avoid confusion, it is recommended that you decide whether to use metric or imperial measurements when beginning any pattern and adhere to the same measurement throughout.

Tension – this is the most important factor in successful knitting. Unless you obtain the tension given for each design, you will not obtain satisfactory results.

Note that when converting inches to centimetres, tension samples will be given to the nearest exact equivalent, i.e. 10cm = 3.9in.

Metrication of knitting needles

As with the measurements of most materials and tools, knitting needles are being converted to metric sizes. The designs in this book have been worked on the existing British sizes but when purchasing new needles, it is essential to check that you obtain the correct size. In order to allow you to become familiar with the new sizes, new needles will bear both the metric sizes in millimetres and the old British number. The following conversion chart has been issued by The Needlemakers' Association and from this you will see that, for example, what is now the new No. 4mm is the old No. 8, and should not be confused with the old No. 4.

English	Metric
14	2mm
13	$2\frac{1}{4}$mm
12	$2\frac{3}{4}$mm
11	3mm
10	$3\frac{1}{4}$mm
9	$3\frac{3}{4}$mm
8	4mm
7	$4\frac{1}{2}$mm
6	5mm
5	$5\frac{1}{2}$mm
4	6mm
3	$6\frac{1}{2}$mm
2	7mm
1	$7\frac{1}{2}$mm
0	8mm
00	9mm
000	10mm

Published by Marshall Cavendish Books Limited
58 Old Compton Street
London W1V 5PA

First printed 1976
Reprinted 1977

Printed in Great Britain by Ben Johnson and Company Ltd., York

ISBN (hardback edition) 0 85685 189 2
ISBN (paperback edition) 0 85685 047 0

AN INTRODUCTION TO KNITTING

In presenting this book my genuine hope is that I can communicate some of my enthusiasm for this most beautiful craft to the reader and whether you approach it as a complete beginner or knowledgeable knitter, arouse your interest in its almost limitless possibilities.

For the first half of this century, knitting was tagged with the fuddy-duddy image it had acquired during the Victorian era and suffered an undeserved decline in popularity. Today it has rightly taken its place as a unique and practical way of interpreting fashion but, even now, most knitters are still not aware of its tremendous scope. In no other field of fashion or craft, other than the allied craft of crochet, do you have such complete control not only over the shape of the ultimate design, but the texture and colour of the fabric. In this craft, you as the knitter, combine both the skill of a weaver and the practical knowledge of a dressmaker – and all for the price of a pair of needles and a few balls of yarn. Of all the crafts and skills acquired by man – and I use the word 'man' advisedly, in that women's skill in this field is only recent in terms of history – knitting has proved to be one of the most fascinating and enduring. It has survived, sometimes through countless centuries without any record, either written or visual, and has developed and evolved by word of mouth from one generation to the next.

The first steps in knitting are as simple as those required for basic cookery, but its ultimate variety is akin to the art of cordon bleu cooking, where nothing that individual taste, ability and imagination can devise is impossible. The only manufactured materials required are a pair of needles and a ball of spun thread but, with sufficient knowledge and time to experiment, even these are comparatively easy to produce by hand. The simple talents needed to encompass its full range are a willing pair of hands, an eye for colour and fabric, some simple mathematical skill and basic dressmaking knowledge. Armed with these attributes the world of knitting is your oyster and you can begin to design garments to suit your own individual shape and taste, without being tied to existing patterns.

The main purpose of this book is to take the technical knowledge it contains and apply this to the basic guide to designing, which is also explained. You can, of course, accept it as it stands and still acquire the necessary skill to become a proficient knitter, but taking the step from knitter to designer is a relatively small one and out of all proportion to the exciting and creative field it opens up for you.

With the present necessity to conserve all natural resources and survive an unhealthy economic period, it is important to know how to make warm, wearable and fashionable garments for the minimum of outlay, both in costs and materials. Knitting is the most practical and satisfying solution to these problems and has the added bonus of extending your own latent creative talents and the therapeutic benefit of making something beautiful with your own hands.

Pam Dawson

HISTORY OF KNITTING

Knitting is an ancient craft, first developed in the deserts of Arabia among the nomadic tribes who lived there 3,000 years ago. It may even have been a familiar technique in pre-biblical times, for knitting of high quality, well advanced in both technique and design, was certainly being produced in Arabia 1,000 years before the death of Christ. No one can date the birth of knitting exactly. It has grown up with civilization. The early knitters were the men of the tribes, and they were very skilled at their craft. As these people kept straggling herds of sheep and goats there was no shortage of material. The women gathered wool from the animals and spun it into yarn for the men, who would sit for hours, tending the flocks and knitting. The articles they produced were simple scarves, robes and socks to wear with sandals.

Ancient knitting

Very few examples of really early knitting are still in existence, but a pair of red sandal socks, pre-Christian in origin, still survive. They are beautifully made, with expertly turned heels. It is interesting to note that stitches have been carefully divided for the big toe, so that the socks were comfortable to wear with sandals.

The socks were knitted in the round on a circular frame, probably made of thin wire. Pins were inserted all round the edge of the circle, and loops were made on the pins. When the wool was wound around the outside of the pins and the loops drawn over it, circular knitting of a rather loose tension was produced.

A spectacular fragment

Twin needles, hooked at the ends rather like today's crochet hooks, were used to make another surviving fragment of Arabic knitting. This piece of work was discovered at Fustat, an ancient ruined city near Cairo in Egypt, and it has been dated at between the 7th and the 9th centuries. From beneath the sand and dust of centuries a fragile piece of knitted silk fabric was retrieved. Worked with exquisite care on a pair of fine wire needles, to an easily-checked tension of 36 stitches to the inch, the fragment reveals an elaborate design in maroon and gold.

Between the years AD 1000 and 1200 little round knitted caps called Coptic caps were being made in Egypt. They were worn by monks and missionaries and it is possible that these men carried the knowledge of knitting with them out of Egypt. Craftsmen in Spain, then in Italy and France and eventually in England and the New World, were fascinated by this new kind of fabric weaving. Knowledge of the craft quickly spread, each nation adding its own ideas and patterns. By the Middle Ages knitting was a common craft form all over Europe. Italy and France were the great medieval homes of fine knitting, and there the knitters soon formed themselves, under Church patronage, into organized guilds.

The Knitters' Guilds

The Knitters' Guild of Paris was a typical example. Young boys of intelligence and manual ability were carefully selected as apprentices. They were bound for six years, three of which were spent working with a master-knitter at home and three learning new techniques in a foreign country. At the end of this time the apprentice was required to demonstrate his skill to his elders. The test was prodigious. In only thirteen weeks the apprentice had to knit an elaborate carpet eight feet by twelve, with extremely intricate designs incorporating flowers, birds, foliage and animals in natural colours, using between twenty and thirty different coloured wools; a beret, sometimes to be felted and blocked after knitting; a woollen shirt; and a pair of socks with Spanish clocks.

No apprentice was accepted who did not produce masterpieces in all these categories, and when he became a master-knitter he knew that shoddy or skimped work would result in heavy fines and even expulsion from the guild, which meant loss of livelihood. The only women admitted to these guilds were the widows of master-knitters. For the most part, the women still sat at home spinning the wool for the men to knit up.

Knitting in England

By the time of Queen Elizabeth I, England was the world leader in knitting. Fine work was being produced by the master-craftsmen, and, in addition, many poor people were knitting up fabrics for felting into leggings, topcoats and caps. Hand knitting gradually became widespread as an important village industry, particularly in the dales of Yorkshire where the finest wool was always available.

Apart from the domestic and commercial work being produced in England, much exquisite decorative knitting was done in the seclusion of the monasteries and the nunneries. The religious influence on the beautiful silk knitting of the 16th and 17th centuries is very marked.

The hand knitting tradition continued to be strong in England until the Industrial Revolution in the 19th century, the age of mass production when interest in handicrafts declined.

Individuality still flourished, however, notably in

Scotland and the Channel Islands, where traditional jumpers (sweaters) and jerseys were made. The 'guernsey', produced on the Channel Island of Guernsey for centuries, took two forms. The everyday one, in plain stocking stitch, was the one most often seen, but on special occasions the men wore guernseys in heavy cable and bobble patterns, each family or village having its own distinctive design. They were called 'bridal shirts' because a courting girl would start to knit one for her sweetheart's wedding day.

The word 'knitting' comes from an old English word meaning 'a knot', and basic techniques have altered little over the centuries. Today, interest in the craft has revived after its Victorian decline. Machine knitting techniques have gained popularity, but most knitters still practice the craft using needles very little different from those used by the Arab pioneer knitters. Knitting or Knotting, the ancient craft is more popular now than it has ever been before.

Right: An English apron, knitted in multi-coloured wool in the early nineteenth century.
Below: A sandal sock knitted in wool. It is Egyptian in origin and dates from the fifth century AD. However, it is thought that knitting probably originated centuries before this, possibly as much as 1000 years before the birth of Christ.

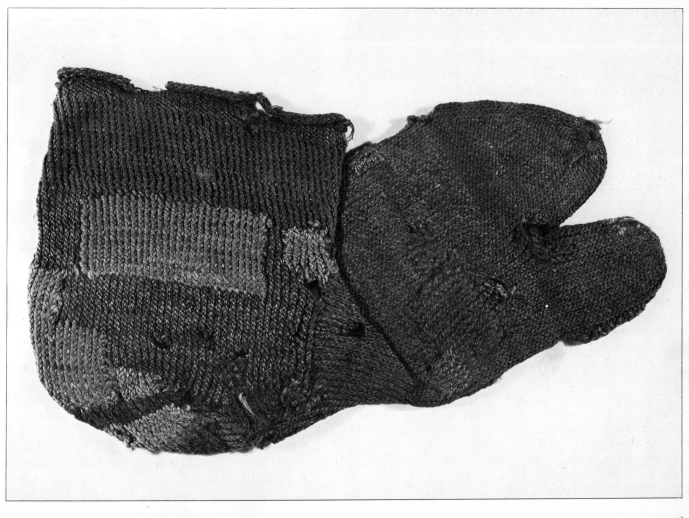

BASIC SKILLS
THE FIRST STEPS

Knitting needles

Modern needles are usually made of lightweight coated metal or plastic and are supplied in a comprehensive range of sizes, both in diameter and length. For British needles, the gauge or diameter of the needle is given as a figure, such as No. 11, No. 10, No. 9 and so on, and the higher the number the smaller the diameter of the needle. The length of the needle is also given and the choice of length will depend on the size and type of garment to be knitted. French and American needle sizes use the reverse of the British system and the highest number is used to denote the largest needle.

For 'flat' knitting – that is, working forwards and backwards on two needles in rows – needles are manufactured in pairs and each needle has a knob at one end to prevent the stitches slipping off.

For 'circular' knitting – that is, working in rounds without a seam – needles are manufactured in sets of four and each needle is pointed at both ends. A flexible, circular needle is also manufactured and the effect is the same as dividing the work between three needles and working with the fourth, but a larger number of stitches may be used.

Holding yarn and needles

Until the art of holding both the yarn and needles comfortably has been mastered, it is impossible to begin to knit. For a right handed person the yarn will be looped around the fingers of the right hand to achieve firm, even knitting. The needle which is used to make the stitches is held in the right hand and the left hand holds the needle with the made stitches ready for working. The reverse of these positions would be adopted by a left handed person.

To hold the yarn correctly, loop the yarn from the ball across the palm of the right hand between the 4th and 3rd fingers, round the 4th finger and back between the 4th and 3rd fingers, over the 3rd finger, between the 3rd and 2nd fingers, under the 2nd finger then over the index finger, leaving the end of the ball of yarn free, in which a slip loop will be made to begin casting on.

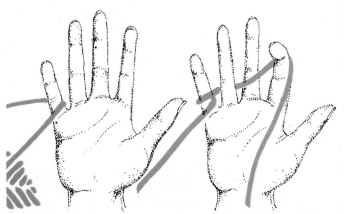

Casting on

This is the first step in hand knitting and it provides the first row of loops on the needle. Different methods of casting on produce different types of edges, each with its own appropriate use, and it is advisable to practise all these variations at some stage.

The thumb method is an excellent way to begin most garments where an edge with some elasticity is required, such as the welt of a jersey, but the two needle method is necessary where extra stitches need to be made during the actual knitting of a garment, such as for buttonholes and pockets. Beginners should practise these two methods. The invisible method gives the appearance of a machine-made edge and is very flexible and neat. The circular method is required for knitting in rounds to produce seamless garments, such as gloves and socks. Experienced knitters will find these methods of interest.

Two needle method of casting on

Make a slip loop in the end of the ball of yarn and put this loop on to the left hand needle. Holding the yarn in the right hand, insert the point of the right hand needle into the slip loop, wind the yarn under and over the point of the right hand needle and draw a new loop through the slip loop. Put the newly made stitch on to the left hand needle. Place the point of the right hand needle between the 2 loops on the left hand needle and wind the yarn under and over the point of the right hand needle again and draw through a new loop. Put the newly made stitch on to the left hand needle. Place the point of the right hand needle between the last 2 loops on the left hand needle and wind the yarn under and over the point of the right hand needle again and draw through a new loop. Put the newly made stitch on to the left hand needle. Continue repeating the last action until the required number of stitches are formed on the left hand needle. This method produces a firm edge and is also used as an intermediate stage in increasing.

Two needle method stage 1

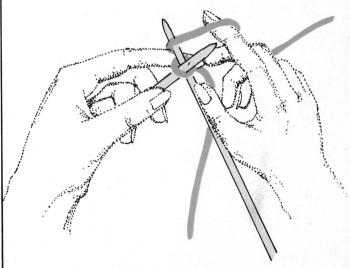

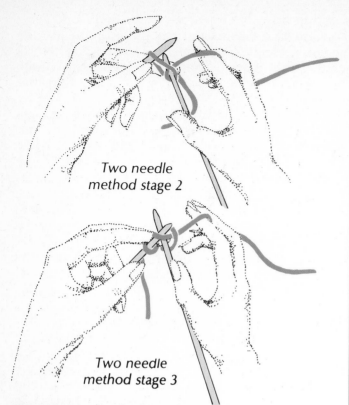

Two needle method stage 2

Two needle method stage 3

Thumb method of casting on using one needle

Make a slip loop in the ball of yarn about 91.5 centimetres (*one yard*) from the end. This length will vary with the number of stitches to be cast on but 91.5 centimetres (*one yard*) will be sufficient for about one hundred stitches.

Put the slip loop on to the needle, which should be held in the right hand. Working with the short length of yarn in the left hand, pass this between the index finger and thumb, round the thumb and hold it across the palm of the hand. Insert the point of the needle under the loop on the thumb and bring forward the long end of yarn from the ball. Wind the long end of yarn under and over the point of the needle and draw through a loop on the thumb, leaving the newly formed stitch on the needle. Tighten the stitch on the needle by pulling the short end of yarn, noting that the yarn is then wound round the left thumb ready for the next stitch. Continue in this way until the required number of stitches are formed on the needle. This method produces an elastic edge which is very hardwearing.

Thumb method stage 1 – making a slip loop

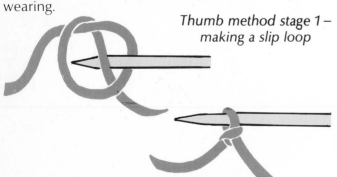

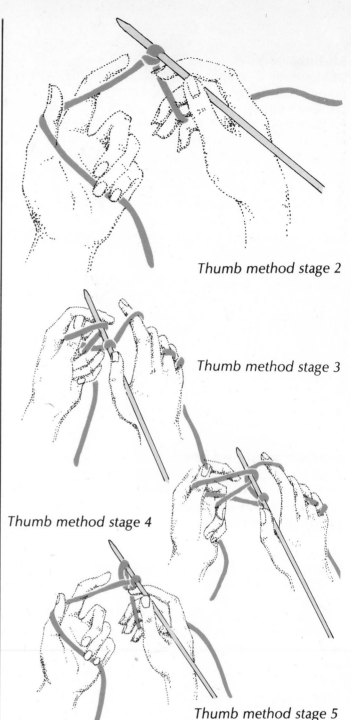

Thumb method stage 2

Thumb method stage 3

Thumb method stage 4

Thumb method stage 5

Invisible method of casting on

Using a length of yarn in a contrast colour which is later removed and the thumb method, cast on half the number of stitches required plus one extra. Using the correct yarn and two needles, begin the double fabric which forms the invisible method.

1st row Holding the yarn in the right hand and the needle with the cast on stitches in the left hand, insert the point of the right hand needle into the first stitch from front to back, wind the yarn under and over the point of the right hand needle and draw through a loop which is kept on the right hand needle – this is a knitted stitch and is called 'K1' –, *bring the yarn forward between the two needles and back over the top of the right hand needle to make a stitch on this row only – this is called 'yarn forward' or 'yfwd' –, K1, repeat from the point marked with a * to the end of the row.

2nd row K1, *yfwd and keep at front of work without taking it back over the right hand needle insert the point of the right hand needle into the front of the next stitch on the left hand needle from right to left, and lift it off the left hand needle on to the right hand needle without working it – this is a slipped stitch and is called 'sl 1' –, bring the yarn across in front of the sl 1 and back between the two needles again – this is called 'yarn back' or 'yb' –, K1, repeat from the point marked with a * to the end of the row.

3rd row Sl 1, *ybk, K1, yfwd, sl 1, repeat from the point marked with a * to the end of the row. Repeat the 2nd and 3rd rows once more. Now continue with the single ribbing which completes this method.

6th row K1, *bring the yarn forward between the two needles, insert the point of the right hand needle into the front of the next stitch on the left hand needle from right to left, wind the yarn over the top of the needle and round to the front and draw through a loop which is kept on the right hand needle – this is a purled stitch and is called 'P1' –, put the yarn back between the two needles, K1, repeat from the point marked with a * to the end of the row.

7th row P1, *put the yarn back between the two needles, K1, bring the yarn forward between the two needles, P1, repeat from the point marked with a * to the end of the row.

Continue repeating the 6th and 7th rows until the rib is the required length, then unpick the contrast yarn used for casting on. This method gives the appearance of the ribbing running right round the edge with no visible cast on stitches.

Increasing on 1st row of invisible casting on

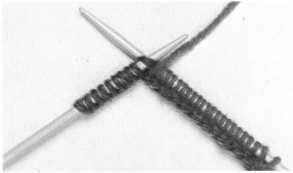

Alternate stitches are slipped on the 4th row

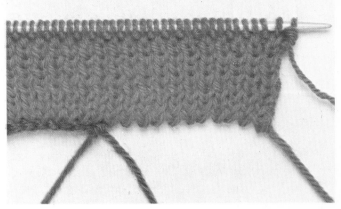

Contrast yarn is unpicked to give ribbed edge

Circular method of casting on using four needles

When working with sets of four needles, one is used for making the stitches and the total number of stitches required is divided between the remaining three needles. Use the two needle method of casting on and either cast on the total number of stitches on to one needle and then divide them on to the 2nd and 3rd needles, or cast on the required number of stitches on to the first needle, then proceed to the 2nd and 3rd needles, taking care that the stitches do not become twisted. Form the three needles containing the stitches into a triangle shape and the fourth needle is then ready to knit the first stitch on the first needle. This method produces a circular fabric without seams.

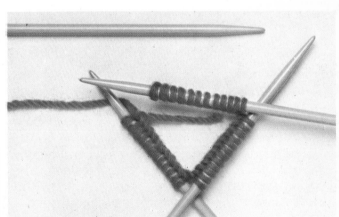

Starting to knit with 4 needles

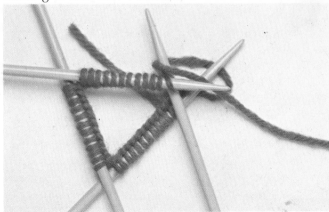

Basic stitches

Once you have cast on your stitches and can hold the yarn and needles comfortably, you can begin to knit – it's as easy as that. All knitting stitches are based on just two methods – knitting and purling – and however complicated patterns may appear they are all achieved by simple, or intricate, arrangements of these two methods to produce an almost infinite variety of fabric and texture. Anything from the finest lace to the thickest carpet can be knitted. The advantages of knitted fabrics are almost too numerous to list and they have been used since time immemorial to achieve examples of exquisite beauty.

Tools of the trade

Before beginning to knit it is essential to ensure that you have all the tools you will require to hand, including yarn and needles. In addition you will need :–
A rigid metal or wooden centimetre/*inch* rule
Scissors
Blunt-ended sewing needles
Rustless steel pins
Stitch holders to hold stitches not in use
Knitting register for counting rows
Knitting needle gauge to check needle sizes
Cloth or polythene bag in which to keep work clean
Iron and ironing surface with felt pad or blanket
Cotton cloths suitable for use when pressing

The basic stitches

To work knitted stitches – hold the needle with the cast on stitches in the left hand and the yarn and other needle in the right hand. Insert the point of the right hand needle through the first stitch on the left hand needle from the front to the back. Keeping the yarn at the back of the work pass it under and over the top of the right hand needle and draw this loop through the stitch on the left hand needle. Keep this newly made stitch on the right hand needle and allow the stitch on the left hand needle to slip off. Repeat this action into each stitch on the left hand needle until all the stitches are transferred to the right hand needle. You have now knitted one row. To work the next row, change the needle holding the stitches to your left hand so that the yarn is again in position at the beginning of the row and hold the yarn and free needle in your right hand.

To work purled stitches – hold the needle with the cast on stitches in your left hand and the yarn and other needle in the right hand. Insert the point of the right hand needle through the first stitch on the left hand needle from right to left, keeping the yarn

at the front of the work pass it over and round the top of the right hand needle and draw this loop through the stitch on the left hand needle. Keep this newly made stitch on the right hand needle and allow the stitch on the left hand needle to slip off. Repeat this action into each stitch on the left hand needle until all the stitches are transferred to the right hand needle. You have now purled one row. To work the next row, change the needle holding the stitches to your left hand so that the yarn is again in position at the beginning of the row and hold the yarn and free needle in your right hand.

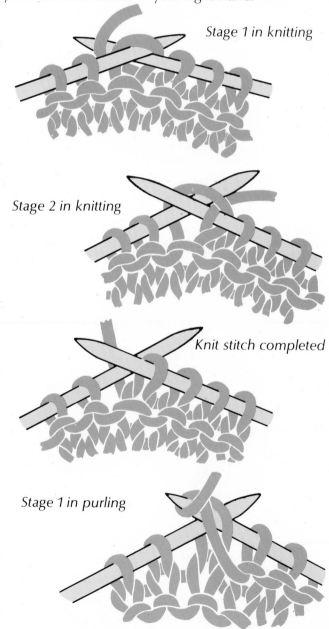

Stage 1 in knitting

Stage 2 in knitting

Knit stitch completed

Stage 1 in purling

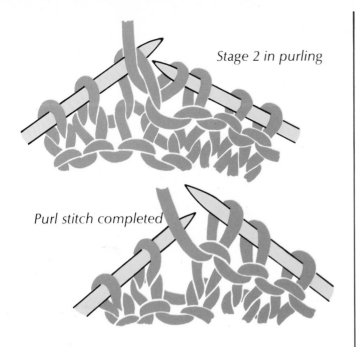

Stage 2 in purling

Purl stitch completed

Garter stitch

This is the simplest of all knitted stitches and is formed by working every row in the same stitch, either knit or purl. If you purl every row, however, you do not produce such a firm, even fabric and unless otherwise stated, wherever you see instructions referring to garter stitch, it is intended that every row should be knitted.

▲*Purled garter stitch* ▼*Knitted garter stitch*

Stocking stitch

This is the smoothest of all knitted stitches and is formed by working one row of knitted stitches and one row of purled stitches alternately. The smooth, knitted side of the fabric is usually called the right side of the work but where a pattern uses the purl

side of stocking stitch as the fabric, it is referred to as reversed stocking stitch.

Stocking stitch

Single rib

This is one of the most useful of all knitted stitches and forms an elastic fabric, ideal for welts, cuffs and neckbands, since it always springs back into shape. It is formed by knitting the first stitch of the first row, bringing the yarn forward to the front of the work between the two needles, purling the next stitch and taking the yarn back between the two needles, ready to knit the next stitch again, then continuing in this way until all the stitches are transferred to the right hand needle. On the next row, all the stitches which were knitted on the first row must be purled and all the stitches which were purled must be knitted. It is essential to remember that the yarn must be brought forward after knitting a stitch so that it is in the correct position ready to purl the next stitch, and taken to the back again after purling a stitch so that it is in the correct position ready to knit the next stitch.

Single rib

Useful hints

Before beginning to knit any pattern, study the list of general abbreviations so that you become familiar with these.
Always wash your hands before beginning to knit and keep them soft and cool.
A bag pinned over the finished work and moved up as it grows will help to keep your knitting clean.
Never leave your knitting in the middle of a row, as this will spoil the line of the work.
Never stick knitting needles through a ball of yarn as this can split the yarn.
When measuring knitting, place it on a flat surface and measure it in the centre of the work, not at the edges.
Always join in a new ball of yarn at the beginning of a row, never in the centre of a row by means of a knot.

Casting off

Casting off is the final stage in knitting and it securely binds off any stitches which remain after all the shaping has been completed, or at the end of the work. It is also used as an intermediate step in decreasing, such as casting off the required number of stitches for an underarm or in the centre of a row for neck shaping.

Where stitches need to be cast off at each end of a row it is usual to do this over two rows by casting off the given number of stitches at the beginning of the first row then working to the end of the row, turning the work and casting off the same number of stitches at the beginning of the next row and then completing this row. If you cast off stitches at the beginning and end of the same row the yarn must then be broken off and rejoined to commence the next row. This is necessary in some designs but the pattern will always clearly state where this method is to be used.

Care must be taken in casting off to keep the stitches regular and even, otherwise the edge will either be too tight or too loose and can pull the whole garment out of shape. In some patterns you will come across the phrase, 'cast off loosely' and, in this case, it is advisable to use one size larger needle in the right hand and work the stitches with this needle, before casting them off.

The normal method of casting off produces a very firm, neat edge, which is not always suitable for some designs, such as the toe of a sock where this line would cause an uncomfortable ridge. In this case, the stitches can be grafted together to give an almost invisible seam. Similarly, a ribbed neckband can be cast off by the invisible method to give a very elastic edge with the appearance of a machine-made garment.

Two needle method of casting off

To cast off on a knit row, knit the first two stitches in the usual way and leave them on the right hand needle, *with the point of the left hand needle lift the first stitch on the right hand needle over the top of the second stitch and off the needle, leaving one stitch on the right hand needle, knit the next stitch and leave it on the right hand needle, repeat from the point marked with a * until the required number of stitches have been cast off and one stitch remains on the right hand needle. If this is at the end of the work, break off the yarn, draw it through the last stitch and pull it up tightly. If stitches have been cast off as a means of shaping, continue working to the end of the row noting that the stitch on the right hand needle will be counted as one of the remaining stitches.

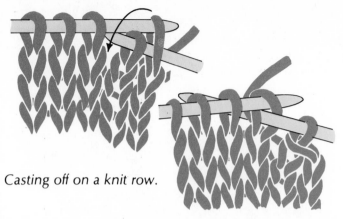

Casting off on a knit row.

To cast off on a purl row, work in exactly the same way but purl each stitch instead of knitting it.

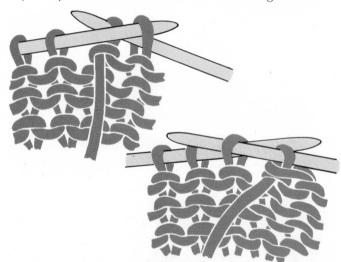

Circular method of casting off using 4 needles

Cast off the stitches on each needle as given for the two needle method of casting off.

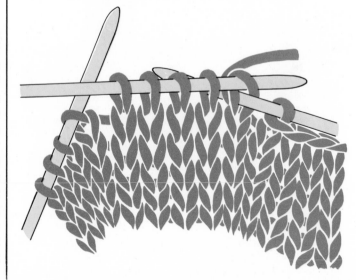

Invisible method of casting off

These instructions are for casting off in single rib when an odd number of stitches has been used and the right side rows begin with K1. Work in ribbing until only two more rows are required to give the finished depth, ending with a wrong side row.

1st row K1, *yfwd, sl 1, ybk, K1, repeat from the point marked with a * to the end of the row.

2nd row Sl 1, *ybk, K1, yfwd, sl 1, repeat from the point marked with a * to the end of the row. Break off the yarn, leaving an end three times the length of the edge to be cast off and thread this into a blunt-ended sewing needle. Hold the sewing needle in the right hand and the stitches to be cast off in the left hand, working throughout from right to left along the row.

1. Insert the sewing needle into the first knit stitch as if to purl it and pull the yarn through, then into the next purl stitch as if to knit it and pull the yarn through, leaving both of the stitches on the left hand needle.

2. *First work two of the knit stitches. Go back and insert the sewing needle into the first knit stitch as if to knit it, pull the yarn through and slip this stitch off the left hand needle, pass the sewing needle in front of the next purl stitch and into the following knit stitch as if to purl it, pull the yarn through.

3. Now work two of the purl stitches. Go back and insert the sewing needle into the purl stitch at the end of the row as if to purl it, pull the yarn through and slip this stitch off the left hand needle, pass the sewing needle behind the next knit stitch and into the following purl stitch as if to knit it, pull the yarn through.

Repeat from the point marked with a * until all the stitches have been worked off. Fasten off the end of yarn.

Grafting stitches

To graft two stocking stitch, or knit edges together have the stitches on two needles, one behind the other, with the same number of stitches on each needle. Break off the yarn, leaving an end three times the length of the edge to be grafted and thread this into a blunt-ended sewing needle. Have the wrong sides of each piece facing each other, with the knitting needle points facing to the right.

*Insert the sewing needle through the first stitch on the front needle as if to knit it, draw the yarn through and slip the stitch off the knitting needle, insert the sewing needle through the next stitch on the front needle as if to purl it, draw the yarn through and leave the stitch on the knitting needle, insert the sewing needle through the first stitch on the back needle as if to purl it, draw the yarn through and slip the stitch off the knitting needle, insert the sewing needle through the next stitch on the back needle as if to knit it, draw the yarn through and leave the stitch on the knitting needle, repeat from the point marked with a * until all the stitches have been worked off both needles.

To graft two edges of purl fabric together, work in the same way as given for stocking stitch, reading knit for purl and purl for knit. It is possible, however, to graft purl edges by turning the work to the wrong side and grafting as given for the stocking stitch method, then turn the work to the right side when the grafting is completed.

To graft two garter stitch edges together, first make certain that the last row knitted on the front needle leaves a ridge on the right side, or outside, of the work and that the last row on the back needle leaves a ridge on the wrong side, or inside, of the work. Work as stocking stitch method, working both needles as given for front needle.

To graft two ribbed edges together. Join each stocking stitch or knit rib to each stocking stitch or knit rib, using the stocking stitch method, and each purl rib to each purl rib, using the purl method.

Variations

The ways of using simple knit and purl stitches to form interesting fabrics are numerous. These basic stitches are simple to work and each one gives a different texture. Use a double knitting yarn and No. 8 needles to practise these stitches.

Reversed stocking stitch

This variation of stocking stitch uses the wrong side, or purl side of the work to form the fabric.
Cast on any number of stitches.
1st row (right side) P to end.
2nd row K to end.
These 2 rows form the pattern.

Twisted stocking stitch

This variation of simple stocking stitch has a twisted effect added on every knitted row by working into the back of every stitch.
Cast on any number of stitches.
1st row K into the back of each stitch to end.
2nd row P to end.
These 2 rows form the pattern.

Broken rib

Cast on a number of stitches divisible by 2+1.
1st row K1, *P1, K1, rep from * to end.
2nd row P1, *K1, P1, rep from * to end.
3rd row K to end.
4th row As 3rd.
These 4 rows form the pattern.

Rice stitch

Cast on a number of stitches divisible by 2+1.
1st row K to end.
2nd row P1, *K1, P1, rep from * to end.
These 2 rows form the pattern.

Moss stitch

Cast on a number of stitches divisible by 2+1.
1st row K1, *P1, K1, rep from * to end.
This row forms the pattern.
Where an even number of stitches are cast on, moss stitch is worked as follows:
1st row *K1, P1, rep from * to end.
2nd row *P1, K1, rep from * to end.
These 2 rows form the pattern.

Irish moss stitch

Cast on a number of stitches divisible by 2+1.
1st row K1, *P1, K1, rep from * to end.
2nd row P1, *K1, P1, rep from * to end.
3rd row As 2nd.
4th row As 1st.
These 4 rows form the pattern.

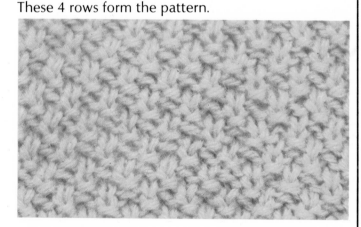

Woven stitch

Cast on a number of stitches divisible by 2+1.
1st row K1, *yfwd, sl 1 P-wise, ybk, K1, rep from * to end.
2nd row P to end.
3rd row K2, *yfwd, sl 1, P-wise, ybk, K1, rep from * to last st, K1.
4th row As 2nd.
These 4 rows form the pattern.

Honeycomb slip stitch

Cast on a number of stitches divisible by 2+1.
1st row P1, *sl 1 P-wise, P1, rep from * to end.
2nd row P to end.
3rd row P2, *sl 1 P-wise, P1, rep from * to last st, P1.
4th row As 2nd.
These 4 rows form the pattern.

Bright and easy knits

When learning a new skill, there is nothing more encouraging than seeing simple articles you make yourself. For each of these ideas you only need to know how to cast on, how to work the basic stitches and how to cast off!

Muffler
Materials
5 × 50grm balls of any Double Knitting yarn
A pair of No.4 needles
To make
Cast on 60 stitches. Work in garter stitch until scarf measures 178.0cm (70in). Cast off.

Evening belt
Materials
1 × 50grm ball of any glitter yarn
A pair of No.9 needles
A 5.0cm (2in) buckle
To make
Cast on 16 stitches. Work in single rib until belt measures required length to go round waist plus approximately 20.5cm (8in). Cast off. Sew on buckle to one end.

Shoulder bag
Materials
2 × 50grm balls of any Double Knitting yarn
A pair of No.8 needles
To make
Cast on 50 stitches. Work in stocking stitch until bag measures approximately 61.0cm (24in). Cast off. Fold bag in half with right sides facing and join side edges. Fold over 5.0cm (2in) at top edge and sew down. Turn bag right side out. Embroider each side or sew on motifs.
Cut remaining yarn into 152·5cm (60in) lengths and plait together, knotting each end of plait. Stitch each end of plait along sides of bag, leaving centre of plait free as shoulder strap.

TENSION

Now that you have mastered the basic steps in knitting, the next stage is to fully understand the significance of achieving the correct tension. It is of such vital importance that it cannot be stressed too often and must not be overlooked, either by the beginner or by the more experienced knitter. It is the simple key to success and no amount of careful knitting will produce a perfect garment unless it is observed.

Tension

Quite simply, the word 'tension' means the number of rows and stitches to a given measurement, which has been achieved by the designer of the garment, using the yarn and needle size stated. As a beginner, it is vital to keep on practising and trying to obtain the correct tension given in a pattern. If it is impossible to hold the yarn and needles comfortably, without pulling the yarn too tightly or leaving it too loose and at the same time obtain the correct tension, then change the needle size. If there are too many stitches to the centimetre (inch), try using one size larger needles; if there are too few stitches to the centimetre (inch), try using one size smaller needles. Too many stitches mean that the tension is too tight and too few stitches mean that the tension is too loose.

This advice applies not only to the beginner but to all knitters beginning a new design. It is so often overlooked on the assumption that the knitter's tension is 'average' and therefore accurate. The point to stress is that although all knitting patterns are carefully checked, the designer of a garment may have produced a tighter or looser tension than average and all the measurements of the garment will have been based on calculations obtained from her tension. With this in mind, it will be readily appreciated that even a quarter of a stitch too many or too few can result in the measurements of the garment being completely inaccurate – through no fault of the designer. It doesn't matter how many times you have to change the needle size – what is important is to obtain the correct tension given in a pattern, before commencing to knit it. Most instructions give the number of stitches in width and the number of rows in depth and if you have to choose between obtaining one and not the other, then the width tension is the most important. Length can usually be adjusted by working more or less rows, as required, but check that the pattern is not based on an exact number of rows but is measured in centimetres (inches).

How to check tension

Before commencing to knit any garment, always work a tension sample at least 10 centimetres (3.9 inches) square, using the yarn, needle size and stitch quoted. Lay this sample on a flat surface and pin it down. Place a firm rule over the knitting and mark out 10 centimetres (3.9 inches) in width with pins. Count the number of stitches between the pins very carefully and make sure that you have the same number as given in the tension. Pin out and count the number of rows in the same way. If there are too many stitches to the given tension measurement then your tension is too tight and you need to use one, or more, size larger needles. If there are too few stitches, then your tension is too loose and you need to use one, or more, size smaller needles.

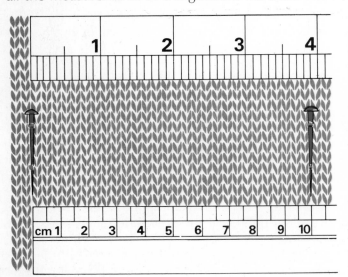

Here the tension is correct

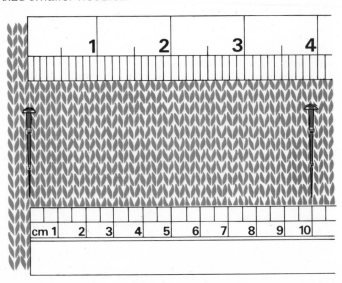

Here the tension is too loose

A decorative cushion cover

An afghan, made from tension samples, is a delightful mixture of colours, patterns and textures

Substituting yarns

Each design has been worked out for the knitting yarn which is quoted in the instructions and this should always be obtained, if possible. If it is impossible to buy the correct yarn, then a substitute may be used but, in this event, it is even more vital to check your tension before beginning the pattern.

To make an afghan or cushion cover

A few minutes spent in the preparation of a tension sample need not be wasted. Similarly, samples of the stitches which interest you can be utilized. As each one is finished it can be laid aside and when you have collected enough, they can be joined together to make a colourful and original afghan or cushion cover. The only requirement is that each sample must be worked to the same size and 10 centimetres *(3.9 inches)* square would be an ideal measurement. In this way you can keep a lasting record of your progress as a knitter, which will eventually serve a very useful purpose.

Afghan

You will require a minimum of 120 squares. Join 10 squares together to form one row, having a total of 12 rows. Bind round all the edges with wool braid or work blanket stitch round all the edges to neaten them.

Cushion cover

You will require 32 squares and a cushion pad or kapok for stuffing. Join 4 squares together to form one row, then 4 rows together to form one side of the cushion. Work the second side in the same way, Place the right sides of each piece facing each other and join 3 sides together. Turn the cover right side out. Insert the cushion pad or stuffing and join the remaining edge, inserting a zip fastener if required.

YARNS

Success in knitting designs is the result of combining two skills in one – those of a weaver and those of a dressmaker – as the fabric and the shape of the garment are produced at the same time. All knitters need to know something about the construction of the many colourful and interesting yarns which are now available. This knowledge, combined with the needle size to be used and the tension obtained, will enable knitters to understand how the right fabric for any garment is achieved. To produce a hard-wearing, textured fabric, using variations of cable stitches, you cannot select a fine baby yarn for the garment, similarly, a thick, chunky yarn would not be suitable for a lacy evening top.

Yarns and ply
'Yarn' is the word used to describe any spun thread, fine or thick, in natural fibres such as wool, cotton, linen, silk, angora or mohair, or in man-made fibres such as Acrilan, Orlon, Nylon or Courtelle. These fibres can be blended together, as with wool and Nylon or Tricel and Nylon, to produce extra hard-wearing yarns which are not too thick.

The word 'ply' indicates a single spun thread of any thickness. Before this thread can be used it must be twisted together to make two or more plys to produce a specific yarn and this process is called 'doubling'. Because each single thread can be spun to any thickness, reference to the number of plys does not necessarily determine the thickness of the finished yarn. Some Shetland yarns, for instance, use only two ply very lightly twisted together to produce a yarn almost comparable to a double knitting quality but, generally speaking, the terms 2 ply, 3 ply, 4 ply and double knitting are used to describe yarn of a recognised thickness.

The following ply classification is applicable to the majority of hand knitting yarns, whether made from natural fibres, man-made fibres or a blend of both.

Baby yarns are usually made from the highest quality fibres and are available in 2 ply, 3 ply, 4 ply and double knitting weights.

Baby Quickerknit yarns are generally equivalent to a 4 ply but as they are very softly twisted, they are light in weight.

2 ply, 3 ply and 4 ply yarns are available in numerous fibres and are usually produced by twisting two or more single spun threads together.

Double Knitting yarns are usually made from four single spun threads – although there are exceptions to this – twisted together to produce yarns virtually double the thickness of 4 ply yarns.

Chunky and Double Double Knitting yarns are extra thick yarns which vary considerably in their construction. They are ideal for outer garments and some are oiled to give greater warmth and protection.

Crepe yarns are usually available in 4 ply qualities – sometimes called 'single crepe' – and Double Knitting weights – called 'double crepe' – and are more tightly twisted than normal yarns. They produce a smooth, firm fabric which is particularly hard-wearing.

Weights and measures
Since there is no official standardisation, yarns marketed by the various Spinners often vary in thickness and in yardage. As most yarns are marketed by weight, rather than length, even the density of dye used to produce certain colours in each range can result in more or less yarn in each ball, although the

structure of the yarn is exactly the same. Although all knitting designs are carefully checked, it would be impossible to make up a separate garment for each colour in the range of yarn quoted and you may sometimes find that you need one ball more or less than given in the instructions because of this difference in dye.

If it is impossible to obtain the correct yarn quoted in the instructions then another comparable yarn may be used, provided the same tension as that given in the pattern is obtained.

Equivalent yarns will knit up to the appropriate tension but do remember that the quantity given will not necessarily apply to another yarn.

Always buy sufficient yarn at one time to ensure that all the yarn used is from the same dye lot. Yarn from a different dye lot may vary slightly in colour, although this may not be noticeable until you have started to knit with it.

Yarns and metrication

When purchasing yarn it is advisable to check the weight of each ball as they now vary considerably, due to the intended introduction of the metric system. Metrication has already been adopted by some Spinners, while others are still in the process of changing over. Also, large stocks of yarns in standard ounces will take some time to run out, so this confused situation will be with us for some time.

Measurements and metrication

The next step in the metric system will be the change-over from imperial measurements in inches and yards to metric measurements in centimetres and metres. To allow readers time to become accustomed to this new system, all measurements will be given in metric sizes followed by the nearest accurate measurements in imperial sizes.

More simple knits

To illustrate how the same stitch worked in a different yarn can produce a variety of fabrics, try making the muffler given earlier in a mohair yarn, to give a lighter, softer version. Or use a yarn which combines a lurex thread to give a glitter effect to make an evening stole. The evening belt also given earlier could equally well be worked in a crisp cotton to make a useful summer accessory. The more you experiment, the more you will be delighted with the fabrics which can be produced.

Shawl

You will need 6 × 25grm balls of 2 ply Baby quality, or super-soft 2 ply, and a pair of No. 9 needles, also 144.0 centimetres (57in) of narrow lace.

Cast on 288 stitches. Work in garter stitch until shawl measures 91.5 centimetres (36in). Cast off loosely. Sew on lace all round edges, gathering it slightly round corners.

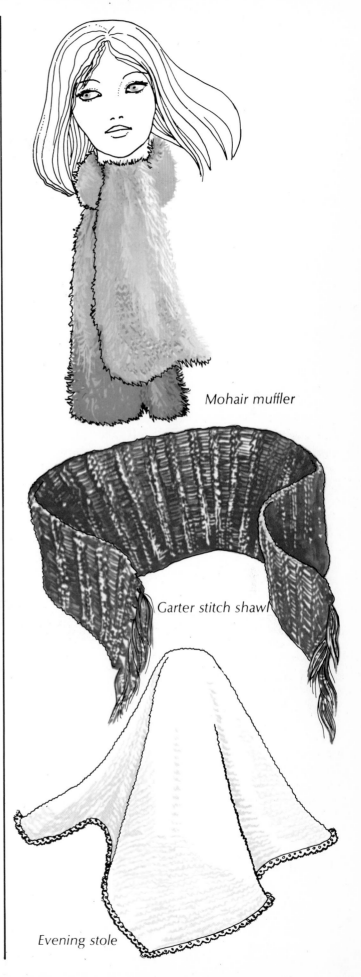

Mohair muffler

Garter stitch shawl

Evening stole

WORKING A PATTERN

A finished knitted garment should look just as attractive and well-fitting as in the illustration and a great deal of care is taken in compiling knitting patterns to ensure that this is possible. The secret lies in being completely objective about the design you choose, just as you would when selecting ready-to-wear clothes. The range of knitting patterns which are available cater for every type of garment in varying sizes. Where a design is only given in smaller sizes, such as a 81.5 (32) or 86.5cm (34 inch) bust, it is usually because the designer feels that it would not be suitable for a more generous figure. Similarly, if only one size is given it is probably because the pattern used for the design covers a large multiple of stitches and another whole repeat of the pattern, to give a larger size, would not be practical.

When you find a design which incorporates all the details you require make sure you read right through all the instructions before beginning to knit. Beginners and experts alike should pay particular attention to the making up section – a deceptively simple shape may require a crochet edging to give it that couture look, or an unusual trimming effect such as a twisted cord belt.

Knitting patterns

Knitting publication styles vary considerably but generally, all instructions fall into three sections:–
1 Materials required, tension, finished sizes and abbreviations.
2 Working instructions for each section.
3 Making up details, edges and trimmings.

Sizes

Check that the size range given in the instructions provides the size you require. If the skirt or sleeve lengths need altering to suit your requirements, read through the working instructions to see if the design allows for these amendments. Some designs are based on an exact number of rows which cannot be altered. After the actual measurements of the design are given, take note that the instructions for the smallest size are given as the first set of figures and that the figures for any other sizes follow in order and are usually shown in brackets. Go through the instructions and underline all the figures which are applicable to the size required, noting that where only one set of figures is given, it applies to all the sizes.

Tension

This section must not be overlooked as it is the vital key to success. Never begin any design without first checking that you can obtain the correct tension.

Materials

Each design will have been worked out for the knitting yarn which is quoted and this should be obtained, if possible. If for any reason it is quite impossible to obtain the correct yarn, you may select a substitute as long as you gain the correct tension but remember that the quantity given will only apply to the original yarn and if a substitute is used, you may require more or less yarn.

Abbreviations

All knitting patterns are abbreviated into a form of shorthand and every knitter soon comes to recognize the terms, 'K2 tog' or 'sl 1, K1, psso' and their meanings. A list of general knitting abbreviations has already been given in the introductory pages of this book but the same terms may not be abbreviated in the same way by other publications and this can sometimes lead to confusion. It is therefore essential to read through any list of abbreviations before beginning a pattern, to make sure you understand them. This is particularly important when they refer to increasing, as the terms, 'make 1' and 'increase 1' can mean two different methods.

In this course, where a specific stitch or technique is given in a pattern, the working method is given out in full for the first time it is used in a row and its abbreviated form given at the end of the working instructions. From that point on, each time the same stitch or technique is used, its abbreviated term will be given.

Working instructions

Each section will be given separately under an appropriate heading, such as, 'Back', 'Front', 'Sleeves' and so on. Each section should be worked in the correct order as it may be necessary to join parts of the garment together at a given point, before you can proceed with the next stage. When measuring knitting

it is necessary to lay it on a flat surface and use a rigid rule. Never measure round a curve but on an armhole or sleeve, measure the depth in a straight line.

Where an asterisk, *, is used in a pattern row it means repeat from that point, as directed. This symbol is also used at the beginning of a section, sometimes as a double asterisk, **, or triple asterisk, ***, to denote a part which is to be repeated later on in the instructions.

When working in rows, always join in a new ball of yarn at the beginning of a row. You can easily gauge whether you have sufficient yarn for another row by spreading out your work and checking whether the remaining yarn will cover its width four times. Any odd lengths of yarn can always be used later for seaming.

If the yarn has to be joined in the middle of the work, which is necessary when working in rounds, then the ends of the old ball of yarn and the new ball should be spliced together. To do this, unravel the end of the new ball and cut away one or two strands from each end. Overlay the two ends from opposite directions and twist them together until they hold. The twisted ends should be of the same thickness as the original yarn. As the join will not be very strong, knit very carefully with the newly twisted yarn for a few stitches. Then carefully trim away any odd ends with a pair of sharp scissors.

Never join in new yarn by means of a knot in the middle of your work, whether working in rows or rounds.

Making up

Most knitters give a sigh of relief when they have cast off the very last stitch and look forward to wearing their new creation. If the finished garment is to be a success however the making up of the separate pieces must be looked upon as an exercise in dressmaking. Details are always given in the instructions as to the order in which the sections are to be assembled, together with any final instructions for edgings or trimmings. Pressing instructions will also be given in this section and if a substitute yarn has been used, it is essential to check whether or not it requires pressing.

Mistakes!

These can happen – a dropped stitch, an interruption in a pattern row which has then been misread and needs unpicking – but don't be tempted to pull the stitches off the needle until you have tried other ways of rectifying the error.

To pick up a dropped stitch on a knit row Insert a crochet hook into the dropped stitch from the front to the back, put the hook under the thread which lies between the two stitches above the dropped stitch and pull this thread through the dropped stitch. Continue in this way until the dropped stitch is level with the last row worked and transfer the stitch to the left hand needle, then continue knitting in the usual way.

To pick up a dropped stitch on a purl row Insert a crochet hook into the dropped stitch from the back to the front, put the hook over the thread which lies between the two stitches above the dropped stitch and pull this thread through the dropped stitch. Slip the stitch on to a spare needle and remove the hook, ready to insert it into the dropped stitch from the back to the front again. Continue in this way until the dropped stitch is level with the last row worked and transfer the stitch to the left hand needle, then continue purling in the usual way.

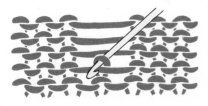

To take back stitches on a knit row Insert the left hand needle from the front to the back into the stitch below the next stitch on the right hand needle, then withdraw the right hand needle from the stitch above and pull the yarn with the right hand to unravel this stitch, keeping the yarn at the back of the work. Continue in this way until the required number of stitches have been unpicked.

To take back stitches on a purl row Insert the left hand needle from the front to the back into the stitch below the next stitch on the right hand needle, then withdraw the right hand needle from the stitch above and pull the yarn with the right hand to unravel this stitch, keeping the yarn at the front of the work. Continue in this way until the required number of stitches have been unpicked.

A BETTER FINISH
Shaping stitches

Knitting may be perfectly straight, as in a scarf, or intricately shaped as in a tailored jacket. This shaping is achieved by means of increasing the number of stitches in a row to make the work wider, or decreasing the stitches in a row to make the work narrower. This is usually done by making two stitches out of one, or by working two stitches together to make one stitch, at a given point in the pattern. Sometimes the shaping forms an integral part of the design and decorative methods of increasing and decreasing are used to highlight the shaping, such as fully-fashioned seams on a raglan jersey.

By means of an eyelet hole method of increasing stitches, carrying the yarn over or round the needle in a given sequence and compensating for these made stitches later on in the row, beautiful lace patterns are produced.

How to increase

The simplest way is to make an extra stitch at the beginning or end of the row, but a pattern will always give exact details where more intricate shaping is required, such as skirt darts.

To make a stitch at the beginning of a row, knit or purl the first stitch in the usual way but do not slip it off the left hand needle. Instead, place the point of the right hand needle into the back of the same stitch and purl or knit into the stitch again. One stitch has been increased.

To make a stitch at the end of a row, work until two stitches remain on the left hand needle, increase into the next stitch and work the last stitch in the usual way. One stitch has been increased.

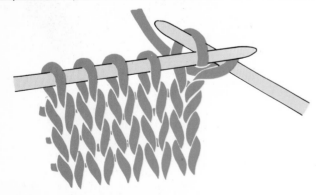

Invisible increasing

Insert the right hand needle into the front of the stitch on the row below the next stitch on the left hand needle and knit a new stitch in the usual way, then knit the next stitch on the left hand needle. One stitch has been increased.

If the increase is on a purl row, insert the right hand needle in the same way and purl a stitch in the usual way, then purl the next stitch on the left hand needle.

Increasing between stitches

With the right hand needle pick up the yarn which lies between the stitch just worked and the next stitch on the left hand needle and place this loop on the left hand needle. Knit into the back of this loop so that the new stitch is twisted and does not leave a hole in the work and place the new stitch on the right hand needle. One stitch has been increased.

If the increase is on a purl row, pick up the yarn between the stitches in the same way and purl into it from the back, then place the new stitch on the right hand needle.

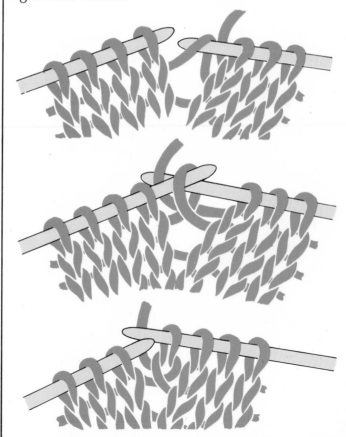

Decorative increasing

To make a stitch between two knit stitches, bring the yarn forward between the needles then back over the top of the right hand needle, ready to knit the next stitch. The abbreviation for this is 'yfwd'.

To make a stitch between a purl and a knit stitch, the yarn is already at the front of the work and is carried over the top of the right hand needle ready to knit the next stitch. The abbreviation for this is 'yon'.

To make a stitch between two purl stitches, take the yarn over the top of the right hand needle and round between the two needles to the front again ready to purl the next stitch. The abbreviation for this is 'yrn'.

To make a stitch between a knit and a purl stitch, bring the yarn forward between the two needles, over the top of the right hand needle then round between the two needles to the front again ready to purl the next stitch. The abbreviation for this is also 'yrn'.

How to decrease

The way to make a simple decrease is by working two stitches together, either at the ends of the row or at any given point. To do this on a knit row, insert the point of the right hand needle through two stitches instead of one and knit them both together in the usual way. This stitch will slant to the right and the abbreviation is 'K2 tog'. One stitch has been decreased.

If the decrease is on a purl row, purl the two stitches together in the same way. This stitch will slant to the left and the abbreviation is 'P2 tog'.

▲*Decreasing on a knit row* ▼*Decreasing on a purl row*

Decreasing by means of a slipped stitch

This method is most commonly used where the decreases are worked in pairs, one slanting to the left and one slanting to the right, as on a raglan sleeve. Slip the stitch to be decreased from the left hand needle on to the right hand needle without working it, then knit the next stitch on the left hand needle. With the point of the left hand needle lift the slipped stitch over the knit stitch and off the needle. This stitch will slant to the left and the abbreviation is 'sl

1, K 1, psso'.

If the decrease is on a purl row, purl the two stitches together through the back of the stitches. This stitch will slant to the right and the abbreviation is 'P2 tog tbl'.

Decorative decreasing

The decorative use of decreasing can be accentuated by twisting the stitches round the decreased stitches to give them greater emphasis. This example shows a decrease which has been twisted and lies in the opposite direction to the line of the seam. The decrease is worked at the end of a knit row for the left hand side and at the end of a purl row for the right hand side.

Knit to the last six stitches, pass the right hand needle behind the first stitch on the left hand needle and knit the next two stitches together through the back of the stitches, then knit the first missed stitch and slip both stitches off the left hand needle and knit the last three stitches in the usual way.

On a purl row, purl to the last six stitches, pass the right hand needle across the front of the first stitch on the left hand needle and purl the next two stitches together, then purl the first missed stitch and slip both stitches off the left hand needle and purl the last three stitches in the usual way.

Decorative decreasing on knit and purl rows

More about shaping

Even the most basic stocking stitch jersey needs careful shaping at the underarm, back and front neck and shoulders, sleeves and top of the sleeves, if it is to fit together correctly. The correct proportions for all these measurements will have been taken into account in every knitting design and the instructions will clearly state where and when the shaping is to be worked.

Where so many knitters come to grief however is in the accurate measuring of each section, so that when a garment is assembled it all fits together without stretching or easing one piece to fit another. The easiest way to overcome this problem is to use a row counter to ensure that the back and front of a garment have exactly the same number of rows before beginning any shaping and that both sleeves match. Many professional knitters prefer to knit both sleeves at the same time, using two separate balls of yarn, to make sure that the shaping for each sleeve is worked on the same row. Another useful tip is to make a note of the number of rows which have been worked for any section, such as the ribbing on the welt of a jersey, before beginning any pattern rows, so that when you come to do the next piece you do not even have to measure the length but can work to the same number of rows.

Whichever method you adopt it is essential to know how to take accurate measurements, if you are to achieve satisfactory results.

Taking measurements

Before taking any measurements it is necessary to lay the section of knitting on a flat surface. If you are sitting comfortably in a chair, it is tempting to try and measure it across your knees, or on the arm of the chair, but this will not give an accurate figure.

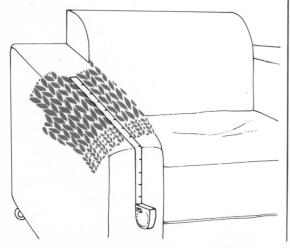

Always measure with a firm rule and not a tape measure and never be tempted to stretch the section to the required length to avoid working a few extra rows before the next stage.

Never measure round a curve but always on the straight of the fabric – a curved measurement is obviously greater and will result in an incorrect depth on armholes or sleeve seams. When measuring an armhole, sleeve or side edge of a section which has been shaped, place the rule on the fabric in a straight line from the commencement of the section to the point you have reached.

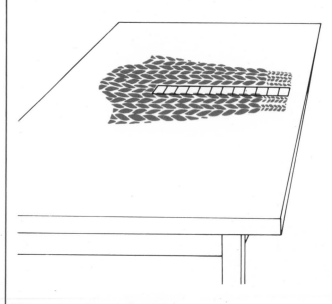

Measurements and tension

It cannot be stressed too often that every design you knit has been calculated on the tension achieved by the designer of the garment and based on the correct proportions for each size. The normal ratio of 5cm (2 in) difference between the bust and hip measurements will have been taken into account, also an allowance of 2.5cm (1 in) or 5.0cm (2 in) for movement, or what is known as tolerance. The width tension, or number of stitches to a given measurement, is vital if you are to obtain an accurate fit. The length tension, or number of rows to a given measurement, is not so important and can be adjusted where a pattern is not given over an exact number of rows and provided you remember that it is even more essential to measure each section accurately. The designer may have achieved more rows to the centimetre (inch) than you are obtaining and her shaping on the sleeves, for instance, will have been calculated to ensure that this is completed well before the point has been reached to shape the head of the sleeve. Where she is increasing on every 6th row in order to complete the shaping inside a certain measurement, you may be working to a looser row tension and will need to increase on every 5th row, in order to end up with the correct number of stitches within the same length. Similarly, if you are working to a tighter row tension, you may need to adjust the shaping and work it on every 7th row, otherwise all the shaping may well be completed before reaching the elbow level and the whole sleeve will be out of shape.

Shaping in rows

Details of casting on or casting off stitches to achieve the correct shape, such as for the underarm, neck or shoulders, will be given in a pattern in detail.

When shaping is required on both side edges of a section, the pattern may simply say, 'decrease one stitch at each end of the next knitted row' and will leave the knitter to adopt whichever method she prefers. In this case, if you use the slip one, knit one, pass slipped stitch over method at the beginning of the row, producing a decreased stitch which slants to the left, when the fabric is facing you, use the knit two together method at the end of the row to make a stitch which slants to the right.

When increasing in a row, whether it is at each end to increase two stitches, or across the row to increase a greater number of stitches, when working twice into a stitch the last stitch made is the increased stitch. If you increase in the first stitch at the beginning of a row, the made stitch will lie inside the first knitted stitch. At the end of the row you should increase in the last but one stitch, so that the made stitch again lies inside the last stitch, which is then knitted in the usual way. Sometimes a pattern will tell you to increase a given number of stitches across a row, without giving exact instructions. To do this you must first work out the exact position for each increased stitch. As an example, say a pattern has commenced

with 80 stitches and at a given point you are required to increase 8 stitches evenly across a row. The accurate way to achieve this would be to increase in the 5th stitch and then into every following 10th stitch 7 times more and knit the last 5 stitches. In this way, each made stitch is evenly spaced across the row.

Shaping in rounds

The same principles apply, whether working in rows or in rounds. A skirt may be worked from the hem to waist in rounds and will need to be shaped by means of decreasing, to lose the extra width at the hem. As an example, if you are working a pattern in wide panels of stocking stitch and narrow panels of reversed stocking stitch, the shaping needs to be worked on the stocking stitch panels to eventually bring them down to the same width as the reversed stocking stitch panels. The pattern may simply say, 'decrease one stitch at each end of every stocking stitch panel' and you should use the slip one, knit one, pass slipped stitch over method at the beginning of each panel and the knit two together method at the end of each panel. In this way, each decreased stitch lies in the same direction as the line of the stocking stitch panels.

Using the same example, when increasing in rounds remember that if you increase in the first stitch of each panel you must increase in the last but one stitch and not in the last stitch.

Casting off and selvedges

Each piece of knitted fabric has selvedge edges which are formed as the work progresses and these edges must be suitable for the fabric produced. Every section of flat knitting has a cast on selvedge, the right and left hand side edges and the cast off edge. Round knitting has only a cast on and cast off selvedge.

Various methods of casting on and off have already been given but the following methods are not so well known. The ways of forming side edge selvedges are also important, as an edge which is too tight or too loose will present difficulties in making up, pulling the garment out of shape.

Double casting on

Two needles are required for this method, which are both held together in the right hand. Make a slip loop in the ball of yarn as given for the thumb method and place this on both needles. Take both ends of the yarn, that is, the end of the yarn from the slip loop and the end from the ball and hold them together in the palm of the left hand, putting the slip loop end round the thumb and the ball end round the forefinger. Using both needles put them up under the first loop on the thumb and over and down through the loop on the forefinger, then through the thumb loop. Release the thumb loop and tighten the stitch on the needles with an upward movement of the right hand, without releasing either end of the yarn held in the palm of the hand. Continue in this way until the required number of stitches are formed on the needles, then withdraw the second needle, transfer the needle holding the stitches to the left hand and have the second needle in the right hand, ready to knit. This forms a very strong yet elastic edge.

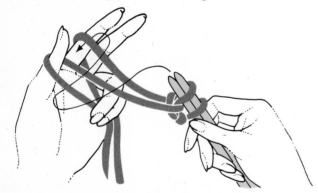

Picot casting on

Two needles are required for this method, one held in each hand. Make a slip loop and place this on the left hand needle then cast on one stitch by the two needle method. Using these two loops make a strip long enough for the number of stitches required by

bringing the yarn forward and ready to take over the top of the right hand needle to make a stitch, slip the first stitch on the left hand needle purlwise, knit the second stitch on the left hand needle and lift the slipped stitch over the knitted stitch and off the right hand needle. Turn and repeat this row until the required number of picot loops are formed by the yarn forward. Pick up these picot loops along one edge with a needle and then continue knitting in the usual way. The other side of the picot edge forms a dainty selvedge ideal for baby garments.

Suspended casting off

Knit the first two stitches in the usual way, then lift the first stitch over the second stitch but instead of allowing it to drop off the right hand needle, retain it on the point of the left hand needle. Pass the right hand needle in front of the held stitch and knit the next stitch on the left hand needle in the usual way, slipping the stitch and the held stitch off the left hand needle together, leaving two stitches on the right hand needle. Continue in this way until all stitches are cast off. This method avoids any tendency to cast off too tightly.

Shaped casting off

Preparation for this method must be made before the final casting off by means of turning the last few rows of knitting without completing them to form a shaped angle, then all the stitches are cast off at once on the final row. It is an ideal way of working shoulder shaping as it does not produce the stepped effect of normal casting off and makes seaming that much easier.

On a right back shoulder edge when the point has been reached for the shoulder shaping, instead of casting off the required number of stitches at the beginning of the next knit row, on the previous purl row work to within this number of stitches then turn the work, slip the first stitch on the left hand needle then knit to the end of the row. Repeat this action the required number of times, then purl across all the stitches. Cast them off on the next knit row in the usual way. Reverse this for a left back shoulder edge by beginning the shaping on a knit row.

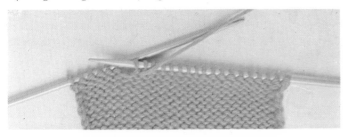

Three stages of shaped casting off

Side selvedges

Where side edges are to be joined together in making up they need to be firm to give a neat edge for seaming. When both edges must show, as in a scarf, they need to be tidy without pulling the sides out of shape.

To work a selvedge for seaming. Slip the first stitch purlwise and knit the last stitch on every row, when working in stocking stitch. On garter stitch, bring the yarn to the front of the work, slip the first stitch on every row purlwise, then take the yarn back between the needles and knit to the end in the usual way.

To work an open selvedge. When working in stocking stitch, slip the first and last stitch on every knit row

knitwise, to form a chain effect, then purl each stitch on the following row in the usual way.

Slipped stitches

Stitches which are slipped from one needle to the other without being worked are used in various ways – as edge stitches, as a means of decreasing and to form part of a pattern. When a slip stitch forms part of a decrease on a knit row, the stitch must be slipped knitwise, otherwise it will become crossed. On a purl row, the stitch must be slipped purlwise, when decreasing. In working a pattern, however, where the slip stitch is not part of a decrease it must be slipped purlwise on a knit row to prevent it becoming crossed when it is purled in the following row.

Slip stitch knitwise on a knit row. Hold the yarn behind the work as if to knit the next stitch, insert the point of the right hand needle into the next stitch from front to back as if to knit it and slip it on to the right hand needle without working it.

Slip stitch purlwise on a knit row. Hold the yarn behind the work as if to knit the next stitch, insert the point of the right hand needle into the next stitch from back to front as if to purl it and slip it on to the right hand needle without working it.

Slip stitch purlwise on a purl row. Hold the yarn at the front of the work as if to purl the next stitch, insert the point of the right hand needle into the next stitch from back to front as if to purl it and slip it on to the right hand needle without working it.

FINISHING TOUCHES
Buttonholes

Details for working buttonholes will always be given in the instructions for a garment but unless they are neatly finished they can spoil the appearance of the garment. Various methods may be used, largely depending on the size of the button required and the overall width of the buttonhole band or border. The buttonholes can be horizontal, vertical or, on a baby garment where a small button is required, simply worked by means of an eyelet hole.

Simple eyelet buttonholes

If the buttonhole is being incorporated in the main fabric, or the buttonhole band, work the front of the garment until the position for the first buttonhole is reached, ending with a wrong side row. On the next row work the first few stitches in the row to the position for the buttonhole, then pass the yarn forward, over or round the needle, depending on the stitch being worked, to make an eyelet hole, work the next two stitches on the left hand needle together to compensate for the made stitch, then work in pattern to the end of the row. On the next row, work across all the stitches in pattern, counting the made stitch as one stitch. Repeat this action for as many buttonholes as are required.

Horizontal buttonholes

These can either be worked as part of the main fabric or on a separate buttonhole band.

Buttonholes worked in one with the main fabric In this case provision will already have been made for a turned under hem and buttonholes will have to be made in the hem and in the main fabric, to form a double buttonhole, which is then neatened with buttonhole stitch on completion. Work until the position for the buttonhole is reached ending at the centre front edge. On the next row work a few

stitches across the hem, cast off the number of stitches required for the buttonhole by the two needle method then continue across the remainder of the hem, work the same number of stitches on the main fabric as were worked on the hem then cast off the same number of buttonhole stitches and work in pattern to the end of the row. On the next row you

need to replace the same number of stitches as were cast off for each buttonhole on the previous row but to avoid spoiling the buttonhole by a loose loop of yarn at one end, which would be the result by merely casting on the same number of stitches, work to the last stitch before the cast off stitches and increase in this last stitch by working into the front and back of it, then cast on one stitch less than was cast off in the previous row. Repeat this action for as many buttonholes as are required. If a turned under hem is not being worked in one with the main fabric, then only a single buttonhole is required.

Buttonholes worked in a separate border Here again, only a single buttonhole is required. Work the band until the position for the buttonhole is reached, ending at the centre front edge. On the next row work a few stitches until the position for the buttonhole is reached, cast off the required number of stitches for the buttonhole and pattern to the end of the row. On the next row, cast on the number of stitches needed to complete the buttonhole as given for working buttonholes in one with the main fabric. Repeat this action for as many buttonholes as are required.

Vertical buttonholes

This method of working buttonholes is ideal when only a narrow band is required and they can also be worked in one with the main fabric. The working instructions are the same for a separate band or when incorporated in the main fabric, remembering to make provision for a double buttonhole if a turned under hem is being worked with the main fabric. Work until the position for the buttonhole is reached, ending at the centre front edge. On the next row

work across a few stitches to the buttonhole opening then turn the work at this point and continue across these stitches only for the required number of rows to take the size of button, ending at the buttonhole opening edge. Break off the yarn and leave these stitches for the time being. Rejoin the yarn to the remaining stitches and work the same number of rows over these stitches, ending at the side edge away from the buttonhole opening. On the next row work across all the stitches to close the buttonhole. Repeat this action for the number of buttonholes required.

Finishing buttonholes

All buttonholes need to be neatened and reinforced when they are completed. This can either be done by working round them in buttonhole stitch, using the same yarn or a matching silk thread, or by means of a ribbon facing.

Buttonhole stitch Work along both sides of the buttonhole opening in buttonhole stitch for a horizontal or vertical buttonhole, neatening each end with three straight stitches. Take care not to work too many stitches round the buttonhole so that the edges become stretched or too few stitches, which would make the hole smaller than intended. Eyelet buttonholes need to be neatened with several evenly spaced buttonhole stitches round the hole, keeping the loops lying towards the centre.

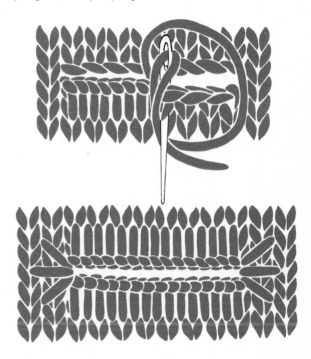

Ribbon facing The ribbon should be straight grained and wide enough to cover the buttonholes with an extra 1.5cm (½ *inch*) on either side and at each end of the band. Take care not to stretch the fabric when measuring the ribbon length and cut the buttonhole and button band facings together so that they match. Fold in the turnings on the ribbon and pin in place on the wrong side of the knitting, easing the fabric evenly and checking that the buttonholes are correctly spaced. Pin the ribbon on each side of every buttonhole to hold it in place. Slip stitch neatly round the edges of the ribbon then cut through the buttonholes in the ribbon making sure that they are exactly the same size as the knitted buttonholes. Work round the knitting and ribbon with buttonhole stitch to neaten the edges.

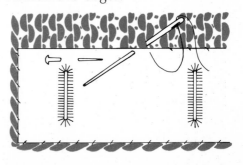

Hems and waistbands

Neat hems and waistbands are very important, particularly on babies' and children's garments where any unnecessary bulk produces an unsightly and uncomfortable edging.

Hems on skirts and dresses may be worked in one with the main fabric, then turned in and slip stitched into place when the garment is completed, or the hem may be knitted in to avoid seaming. Waist bands should be neatly ribbed and either folded in half to form a casing for the elastic, or the elastic may be directly applied to the wrong side of the fabric by means of casing, or herringbone stitch.

Turned under stocking stitch hem

Using one size smaller needles than given for the main fabric, cast on the required number of stitches. Beginning with a knitted row work an odd number of rows in stocking stitch, then change to the correct needle size. On the next row, instead of purling to the end, knit into the back of each stitch to form a ridge which marks the hemline. Beginning with a knitted row again, work one row less in stocking stitch than was worked for the hem, thus ending with a purl row to complete the hem. **. When the garment is completed and the side seams have been joined, turn the hem to the wrong side of the work at the hemline and slip stitch in place.

Knitted in hem in stocking stitch

Work as given for the turned under hem to ** Before continuing with the pattern, use an extra needle and pick up the loops from the cast on edge from left to right, so that the needle point is facing the same way as the main needle. Hold this needle behind the stitches already on the left hand needle and knit to the end of the row, working one stitch from the left hand needle together with one stitch from the extra needle. When the garment is completed, join the side seams working through the double fabric of the hem.

Picot hem

Using one size smaller needles than given for the main fabric cast on an odd number of stitches. Beginning with a knitted row work an even number of rows in stocking stitch. Change to the correct needle size.

Next row (eyelet hole row) *K2 tog, yfwd, rep from * to last st, K1.

Beginning with a purl row work one more row in stocking stitch than was worked for the hem, thus ending with a purl row to complete the hem. When the garment is completed and the side seams have been joined, turn the hem to the wrong side at the eyelet hole row and slip stitch in place.

Ribbed waistband

Using one size smaller needles than those given for the main fabric, work in K1, P1 rib for twice the width of the elastic, plus a few extra rows. If 2.5cm(1in) elastic is being used, work 5cm (2in) plus 2 extra rows, then cast off in rib. When the garment is completed and the side seams have been joined, turn in the waistband to the wrong side and slip stitch in place leaving an opening at one side to thread the elastic through. Insert the elastic and fasten off securely, then neaten the opening.

Casing stitch waistband

When the garment is completed join the side seams. Cut the elastic to the required waist length, allowing 2.5cm (1in) extra for an overlap, and secure the 2 ends to form a circle. Using pins mark off the waistband and elastic into equal sections. Pin the elastic into place on the wrong side of the fabric. Thread a blunt ended sewing needle with matching yarn and secure to the side seam of the waistband. Hold the waistband and elastic, slightly stretched, over the fingers of the left hand then take the sewing needle over the elastic and lightly insert it through the top of the waistband from right to left and pull the yarn through. Take the sewing needle over the elastic again and lightly insert it through the fabric below the elastic from right to left about 2 stitches along to the right and pull the yarn through. Take the sewing needle back over the top of the elastic to the top edge about 2 stitches along to the right, insert the needle lightly through the fabric from right to left and pull the yarn through. Continue in this way right round the waistband until the elastic is secured, taking great care to distribute the knitting evenly, then fasten off.

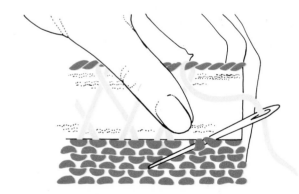

Baby's pants

Size

To fit 51[56:61]cm (20[22:24]in) hips
Length at side, 18[20.5:23]cm (7[8:9]in)
The figures in brackets [ ] refer to the 56 (22) and 61cm (24in) sizes respectively

Tension

30 sts and 40 rows to 10cm (3.9in) over st st worked on No.11 needles

Materials

2[2:3] × 25grm balls of Robin Tricel-Nylon Perle 4 ply
One pair No.11 needles
One pair No.12 needles
Waist length of 2.5cm (1in) wide elastic
Leg lengths of 1.5cm (½in) wide elastic

Pants left side

Using No.11 needles cast on 93[99:105]sts. Beg with a K row work 2 rows st st.

Shape crotch

Cont in st st, cast off for back edge 3 sts at beg of next and foll alt row then dec one st at same edge on every foll 4th row 4 times in all, *at the same time* cast off 2 sts for front edge on foll alt row and dec one st at same edge on every alt row 8 times in all. 73[79:85]sts. Cont without shaping until work measures 15[18:20.5]cm (6[7:8]in) from beg, ending with a P row.

Shape back

Next row K to last 24 sts, turn.
Next row Sl 1, P to end.
Next row K to last 32 sts, turn.
Next row Sl 1, P to end.
Cont working 8 sts less in this way on next and every alt row 4[5:6] times more. Change to No.12 needles.

Waistband

Next row K1, *P1, K1, rep from * to end.
Next row P1, *K1, P1, rep from * to end.
Rep last 2 rows 4 times more. Cast off in rib.

Pants right side

Work as given for left side, reversing all shaping.

Leg bands

Using No.12 needles and with RS of work facing, K up 93[99:105]sts round leg. Work 2.5cm (1in) K1, P1 rib as given for waistband. Cast off in rib.

To make up

Press each piece under a dry cloth with a cool iron. Join front, back and leg seams. Sew elastic inside waistband using casing st. Fold leg bands in half to WS and sl st down. Thread elastic through leg bands and fasten off. Press seams.

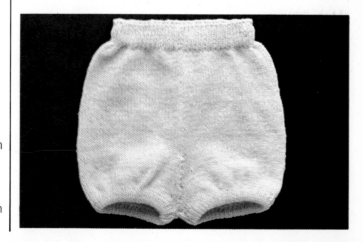

Pockets

Pockets are always a practical addition, particularly on men's and children's garments. They can be easily added to any chosen design, and inserted horizontally or vertically, as part of the main fabric, or applied as patch pockets when the garment is completed. In each case, a certain amount of planning is required before beginning the garment, to work out the exact positioning for each pocket. It must also be remembered that they will use extra yarn, so it would be as well to buy an extra ball.

If you have, for example, a favourite cardigan pattern for a man but would like to add inserted horizontal pockets above the welt, first check the given length to the underarm and work out the depth of pocket required. About 10cm (*4in*) by 10cm (*4in*) would be a reasonable size and this should be calculated to allow the pocket lining to come above any ribbed welts or inside any front edges. The same measurements apply to a patch pocket.

For an inserted vertical pocket, the same calculations must be made to ensure that the opening is correctly positioned and that the pocket lining has sufficient room to lie flat inside any front edges.

Patch pockets are the simplest to work and easy to apply, see later. They can be used as breast pockets on an otherwise plain jersey, applied to the sleeves above elbow level on a teenage jacket, or on the skirt of a dress at hip level. A straight turned down, buttoned flap can be added, or a plain square pocket can be given a highly individual touch if it is worked in a contrasting stitch or finished with embroidery.

Inserted horizontal pockets
First check the number of stitches you need to make the size of pocket required – on a tension of 6 stitches

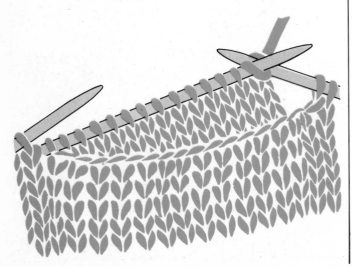

to 2.5cm (*1in*), a 10cm (*4in*) pocket would need 24 stitches. Cast on this number of stitches and make the inside pocket flap first, working in stocking stitch until it is the required depth, ending with a wrong side row, then leave these stitches on a holder. Now work the main fabric of the garment until the required depth for the pocket has been reached, ending with the right side of the work facing you. On the next row work until the position for the pocket opening is reached, slip the required number of stitches for the pocket top on to a holder, with the right side of the pocket lining stitches facing the wrong side of the main fabric, work across the pocket lining stitches, then work to the end of the row across the main fabric. Complete the section as given in the instructions. With the right side of the work facing, rejoin the yarn to the pocket top stitches on the holder and work 1.5cm (½*in*) to 2.5cm (*1in*) in rib or garter stitch

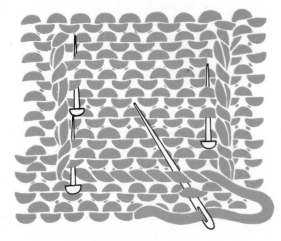

to complete the pocket. To make up the pocket, stitch the lining in place on the wrong side and neaten the side edges of the pocket top by slip stitching the edges to the main fabric.

Inserted vertical pockets
First check the number of rows you need to make the size of pocket required – if a tension of 8 rows to 2.5cm (*1in*) is given, a 10cm (*4in*) pocket will require 32 stitches. Cast on this number of stitches and make the inside pocket flap first, working in stocking stitch until it is the required depth, then leave these stitches on a holder. Work the main fabric of the garment until the required position for the pocket opening has been reached, ending with the right side of the work facing you. On the next row work until the position for the pocket opening is reached, turn at this point and work the required number of rows on

this section only, ending with a wrong side row. Break off the yarn. Return to where the work was divided, rejoin the yarn to the remaining stitches and work the same number of rows on this section, ending with a

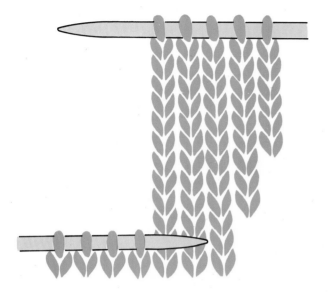

wrong side row. Break off the yarn. Return to the first section, rejoin the yarn and work across all the stitches to close the pocket opening, then complete the section as given in the instructions. With the right side of the work facing you, rejoin the yarn along the edge of the first pocket section worked on the right front of a garment, or along the second pocket section worked on the left front of a garment, and

pick up the required number of stitches. Work 1.5cm ($\frac{1}{2}in$) to 2.5cm ($1in$) rib or garter stitch to complete the pocket opening. With the right side of the pocket flap against the wrong side of the main fabric, join the flap to the other edge of the pocket opening and sew round the other 3 edges. Neaten the pocket opening by slip stitching the edges to the main fabric.

Patch pocket

Check the number of stitches and rows required to give the correct size for the pocket. If using a patterned stitch, such as cable, make sure that the pattern will work out exactly over the number of stitches and adjust them accordingly – it is better to have a slightly smaller or larger pocket than an incorrect pattern repeat. Cast on the stitches and work the number of rows to give the required depth, then cast off. With the wrong side of the patch pocket facing the right side of the main fabric, sew round 3 sides of the pocket.

Patch pocket with flap

Work as given for patch pocket until the required depth has been reached but do not cast off. Unless a completely reversible stitch, such as ribbing or garter stitch, has been used for the pocket, the pattern must now be reversed so that when the flap is turned down, the right side of the fabric will be showing. To do this if you have ended with a wrong side row, simply work another wrong side row for the first row of the flap, then continue in pattern for the required depth of the flap and cast off. Similarly, if you have ended with a right side row, work another right side row and complete in the same way. Sew on the pocket as given for patch pockets, turn the flap over to the right side and trim with one button at each end, if required.

Patch pockets with cable trim on a slip-over and patch pockets with flaps on a plain sweater

Neckbands and collars

Neckbands and collars

The neck opening on any garment, where the necessary shaping to give a good fit has been worked as part of the main fabric, will require neatening, either by means of a neckband or a collar. The most usual method of working a neckband on a round-necked jersey is to pick up the required number of stitches round the neck opening and work a few rows, or rounds, in single or double rib. This forms a neat edge with sufficient elasticity to hold its shape when it is pulled on or off over the head.

Collars may be added to a jersey or cardigan, either by picking up stitches round the neck edge or by making a separate section, which is then sewn round the neck edge to complete the garment. When working either a neckband or collar where the stitches must be picked up, see section on Making Up to ensure that stitches are picked up neatly and evenly round the opening.

Neckbands

To complete a round neck on a jersey, provision for an opening must be made if the neckband is to be worked on two needles. If a back or front neck opening has not been worked as part of the main fabric, only one shoulder seam should be joined, leaving the other seam open until the neckband has been completed. When a round neckband is worked on 4 needles, no opening is required and the stitches are simply picked up and worked in rounds to the required depth. When working a ribbed neckband, the depth can quite easily be adjusted to suit personal taste, to form either a round, crew or polo neck. If a polo neck is required, however, it must be remembered that this will take extra yarn and provision should be made for this when purchasing the yarn.

To complete a square neck on a jersey or cardigan, each corner must be mitred to continue the square shape and allow the neckband to lie flat. The neatest way to do this is to pick up the required number of stitches and mark each corner stitch with coloured thread. Keep these marked stitches as knitted stitches on the right side of the work, whether working in rows or rounds, and decrease one stitch on either side of each marked stitch on every row or round, making sure that the decreased stitches slant towards the corner stitch. As an example, when working in rows of garter stitch with the right side of the work facing, work to within 2 stitches of the corner stitch, sl 1, K1, psso, K corner st, K2 tog, then K to within 2 stitches of the next corner. On the following row, the decreased stitches will be worked in the same way but the corner stitch must be purled.

Collars

Collars come in all styles and sizes but to sit correctly round the neck, they must be carefully shaped. They can be worked in 2 sections to form a divided collar, where a jersey has a centre back neck opening, or in one piece to complete a jersey or a cardigan. Where the fabric used for the collar is reversible, such as garter stitch or ribbing, the stitches should be picked up round the neck in the usual way with the right side of the work facing. Where a fabric such as stocking stitch is used for a collar, however, the stitches must be picked up with the wrong side of the work facing, to ensure that the correct side of the fabric is shown when the collar is turned down.

Jersey with ribbed neckband or shirt collar

Sizes

To fit 86.5[91.5:96.5]cm (34[36:38]in) bust
Length to shoulder, 58.5[59.5:61]cm (23[23½:24]in)
Sleeve seam, 43[44.5:45.5]cm (17[17½:18]in)
The figures in brackets [] refer to the 91.5 (36) and 96.5cm (38in) sizes respectively

Tension

30 sts and 38 rows to 10cm (3.9in) over st st worked on No.11 needles

Materials

7[7:8] × 50 grm balls of any 4 ply plus 1 extra ball if collar is required
One pair No.11 needles
One pair No.12 needles
5 buttons

Back

Using No.12 needles cast on 134[142:150] sts. Work 5cm (2in) K1, P1 rib. Change to No.11 needles. Beg with a P row cont in reversed st st until work measures 40.5cm (16in) from beg, ending with a K row.

Shape armholes

Cast off 5[6:7] sts at beg of next 2 rows. Dec one st at each end of next and every alt row until 102[108:114] sts rem. Cont without shaping until armholes measure 18[19:20.5]cm (7[7½:8]in) from beg, ending with a K row.

Shape shoulders

Cast off at beg of next and every row 12 [12:13] sts twice, 12[13:13] sts twice and 12[13:14] sts twice. Leave rem 30[32:34] sts on holder.

Front

Work as given for back until front measures 39.5cm (15½in) from beg, ending with a P row.

Divide for front opening

Next row K62[66:70] sts, cast off 10 sts, K to end.
Complete this side first. Cont in reversed st st until work measures same as back to underarm, ending at armhole edge.

Shape armhole

Cast off 5[6:7] sts at beg of next row. Dec one st at armhole edge on every alt row until 46[49:52] sts rem. Cont without shaping until armhole measures 14cm (5½in) from beg, ending at centre front edge.

Shape neck

Cast off 3[4:5] sts at beg of next row. Dec one st at neck edge on every alt row until 36[38:40] sts rem. Cont without shaping until armhole measures same as back to shoulder, ending at armhole edge.

Shape shoulder

Cast off at beg of next and every alt row 12[12:13] sts once, 12[13:13] sts once and 12[13:14] sts once.

With RS of work facing, rejoin yarn to rem sts and complete to match first side, reversing shaping.

Sleeves

Using No.12 needles cast on 64[68:72] sts. Work 7.5cm (3in) K1, P1 rib. Change to No.11 needles. Beg with a P row cont in reversed st st, inc one st at each end of 7th and every foll 8th row, until there are 96[100:104] sts. Cont without shaping until sleeve measures 43[44.5:45.5]cm (17[17½:18]in) from beg, ending with a K row.

Shape top

Cast off 5[6:7] sts at beg of next 2 rows. Dec one st at each end of next and every alt row until 60 sts rem, ending with a K row. Cast off 4 sts at beg of next 10 rows. Cast off rem 20 sts.

Button band

Using No.12 needles cast on 12 sts. Beg 1st row with P1, work in P1, K1 rib until band fits up left front edge to beg of neck shaping, when slightly stretched. Leave sts on holder. Mark positions for 4 buttons with 5th to come in neckband.

Buttonhole band

Work as given for button band, beg 1st row with K1 and making buttonholes as markers are reached, as foll:

Next row (buttonhole row) Rib 5, cast off 2, rib 5.
Next row Rib to end, casting on 2 sts above those cast off in previous row.

Ribbed neckband

Join shoulder seams. Sew on button and buttonhole bands, making sure that next row will beg and end with K1. Using No.12 needles and with RS of work facing, rib across buttonhole band, K up 28[30:32] sts up right side of neck, K across back neck sts inc 5 sts evenly across sts and K up 28[30:32] sts up left front neck, then rib across button band. 115[119:123] sts. Work 9 rows K1, P1 rib, making buttonhole as before on 5th and 6th rows. **. Cast off.

Collar

Work as given for neckband to **.

Next row Cast off 6 sts, rib 5 sts and leave on holder, rib to last 11 sts, rib 5 sts and leave on holder, cast off 6 sts. Break off yarn.

Change to No.11 needles. Using 2 strands of yarn, work 15 more rows rib, inc one st at each end of every row. Dec one st at each end of next 6 rows. Cast off 3 sts at beg of next 6 rows. Cast off rem sts.

Edging

Using No.12 needles and one strand of yarn, rejoin yarn to WS of first set of 5 sts. Work in rib until edging fits round outer edge of collar to centre back. Cast off. Work other side in same way. Sew edging round collar, joining at centre back.

To make up

Press as required. Join side and sleeve seams. Set in sleeves. Sew on buttons.

MAKING UP
YARNS AND SEAMS

The making up of a garment requires as much care and skill as the actual knitting of each section. The technical knowledge which has been involved in producing an interesting fabric and the correct shape and proportions of the garment will be of no avail if the pieces are hurriedly assembled, or if scant attention is paid to the specific instructions for handling the yarn used. Some yarns do not require pressing, in fact, they lose their character if they are pressed and the texture of certain stitches, such as Aran patterns, can be completely ruined by over-pressing. Read the instructions carefully before beginning any making up and if you have not used the yarn specified, check whether or not the substitute requires pressing by referring to the instructions given on the ball band.

Handling yarns

Each yarn, whether it is made from natural fibres, man-made fibres, or various blends of both, requires a different method of handling in making up. The Home Laundering Consultative Council has compiled an ironing and dry-cleaning code in respect of hand knitting yarns and the relative symbols are shown on most ball bands. The following list gives a guide to the correct method of handling various qualities but with so many new and exciting yarns becoming available, it is even more essential to check the specific requirements of each yarn.

Pure wool This quality should be pressed under a damp cloth with a warm iron.

Blends of wool and nylon fibres Provided the wool content is greater than the nylon content, such as 60% wool and 40% nylon, these qualities should be pressed lightly under a damp cloth with a warm iron.

Blends of wool and acrylic fibres Do not press.

Nylon Press under a dry cloth with a cool iron.

Courtelle Do not press.

Acrylic fibres Do not press.

Cotton Press under a damp cloth with a fairly hot iron.

Mohair Press very lightly under a damp cloth with a warm iron.

Blends of mohair and acrylic fibres Do not press.

Blends of tricel and nylon Press lightly under a dry cloth with a warm iron.

Glitter yarns Do not press, unless otherwise clearly stated on the ball band.

Angora Steam press under a very damp cloth with a warm iron, by holding the iron over the cloth to make steam but not applying any pressure.

Embossed stitches Heavy cables, Aran patterns and any fabric with a raised texture should be steam pressed. This will neaten the fabric without flattening the pattern.

Warning! If in doubt, do not press.

Blocking

As so many yarns now available do not require pressing, it is not always necessary to block out each piece to the correct size and shape. If pressing is required however place each piece right side down on an ironing pad and pin it evenly round the edges to the pad. Use rustless tailor's pins and never stretch the knitting, or the pins will tend to make a fluted edge.

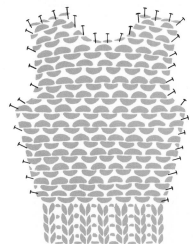

Take care to see that the stitches and rows run in straight lines and that the fabric is not pulled out of shape. Once the pieces are pinned into place, check with a firm rule that the width and length are the same as those given in the instructions.

	HOT	WARM	COOL	DO NOT IRON
IRONING	⌁	⌁	⌁	⌁
DRYCLEAN	Ⓐ	Ⓟ	Ⓕ	⊗
	Usual dry cleaning	Normally drycleanable in most solvents. If drycleaned inform cleaner of composition of yarn.	Drycleanable in some solvents It is important that the cleaner is informed of the composition of the yarn if dry-cleaning is to be undertaken.	DO NOT DRYCLEAN

Pressing

Use a clean cloth and place it over the piece to be pressed, then press the iron down on top of the cloth and lift it up again, without moving it over the surface of the cloth as you would if you were actually ironing. Each area should be pressed evenly but not too heavily before lifting the iron to go on to the next area. Ribbed or garter stitch edges on any piece do not require pressing, or they will lose their elasticity.

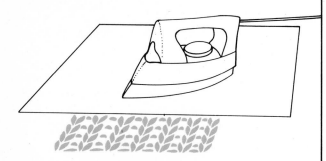

Seams

The choice of seaming method will largely depend on the type of garment being assembled. A baby's vest needs invisible seams without any hard edges and the flat seam method is normally used to join any ribbed edges where a neat, flat edge is required. Use a blunt ended wool needle and the original yarn for joining pieces together. If the yarn is not suitable for sewing purposes, as with mohair, use a finer quality such as 3 ply in the same shade.

Invisible seam Secure the sewing yarn to one side of the pieces to be joined. With the right sides of both pieces facing you, pass the needle across to the other side of the work, pick up one stitch and pull the yarn through. Pass the needle across the back to the first side of the work, pick up one stitch and pull the yarn through. Continue working in this way, making rungs across from one piece to the other and pulling each stitch up tightly so that it is not seen on the right side of the work when the seam is completed.

Back stitch seam Place the right sides of each piece to be joined together and work along the wrong side of the fabric about one stitch in from the edge. Keep checking the other side of the seam to make sure that you are working in a straight line. Begin by securing the sewing yarn, making two or three small running stitches one on top of the other, *with the needle at the back of the work move along to the left and bring the needle through to the front of the work the width

of one stitch from the end of the last stitch, and pull the yarn through, take the needle back across the front of the work to the right and put it through to the back of the work at the end of the last stitch and pull the yarn through. Continue in this way repeating from * until the seam is completed, taking care to pull each sewing stitch firmly through the knitting, without stretching the pieces or drawing up the seaming stitches too tightly.

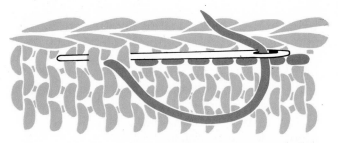

Flat seam Place the right sides of each piece to be joined together and place your forefinger between the two pieces. Secure the sewing yarn to one side of the pieces to be joined then pass the needle through the edge stitch on the underside piece directly across to the matching stitch on the upper-side piece and pull the yarn through. Turn the needle and work back through the next stitch on the upper-side piece directly across to the matching stitch on the underside piece, again pulling the yarn through. Continue in this way until the seam is completed.

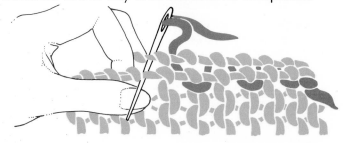

Slip stitch seam This is required for turning in hems and facings to the wrong side of the work. Turn in the hem or facing so that the wrong side of the main fabric is towards you. Secure the sewing yarn at a seam then insert the needle and lightly pick up one stitch from the main fabric and pull the yarn through, move along to the left the width of one stitch, insert the needle into the edge stitch of the hem or facing and pick up one stitch, then pull the yarn through. Move along to the left the width of one stitch and continue in this way until the seam is completed.

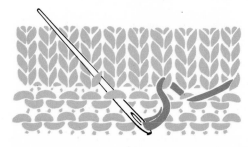

SETTING IN

More about making up! As we have already explained in the previous chapter, the care and attention to detail required in making up are as essential as in knitting the actual pieces. The correct seaming method, the correct handling and pressing of yarns, the correct method of finishing hems, applying pockets, completing edgings – all these techniques mean the difference between a hand-made garment and a couture design. Here are more tricks of the trade which will enable you to give all your garments the finish and flair of a ready-to-wear design.

Sewn on bands

Where bands are worked separately and are not incorporated in the working instructions for the main sections, such as button and buttonhole bands, use a flat seam to apply the bands. Each band should be slightly less than the finished length of the main fabric and should be slightly stretched and pinned into position before seaming.

Applying the pocket

Shoulder seams

Use a firm back stitch seam, taking the stitches across the steps of shaping in a straight line. On heavy outer garments, school or sports jerseys, or any garment where extra strength is needed, reinforce these seams with ribbon or tape.

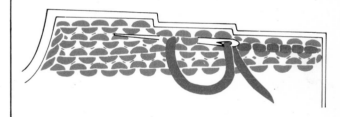

Set-in sleeves

Mark the centre top of the sleeve head and pin this to the shoulder seam, then pin the cast off underarm stitches to the underarm stitches of the body. Use a back stitch seam, working in a smooth line around the curve of the armhole and taking care not to pull the stitches too tightly.

Sewn on pockets

Use a slip stitch seam to apply the pocket, taking care to keep the line of the pocket and main fabric straight. A useful tip is to use a fine knitting needle, pointed at both ends, to pick up every alternate stitch along the line of the main fabric, then catch one stitch from the edge of the pocket and one stitch from the needle alternately. Make sure that the lower edge of the pocket lies in a straight line across a row of the main fabric.

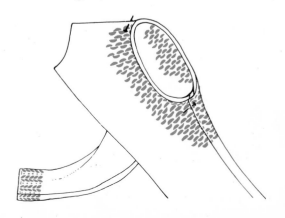

Side and sleeve seams
Use a back stitch seam and join in one piece, working extra stitches across the underarm join to secure it firmly.

Sewing in zip fasteners
Pin the zip fastener into the required opening, taking care not to stretch the knitting. With the right side of the work facing, sew in the zip using a back stitch seam and keeping as close to the edge of the knitting as possible. On something like a back neck opening or skirt side seam, work in a straight line down the zip from top to bottom, then work extra stitches across the end of the zip to secure it and continue up the other side of the zip.

When inserting an open-ended zip, keep the fastener closed and insert it as for an opening from top to lower edge, fastening off securely at the end. Break off the yarn and work along the other side in the same way. This ensures that both sides match and that one side is not pulled out of shape, making it difficult to operate the zip smoothly.

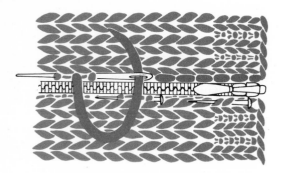

Knitting up edges
You will frequently come across the phrase, 'knit up stitches', such as round a neckline, along a front edge or pocket top, as a means of neatening an unfinished edge. This is usually worked with the right side of the garment facing you. The instructions will always clearly state where stitches are required to be picked up with the wrong side facing you, such as would be needed for a stocking stitch collar, where the turned down collar fabric must match the main fabric. You can either pick up these stitches directly on to a knitting needle, or use a crochet hook to pick up the stitches and then transfer them to a knitting needle.

Knitting up stitches across the line of main fabric

Knitting up stitches across the line of main fabric
Have the right side of the fabric facing you and hold the yarn at the back of the work. Use a crochet hook and put this through the work from the right side to the wrong side and pick up a loop of yarn from the back, bring this loop through to the right side and transfer the stitch to a knitting needle. Continue in this way until the required number of stitches have been picked up.

Knitting up stitches round a curved edge This could be a neckband or armhole band. Have the yarn at the back of the work and the right side of the fabric facing you. Put a knitting needle through from the front to the back of the fabric and pick up a loop of yarn, bring this loop through to the right side of the work and leave the stitch on the needle. If a crochet hook is used, pick up the loop in the same way with the hook then transfer the stitch to a knitting needle. Continue in this way until the required number of stitches have been picked up.

An easy way to ensure that stitches are picked up evenly is to pin out the main section of fabric at regular intervals of, say, 5cm (*2in*) and pick up the same number of stitches inside each pin. As a guide, make sure that where you are picking up stitches across stitches you pick up one loop for each stitch and across rows, approximately one stitch for every two rows.

Knitting up front bands Count the number of rows on the main fabric then check this against the number of stitches to be picked up and make sure that you knit them up evenly. Pin out sections as given for knitting up stitches round a curved edge and pick up the same number of stitches between each pin. Unless otherwise stated in the instructions, always work the button band first so that you can mark the exact position for each button and then work the appropriate buttonhole on the buttonhole band, as these markers are reached.

TAKING CARE

The correct after-care of all knitted garments is extremely important if they are to retain their original texture and shape. Many of the yarns available today are machine-washable and the ball band will clearly indicate where this is applicable. If you are in any doubt at all, however, always hand wash rather than risk ruining the garment. Similarly, check whether the yarn can be dry cleaned from the ball band, referring to the Home Laundering chart earlier for details.

Care in washing

Whether you are machine washing or hand washing a garment, it is essential that the minimum amount of handling occurs when the fabric is wet. Before washing, turn the garment inside out. Never lift the garment by the shoulders, thus allowing the weight of the water to pull the design out of shape. Squeeze out any excess moisture very gently but never wring the garment, supporting the whole weight with both hands.

Always rinse two or three times, making sure that all soap or detergent deposits have been thoroughly removed, using a fabric conditioner if required. Once the garment has been rinsed, gently lift it on to a draining board, again supporting the weight, while you prepare a drying area.

Care in drying

Very few yarns take kindly to contact with direct heat or sunlight and the garment should always be allowed to dry out naturally. You also run the risk of pulling the whole garment out of shape if you peg it on to a line while it is still wet, however carefully. The best possible way of drying any garment, whatever the composition of the yarn used, is on a flat surface – a kitchen table top is ideal.

First place 3 or 4 old newspapers over the surface which is to be used for drying, spreading them out well beyond the full extent of the garment. Cover the newspapers completely with one or two clean towels which are colour-fast – a white garment placed on a red towel which is not completely colour-fast could result in some unsightly pink patches! Gently lift the garment on to the centre of the towel. Spread it into its original size and shape and gently pat it flat on to the towel, smoothing out any creases. Leave the garment until all the excess moisture has been absorbed by the towels and newspapers. Then – and only then – should it be carefully lifted and placed over a line for the final airing, pegging the

garment at the underarms only and never from the shoulders.

Care in pressing

If the garment has been well smoothed out and allowed to dry in shape it should not require any pressing. If it does need ironing, however, first check the instructions given on the ball band, then refer to the beginning of this section for handling details.

Care in wear

However careful you are, a garment may become snagged or the yarn may 'pill' into little balls of fluff. It is a simple matter to remedy these faults before too much damage is done.

To prevent the risk of snagging, do not put on a garment while you are wearing any jewellery which could catch in the yarn and pull a thread. Should you discover a snag in a garment, however, never cut it off or you will run the risk of the fabric unravelling. Using a blunt ended sewing needle, push the snagged end of yarn through to the wrong side of the fabric and gently tighten the yarn until the stitch is the correct size, then knot the end of yarn and leave it on the wrong side.

Where pilling occurs in the yarn, gently pull off these

little balls of fluff, taking care not to snag the yarn. If the pilling is excessive, the fabric should be gently brushed over with a teasel to remove the fluff.

Make do and mend

Hand knitting need never be wasted, even if the original garment has outgrown its use. Unpick the seams of the garment, taking great care not to cut the fabric, and unravel each section winding the yarn into hanks by passing it round the backs of two chairs. To remove any crinkles from the yarn, either hand wash each hank and hang out to dry, or hold them taut in front of the spout of a gently steaming kettle, moving them backwards and forwards through the steam until the kinks have disappeared. Some areas of knitting may wear thin in use particularly on children's garments. These can easily be re-inforced by means of Swiss darning. It doesn't matter if you cannot match the original yarn – a contrasting colour darned into a motif will give an interesting new lease of life to the design.

Elbows which are worn through can easily be covered with a patch of leather or suede, applied to the right side of the fabric. To disguise the fact that these are patches, add new interest to the garment by making leather patch pockets to match.

KNITTING IN ROUNDS
BASIC TECHNIQUES

Knitting in rounds, as opposed to knitting in rows to produce flat knitting, literally means producing a seamless, tubular piece of fabric. This method may be worked on sets of needles, usually 4, which are pointed at both ends and manufactured in varying lengths and the length of needle will be determined by the total number of stitches required.

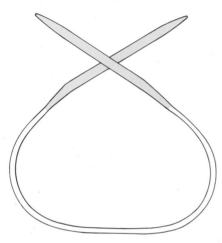

Circular needles are also obtainable and those manufactured by Aero, called Twin-Pins, comprise two rigid, shaped needle sections pointed at one end, with the other end of each section being joined into one continuous length by a light-weight, flexible strip of nylon. Before using Twin-Pins the twist which the nylon strip may develop through packing may be removed by immersing it in fairly warm water and then drawing it between the fingers until it lies in a gradual curve. These are also manufactured in varying lengths and the chart gives a guide to the minimum number of stitches required for each length, to reach from needle point to needle point without stretching. The advantage of circular needles over sets of needles is that they may also be used as an ordinary pair of needles for working to and fro in rows.

As knitting in rounds dispenses with seaming, it is the ideal way of making socks and stockings, gloves and mittens, hats, skirts and even jerseys. The minimum of seaming on a jersey is possible by working the body in one piece to a point where the work can be divided and continued in rows.

Casting on
Details of casting on with more than two needles have already been given in Chapter 1. The total number of stitches required can either be cast on to one needle and then divided between three of the needles, leaving the fourth needle to knit with, or can be cast on to each of the three needles separately.

When casting on with a circular needle, simply use each shaped section as a pair of needles, having one section in the left hand and one in the right.

Whether using sets of needles or a circular needle, the important point to remember is that the cast on stitches must not become twisted before joining them into a round.

Knitting in rounds
Once you have cast on the required number of stitches, using sets of needles, form them into a circle by putting the spare needle into the first stitch on the left hand needle and knit this stitch in the usual way. Continue to knit all the stitches on the first needle and once this is free use it to knit the stitches of the second needle, then use the second needle to knit the stitches of the third needle. Always pull the yarn tightly across to the first stitch of each needle to avoid a loose stitch.

With a circular needle, simply continue knitting each stitch until you come to the beginning of the round again.

TENSION	LENGTHS OF AERO CIRCULAR TWIN-PIN NEEDLES AVAILABLE AND MINIMUM NUMBER OF STITCHES REQUIRED						
Stitches to 2.5 cm(1in.)	40.5 cm 16"	51.0 cm 20"	61.0 cm 24"	68.5 cm 27"	70.6 cm 30"	91.5 cm 36"	106.5 cm 42"
5	80	100	120	135	150	180	210
5½	88	110	132	148	165	198	230
6	96	120	144	162	180	216 .	250
6½	104	130	156	175	195	234	270
7 ·	112	140	168	189	210	252	294
7½	120	150	180	202	225	270	315
8	128	160	192	216	240	288	336
8½	136	170	204	220	255	306	357
9	144	180	216	243	270	324	378

As it is easy to lose track of where each round of knitting begins, mark the beginning of the round with a knotted loop of contrast yarn on the needle before the first stitch of every round and slip this loop from the left hand needle to the right hand needle without knitting it.

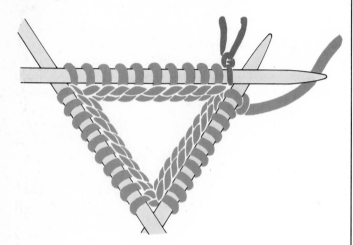

Stocking stitch in rounds
Since the right side of the fabric is always facing the knitter and the work is not turned at the end of each row as in flat knitting, stocking stitch in rounds is produced by knitting every round. This has a great advantage when working complicated, multi-coloured patterns.

Garter stitch in rounds
Because the work is not turned, to produce garter stitch in rounds the first round must be knitted and the second round purled, to form the ridged effect.

Ribbing in rounds
Here again, the right side of the fabric is facing so each knit stitch must be knitted on every round and each purl stitch purled on every round. When working in rounds of ribbing, remember that if you begin a round with one or more knitted stitches, you must end with one or more purled stitches to complete the round exactly.

Socks without heel shaping
This practical way of producing socks without heel shaping must be worked on sets of needles.

Size
Round top of sock, 20.5cm (8in)
Length to toe, 58.5cm (23in), adjustable

Tension
32 sts and 36 rows to 10.0cm (3.9in) over patt worked on No.12 needles

Materials
5 × 1oz balls of Patons Nylox 4 ply
Set of 4 No.12 needles pointed at both ends

Socks
Using set of 4 No.12 needles cast on 80 sts, 26 each on 1st and 2nd needles and 28 on 3rd needle. Mark beginning of round with coloured thread.
1st round *K1, P1, rep from * to end.
Rep 1st round for single ribbing until work measures 10.0cm (4in) from beg. Commence patt.
1st patt round *K3, P2, rep from * to end.
Rep 1st patt round 3 times more.
5th patt round P1, *K3, P2, rep from * to last 4 sts, K3, P1.
Rep 5th patt round 3 times more.
9th patt round *P2, K3, rep from * to end.
Rep 9th patt round 3 times more.
13th patt round K1, *P2, K3, rep from * to last 4 sts, P2, K2.
Rep 13th patt round 3 times more.
17th patt round K2, *P2, K3, rep from * to last 3 sts, P2, K1.
Rep 17th patt round 3 times more. These 20 rounds form patt. Cont in patt until work measures 52.0cm ($20\frac{1}{2}$in) from beg, or required length less 6.5cm ($2\frac{1}{2}$in). Cont in st st, K each round.
Shape toe
1st round *K8 sts, K2 tog, rep from * to end.
Work 2 rounds st st without shaping.
4th round *K7 sts, K2 tog, rep from * to end.
Work 2 rounds st st without shaping.
7th round *K6 sts, K2 tog, rep from * to end.
Work 2 rounds st st without shaping.
10th round *K5 sts, K2 tog, rep from * to end.
Work 2 rounds st st without shaping.
13th round *K4 sts, K2 tog, rep from * to end.
Work 2 rounds st st without shaping.
16th round *K3 sts, K2 tog, rep from * to end.
Work 2 rounds st st without shaping.
19th round *K2 sts, K2 tog, rep from * to end.
Work 2 rounds st st without shaping.
22nd round *K1 st, K2 tog, rep from * to end.
23rd round *K2 tog, rep from * to end.
Break off yarn, thread through rem sts, draw up and fasten off securely.

DOUBLE FABRICS

A double stocking stitch fabric can quite easily be produced by working in rounds and using this tube of material as a double sided fabric. Alternatively, double fabric can also be worked in rows on two needles by the simple means of a slipped stitch and this method is most effective when two different yarns, giving the same tension, are used for each side of the material.

The ideas shown here will enable you to practise both these methods to make a warm scarf or a glamorous evening hood.

Scarf

We have made our scarf in stocking stitch, knitting every round, in wide stripes. You can just as easily work narrow stripes in more than two colours or a simple, all-over patterned stitch in one colour, provided you check the multiples of stitches required for the pattern and amend the number of stitches cast on accordingly. The total quantity of yarn given will be a guide to the amount required but remember that a patterned stitch may need more yarn.

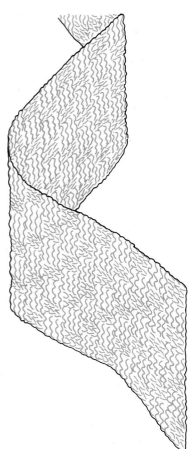

Scarf knitted in all-over patterned stitch.

Size

23cm (*9in*) wide by 152.5cm (*60in*) long

Tension

22 sts and 28 rows to 10cm (*3.9in*) over st st worked on No.8 needles.

Materials

4 × 50 grm balls of Jaeger Spiral-Spun in main shade, A
4 balls of same in contrast colour, B
Set of 4 No.8 needles pointed at both ends *or*
One No.8 circular Twin-Pin

Scarf

Using set of 4 No.8 needles or No.8 circular Twin-Pin and A, cast on 100 sts. Work in rounds of st st, every round K, until work measures 10cm (*4in*) from beg. Break off A and join in B. Work a further 10cm (*4in*) st st. Cont working stripes in this way until work measures 152.5cm (*60in*) from beg. Cast off.

To make up

Press under a damp cloth with a warm iron. Cut rem yarn into 30.5cm (*12in*) lengths and knot fringe along each short end, working through double fabric and using A and B alternately. Trim fringe.

Evening hood

We have used a glitter yarn and mohair to make this double sided hood for evening. Using a plain yarn and repeating the first pattern row only, a snug, day-time version can quite easily be made. The total quantity of yarn given will be a guide to the amount required but make sure that you can achieve the same tension.

Size
28cm (*11in*) wide by 142cm (*56in*) long

Tension
16 sts and 28 rows to 10cm (*3.9in*) over double fabric worked on No.8 needles

Materials
5 × 1oz balls of Jaeger Mohair-Spun in main shade, A
5 × 25 grm balls of Jaeger Astral-Spun in contrast colour, B
One pair No.8 needles pointed at both ends
One pair No.10 needles

Evening hood
Using No.10 needles and A, cast on 88 sts. Change to No.8 needles.
1st row (RS) Using A, *K1, yfwd, sl 1 P-wise, ybk, rep from * to end. Join in B.
(**Note:** When using one colour, turn and rep this row throughout.)

2nd row Do not turn work but return to beg of row, using B, *sl 1 P-wise, yfwd, P1, ybk, rep from * to end. 44 sts each in A and B.
3rd row Turn work and cross A and B to close side edge, using B, *K1, yfwd, sl 1 P-wise, ybk, rep from * to end.
4th row Do not turn work but return to beg of row, using A, *sl 1 P-wise, yfwd, P1, ybk, rep from * to end. Turn and cross A and B to close side edge.
These 4 rows form the patt. Cont in patt until work measures 61cm (*24in*) from beg, ending with a 2nd or 4th patt row.
Shape top
Next row Dec one st at beg of row in A and B by using both strands tog and (K2 tog) twice, patt to end.
Next 3 rows Patt to end.
Rep last 4 rows 13 times more. 30 sts each in A and B.
Next row Using A and B tog, (inc in next st) twice, patt to end.
Next 3 rows Patt to end.
Rep last 4 rows 13 times more. 44 sts each in A and B. Cont in patt without shaping until work measures 61cm (*24in*) from last inc row. Cast off K2 tog along row.

To make up
Do not press. Join back shaping seam and 15cm (*6in*) of straight edges.

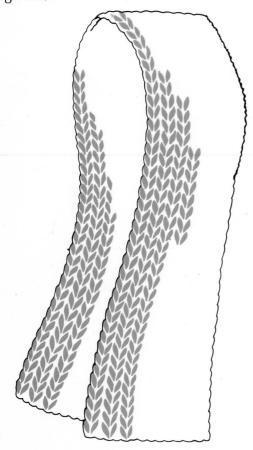

Hood worked in same yarn and colour throughout

44

GLOVES AND MITTENS

When knitting in rounds to produce gloves, mittens, socks and stockings, the most difficult part to master is the shaping required to give a perfect fit to fingers and thumbs or heels and toes. To do this correctly, at a given point in the pattern some of the stitches will be left unworked and held in abeyance on a stitch holder, while the first section is completed. then the unworked stitches will be picked up, together with additional stitches in some instances, to complete the work.

All these shaping details will be given out in full in any pattern and in the sequence in which they are to be worked. This chapter deals with gloves and mittens, which can be worked entirely in rounds without seaming, and includes a pair of mittens for a baby – ideal for a first attempt.

Both the designs given here begin at the wrist, where a firm ribbed edge is required to give a snug fit, and stocking stitch has been used for the main sections. They can both be made in one colour only but, as a way of using up oddments of the same quality yarn, we have worked the wrist and thumb of the mittens in a contrasting colour, and the wrist, thumb, and each finger of the gloves in a different colour, for a really jazzy, fun effect.

Babies' mittens
Size
To fit 9/18 months

Tension
28 sts and 36 rows to 10cm (*3.9in*) over st st worked on No.10 needles

Materials
1 × 25 grm ball of 4 ply yarn in main shade, A
Oddment of contrast colour, B
Set of 4 No.10 needles pointed at both ends
Set of 4 No.12 needles pointed at both ends

Mittens
Using set of 4 No.12 needles and B, cast on 36 sts, 12 on each of 3 needles. Mark beg of round with coloured thread.
1st round *K1, P1, rep from * to end.
Rep this round until work measures 2.5cm (*1in*) from beg. Break off B. Join in A. Change to set of 4 No.10 needles. Beg with a K round work in rounds of st st until work measures 4cm (*1½in*) from beg.
Shape thumb
Next round K17, pick up loop lying between sts and K tbl – called inc 1 –, K2, inc 1, K17.
Next round K to end.

Next round K17, inc 1, K4, inc 1, K17. 40 sts.
Next round K to end.
Cont inc in this way on next and every alt round until there are 46 sts.
Divide for thumb
Next round K18, sl next 10 sts on to holder and leave for thumb, turn and cast on 2 sts, turn and K18. 38 sts.
Cont in rounds of st st until work measures 10.5cm (*4¼in*) from beg.
Shape top
Next round K1, sl 1, K1, psso, K13, K2 tog, K2, sl 1, K1, psso, K13, K2 tog, K1. 34 sts.
Next round K to end.
Next round K1, sl 1, K1, psso, K11, K2 tog, K2, sl 1, K1, psso, K11, K2 tog, K1. 30 sts.
Cont dec 4 sts in this way on every alt round until 14 sts rem. Arrange sts on 2 needles and cast off tog or graft sts.
Thumb
Using set of 4 No.10 needles, B and with RS of work facing, arrange 10 thumb sts on 3 needles, then K up 2 sts from base of cast on sts. 12 sts. Cont in rounds of st st until thumb measures 2cm (*¾in*) from beg.
Shape top
Next round *K2 tog, rep from * to end. 6 sts.
Rep last round once more. Break off yarn, thread through rem sts, draw up and fasten off.

Children's gloves
Size
To fit 15.5cm (6¼in) all round hand

Tension
30 sts and 38 rows to 10cm (3.9in) over st st worked on No.11 needles.

Materials
1 × 25 grm ball of 4 ply in main shade, A
1 ball each, or oddments of contrast colours, B, C, D, E and F.
Set of 4 No.11 needles pointed at both ends
Set of 4 No.12 needles pointed at both ends

Gloves
Using set of 4 No.12 needles and B, cast on 48 sts and arrange on 3 needles. Mark beg of round with coloured thread. Work 6.5cm (2½in) rib as given for mittens. Break off B. Join in A. Change to set of 4 No.11 needles. Work 4 rounds st st.
Shape thumb
Next round K23, inc 1 as given for mittens, K2, inc 1, K23.
Work 3 rounds st st without shaping.
Next round K23, inc 1, K4, inc 1, K23.
Cont inc in this way on every foll 4th round until there are 60 sts, ending with 3 rounds st st after last inc round.

Divide for thumb
Next round K24, sl next 12 sts on to holder and leave for thumb, turn and cast on 2 sts, turn and K24. 50 sts.
Cont in st st until work measures 15cm (6in) from beg.
First finger
Next round Sl first 18 sts of round on to holder, join C to next st and K14, turn and cast on 2 sts, leave rem 18 sts on 2nd holder.
Cont in st st on these 16 sts until finger measures 5.5cm (2¼in) from beg.
Shape top
Next round K1, *K2 tog, K1, rep from * to end. 11 sts.
Next round K to end.
Next round K1, *K2 tog, rep from * to end. 6 sts.
Break off yarn, thread through rem sts, draw up and fasten off.
Second finger
Next round Using D and with RS of work facing, leave first 11 sts on holder and K across last 7 sts on first holder, K up 2 sts from base of first finger, K across next 7 sts on 2nd holder, turn and cast on 2 sts. 18 sts.
Cont in st st until finger measures 6.5cm (2½in) from beg.
Shape top
Next round *K1, K2 tog, rep from * to end. 12 sts.
Next round K to end.
Next round *K2 tog, rep from * to end. Complete as given for first finger.
Third finger
Next round Using E and with RS of work facing, leave first 6 sts on holder and K across last 5 sts on first holder, K up 2 sts from base of 2nd finger, K across next 5 sts on 2nd holder, turn and cast on 2 sts. 14 sts.
Cont in st st until finger measures 5.5cm (2¼in) from beg.
Shape top
Next round K1, *K2 tog, K1, rep from * to last st, K1. 10 sts.
Complete as given for 2nd finger.
Fourth finger
Next round Using F and with RS of work facing, K across rem 6 sts on first holder, K up 2 sts from base of 3rd finger, K across rem 6 sts on 2nd holder. 14 sts.
Cont in st st until finger measures 5cm (2in) from beg.
Shape top
Work as given for 3rd finger.
Thumb
Next round Using B and with RS of work facing, K across 12 thumb sts, then K up 4 sts from base of cast on sts. 16 sts.
Cont in st st until thumb measures 4.5cm (1¾in) from beg.
Shape top
Work as given for 1st finger.

SOCKS AND STOCKINGS

The previous chapter dealt with knitting in rounds to produce gloves and mittens, where the complete design can be worked without seaming. This chapter shows how simple it is to make socks and stockings, where the leg and foot can be worked in rounds and the stitches are divided at the heel and worked in rows, to produce the heel gusset shaping.

A plain basic sock design can be adapted in a variety of ways, either by using stripes for the leg and instep, keeping the top, heel and sole in a plain colour, or by introducing a patterned stitch for the leg and instep but, in this event, make sure that the pattern chosen will divide evenly into the total number of stitches cast on. Alternatively, men's socks look most effective when a small, two-colour motif is used as a clock on either side of the leg.

Here we give instructions for a pair of hard-wearing socks for children and a pair of beautiful, lacy stockings as a fashion accessory.

Socks
Sizes
To fit 18cm (7in) foot
Length of leg from top of heel, 20.5cm (8in)

Tension
32 sts and 40 rows to 10cm (3.9in) over st st worked on No.12 needles

Materials
4 × 25 grm balls of Wendy 4 ply Nylonised
Set of 4 No.12 needles pointed at both ends

Socks
Using set of 4 No.12 needles cast on 56 sts and arrange on 3 needles. Mark end of round.
1st round *K1, P1, rep from * to end.
Rep this round until work measures 4cm (1½in) from beg. Beg with a K round cont in rounds of st st until work measures 7.5cm (3in) from beg.
Shape leg
Next round K1, sl 1, K1, psso, K to last 3 sts, K2 tog, K1.
Work 4 rounds st st without shaping. Rep last 5 rounds until 42 sts rem. Cont without shaping until work measures 20.5cm (8in) from beg. Break off yarn.
Divide for heel
Next row Sl first and last 11 sts of round on to one needle, rejoin yarn and P to end. 22 sts.
Beg with a K row work 16 rows st st, ending with a P row.

Turn heel
Next row K14 sts, sl 1, K1, psso, turn.
Next row P7 sts, P2 tog, turn.
Next row K7 sts, sl 1, K1, psso, turn.
Next row P7 sts, P2 tog, turn.
Rep last 2 rows until all sts are on one needle.
Next round K4 sts, using 2nd needle K rem 4 heel sts, K up 10 sts down side of heel, using 3rd needle K across 20 sts of instep, using 4th needle K up 10 sts up other side of heel then K the first 4 sts on to this needle.

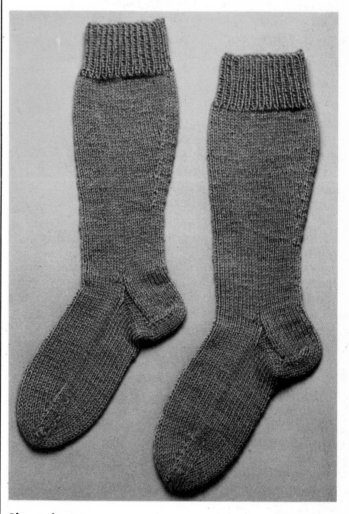

Shape instep
1st round K to end.
2nd round 1st needle K to last 3 sts, K2 tog, K1; 2nd needle K to end; 3rd needle K1, sl 1, K1, psso, K to end.
Rep last 2 rounds until 42 sts rem. Cont without shaping until work measures 10cm (4in) from where sts were picked up at heel.

Shape toe
1st round 1st needle K to last 3 sts, K2 tog, K1; 2nd needle K1, sl 1, K1, psso, K to last 3 sts, K2 tog, K1; 3rd needle K1, sl 1, K1, psso, K to end. Work 2 rounds st st without shaping. Rep last 3 rounds until 22 sts rem, then K across sts on 1st needle. Cast off sts tog or graft sts.

Lacy stockings
Sizes
To fit 21.5[24]cm ($8\frac{1}{2}$[$9\frac{1}{2}$]in) foot
Leg length to top of heel, 71cm (28in), adjustable
The figures in brackets [] refer to the 24cm ($9\frac{1}{2}$in) size only

Tension
28 sts and 30 rows to 10cm (3.9in) over patt worked on No.5 needles

Materials
3 × 1 oz balls Jaeger Faerie-Spun 2 ply
Set of 4 No.6 needles pointed at both ends
Set of 4 No.7 needles pointed at both ends
Set of 4 No.9 needles pointed at both ends
Set of 4 No.10 needles pointed at both ends

Stockings
Using set of 4 No.6 needles cast on 68 sts very loosely and arrange on 3 needles. Mark beg of round with coloured thread. Work 8 rounds K1, P1 rib. Commence patt.
1st round *(K2 tog) 3 times, yfwd, (K1, yfwd) 5 times, (K2 tog tbl) 3 times, rep from * to end.
2nd and 3rd rounds K to end.
4th round P to end.
These 4 rounds form patt, noting that sts should be arranged on needles as required. Rep 4 patt rounds 17 times more, adjusting length at this point and noting that work will stretch to 81.5cm (32in). Change to set of 4 No.7 needles and rep patt rounds 16 times. Change to set of 4 No.9 needles and rep patt rounds 16 times. Change to set of 4 No.10 needles and rep patt rounds 8 times.
Shape heel
Next round K15, K into front and back of next st – called inc 1 –, K1, patt 34 sts, inc 1, K16.
Next round K18, patt 34, K18.
Next round K16, inc 1, K1, patt 34, inc 1, K17.
Next round K19, patt 34, K19.
Keeping heel sts in st st and centre 34 sts in patt, cont to inc in this way on next and every alt round until there are 80 sts, then work 4 rounds without shaping.
Next round Still keeping centre 34 sts in patt, K21, K2 tog, patt 34, sl 1, K1, psso, K21.
Next round K22, patt 34, K22.
Next round K20, K2 tog, patt 34, sl 1, K1, psso, K20.
Next round K21, patt 34, K21.
Cont dec in this way on next and every alt round

until 56 sts rem, then cont without shaping until foot measures 18[20.5]cm (7[8]in) from centre of heel, or required length less 4cm ($1\frac{1}{2}$in).
Shape toe
Next round K12, K2 tog, sl 1, K1, psso, K24, K2 tog, sl 1, K1, psso, K12.
Next round K to end.
Next round K11, K2 tog, sl 1, K1, psso, K22, K2 tog, sl 1, K1, psso, K11.
Next round K to end.
Cont dec in this way on next and every alt round until 20 sts rem. K sts from 3rd needle on to 1st needle and graft sts.

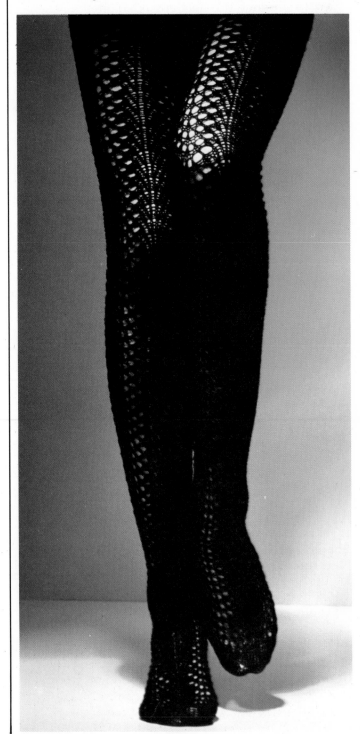

MOTIFS IN ROUNDS

We have already explained earlier how knitting in rounds produces seamless, tubular fabric. This section deals with knitting in rounds to form flat, circular medallion shapes, which have a variety of uses.

Fine cotton yarn and lacy stitches can be used to make delicate table mats, or a thick cotton yarn and a simple stitch can be used for a hard-wearing rug. Oddments of double knitting yarns can also be utilized for colourful, circular cushions or afghans.

Simple hexagonal medallion
Using set of 4 needles cast on 6 sts, having 2 sts on each of 3 needles. Join needles into a round and K all sts tbl to keep centre flat. Commence patt.

1st round *K into front then into back of next st – called inc 1 –, rep from * to end. 12 sts.
2nd round *Inc 1, K1, rep from * to end. 18 sts.
3rd round *Inc 1, K2, rep from * to end. 24 sts.
4th round *Inc 1, K3, rep from * to end. 30 sts.
5th round *Inc 1, K4, rep from * to end. 36 sts.
6th round *Inc 1, K5, rep from * to end. 42 sts.
Cont inc 6 sts in this way on every round until medallion is required size. Cast off loosely.

To make a cushion cover
Size
40.5cm (16in) diameter

Tension
24 sts and 32 rows to 10cm (3.9in) over st st worked on No.8 needles

Materials
1 × 50grm ball each of Jaeger Spiral Spun in 4 contrast colours, A, B, C and D
Set of 4 No.8 needles
One No.8 circular Twin Pin
40·5cm (16in) diameter circular cushion pad

Cover
Work as given for hexagonal medallion, working 2 rounds each in A, B, C and D throughout and changing to circular Twin Pin when required, until work measures 40.5cm (16in) diameter. Cast off loosely. Make another hexagonal medallion in same way.

To make up
Press each piece under a damp cloth with a warm iron. With RS facing, join medallions tog leaving an opening large enough to insert cushion pad. Turn RS out. Insert pad and complete seam. Sew one button to centre of each side, if required.

To make a circular lace table mat
Size
25.5cm (10in) in diameter

Materials
1 × 20grm ball of Twilley's Twenty
Set of 4 No.12 needles

Table mat
Using set of 4 No.12 needles cast on 8 sts, having 2 sts on 1st needle and 3 sts each on 2nd and 3rd needles. Join needles into a round and K all sts tbl to keep centre flat. Commence patt.

1st round *Yfwd, K1, rep from * to end. 16 sts.
2nd and every alt round K to end.
3rd round *Yfwd, K2, rep from * to end. 24 sts.
5th round *Yfwd, K3, rep from * to end. 32 sts.
7th round *Yfwd, K4, rep from * to end. 40 sts.
9th round *Yfwd, K5, rep from * to end. 48 sts.
11th round *Yfwd, K6, rep from* to end. 56 sts.
13th round *Yfwd, K1, K2 tog, y2rn, K2 tog, K2, rep from * to end.
Note that on next and subsequent rounds where y2rn has been worked on previous round, you must K1 then P1 into y2rn.
15th round *Yfwd, K8, rep from * to end.
17th round *Yfwd, K9, rep from * to end.

19th round *Yfwd, K1, K2 tog, y2rn, (K2 tog) twice, y2rn, K2 tog, K1, rep from * to end.

21st round *Yfwd, K11, rep from * to end.

23rd round *Yfwd, K12, rep from * to end.

25th round *Yfwd, K5, K2 tog, y2rn, K2 tog, K4, rep from * to end.

27th round *Yfwd, K4, K2 tog, y2rn, (K2 tog) twice, y2rn, K2 tog, K2, rep from * to end.

29th round *Yfwd, K7, K2 tog, y2rn, K2 tog, K4, rep from * to end.

31st round *Yfwd, K1, yfwd, K2 tog, K3, K2 tog, y2rn, (K2 tog) twice, y2rn, K2 tog, K2, rep from * to end.

33rd round *Yfwd, K1, K2 tog, yfwd, K2 tog, K4, K2 tog, y2rn, K2 tog, K4, rep from * to end.

35th round *Yfwd, K1, yfwd, K2, yfwd, K1, yfwd, K2 tog, K11, rep from * to end.

37th round *Yfwd, K2, yfwd, K1, K2 tog, yfwd, K1, K2 tog, yfwd, K2 tog, K10, rep from * to end.

39th round *Yfwd, K1, yfwd, K2 tog, K1, yfwd, K2 tog, K1, yfwd, K2 tog, yfwd, K1, yfwd, (K2 tog) twice, y2rn, (K2 tog) twice, y2rn, K2 tog, K1, rep from * to end.

41st round *Yfwd, K2 tog, K1, yfwd, K1, K2 tog, yfwd, K2 tog, K1, yfwd, (K2 tog) twice, yfwd, K2 tog, K8, rep from * to end.

43rd round *Yfwd, K1, K2 tog, yfwd, (K2 tog) twice, yfwd, K1, K2 tog, yfwd, K1, K2 tog, yfwd, K2 tog, K7, rep from * to end.

45th round *Yfwd, K1, yfwd, K2 tog, K1, yfwd, K2 tog, K1, yfwd, K2 tog, K1, yfwd, K2 tog, yfwd, K1, yfwd, (K2 tog) twice, y2rn, K2 tog, K2, rep from * to end.

47th round *(Yfwd, K2 tog, K1) 3 times, yfwd, K1, K2 tog, yfwd, K2, yfwd, K2 tog, yfwd, K2 tog, K5, rep from * to end.

49th round *Yfwd, (K2 tog) twice, yfwd, K2 tog, (K1, yfwd, K2 tog) 3 times, K1, yfwd, K2, yfwd, K2 tog, K4, rep from * to end.

51st round *Yfwd, (K2 tog) twice, (yfwd, K2 tog, K1) 5 times, yfwd, K2 tog, K3, rep from * to end.

53rd round *Yfwd, (K2 tog) twice, (yfwd, K2 tog, K1) 5 times, yfwd, K2 tog, K2, rep from * to end.

55th round *Yfwd, K3 tog, K1, (yfwd, K2 tog, K1) 5 times, yfwd, K2 tog, K1, rep from * to end.

57th round *Yfwd, (K2 tog) twice, (yfwd, K2 tog, K1) 5 times, yfwd, K2 tog, rep from * to end.

58th round As 2nd.

Cast off loosely.

Edging

Using 2 No.12 needles cast on 9 sts.

1st row Sl 1, K1, yfwd, K2 tog, K1, yfwd, K2 tog, yfwd, K2.

2nd and every alt row K to end.

3rd row Sl 1, K1, yfwd, K2 tog, K2, yfwd, K2 tog, yfwd, K2.

5th row Sl 1, K1, yfwd, K2 tog, K3, yfwd, K2 tog, yfwd, K2.

7th row Sl 1, K1, yfwd, K2 tog, K1, yfwd, K2 tog, K1, yfwd, K2 tog, yfwd, K2.

9th row Sl 1, K1, yfwd, K2 tog, K2, yfwd, K2 tog, K5.

10th row Cast off 4 sts, K to end.

Rep 1st to 10th rows until edging fits round table mat. Cast off.

To make up

Press under a damp cloth with a warm iron. Sew cast on edge of edging to cast off edge. Sew round table mat. Press.

More motifs

The same technique which produces flat, circular shapes can be used to form other geometric medallions, such as triangles, squares and octagons. It is simply a matter of working out how many sides you need and spacing the shaping on each side to increase the size of the medallion.

Because you are working on 3 needles with numbers of stitches which will not always divide by 3, the number of stitches cast on to each needle will not always be equal. When the number of stitches become too many to hold comfortably on 3 needles, change to a circular Twin Pin. Always mark the beginning of the round with a coloured marker and, if you find it easier, cast on the full number of stitches on to one needle and knit each stitch through the back of the loop, before dividing them on to 3 needles.

Triangular medallion

Using set of 4 needles cast on 6 sts, having 2 sts on each needle. Join needles into a round and K all sts tbl to keep centre flat.

1st round *K into front then into back of next st – called inc 1 –, rep from * to end. 12 sts.

2nd round *Inc 1, K2, inc 1, rep from * to end. 18 sts.
3rd round * Inc 1, K4, inc 1, rep from * to end. 24 sts.
4th round *Inc 1, K6, inc 1, rep from * to end. 30 sts.

5th round *Inc 1, K8, inc 1, rep from * to end. 36 sts.
Cont inc 6 sts in this way on every round until medallion is required size. Cast off loosely.

Square medallion

Using set of 4 needles cast on 8 sts, having 2 sts on 1st needle and 3 sts each on 2nd and 3rd needles. Join needles into a round and K all sts tbl to keep centre flat. Commence patt.
1st round *K into front then into back of next st – called inc 1 –, rep from * to end. 16 sts.

2nd and every alt round K to end.
3rd round *Inc 1, K2, inc 1, rep from * to end. 24 sts.
5th round *Inc 1, K4, inc 1, rep from * to end. 32 sts.
7th round *Inc 1, K6, inc 1, rep from * to end. 40 sts.
8th round K to end.
Cont inc 8 sts in this way on next and every alt round until medallion is required size. Cast off loosely.

Octagonal medallion

Cast on and work 1st and 2nd rounds as given for square medallion.
3rd round As 1st. 32 sts.
4th and 5th rounds K to end.
6th round *Inc 1, K2, inc 1, rep from * to end. 48 sts.
7th and 8th rounds K to end.
9th round *Inc 1, K4, inc 1, rep from * to end. 64 sts.
10th and 11th rounds K to end.

12th round *Inc 1, K6, inc 1, rep from * to end. 80 sts.
13th and 14th rounds K to end.
Cont inc 16 sts in this way on next and every foll 3rd round until medallion is required size. Cast off loosely.

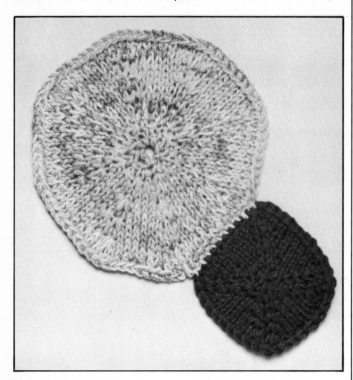

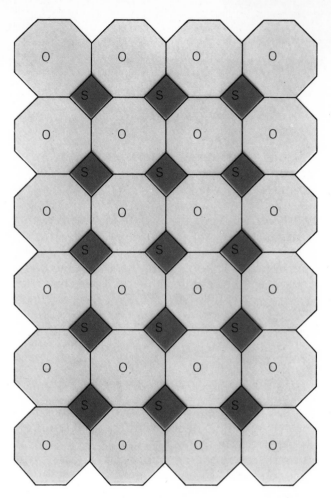

24 octagonal medallions = O
15 square medallions = S

Bath mat
Size
51cm (*20in*) wide by 76cm (*30in*) long

Tension
Each octagonal medallion measures 12.5cm (*5in*) diameter worked on No.8 needles and using 2 strands of yarn

Materials
6 × 50grm balls of Twilley's Stalite in main shade, A
2 × 50grm balls of contrast colour, B
Set of 4 No.8 needles

Note
Yarn is used double throughout

Bath mat
Using set of 4 No.8 needles and A, make 24 octagonal medallions, working 14 rounds only for each one.
Using set of 4 No.8 needles and B, make 15 square medallions, working 8 rounds only for each one.

To make up
Press each piece under a damp cloth with a warm iron. Join medallions as shown in diagram. Press.

Another way of using instructions for the bath mat would be to use up oddments of double knitting yarn in as many colours as possible to make a cheerful and practical pram rug.

ACHIEVING EXPERTISE
ADJUSTING PATTERNS

Making amendments to an existing pattern is quite an easy matter, provided you take the time to work out the correct positioning of these alterations before commencing any knitting. A plain cardigan can be given an entirely different look by the addition of picot edgings instead of ribbed edges. Slimming bust darts may be incorporated into a basic jersey to achieve a better fit for the fuller figure. With a little care even the proportions of armholes and shoulders may be altered to suit your own individual requirements. Once you have the know-how, it is a simple matter to apply it and so gain even greater satisfaction from your knitting.

Edges

With knitting, the same basic shape can always be worked in a variety of stitches (see Bobble Stitches). Similarly, an existing pattern for a plain jersey or cardigan does not always need to have ribbed edges. Instead, try a picot edging on the welt, cuffs and neck-band of a jersey, or even the front bands of a cardigan. On a straight edge first check the number of stitches for each piece of the original pattern, after the ribbing has been completed. This will be the correct number of stitches to cast on to begin the picot edging. Beginning with a knit row work the required depth for a turned-under hem, say 2.5cm (1 inch), ending with a purl row. On the next row make a picot edge by knitting two stitches together, then bring the yarn forward and over the needle to make a stitch and continue in this way to the end of the row, making sure that you end with the correct number of stitches. Beginning with a purl row work one row less than the hemline to complete the edging, then either continue in stocking stitch or pattern as directed in the instructions, remembering to adjust the total length which will have taken the ribbing into account.

Where these picot edges need to be joined at right angles, such as the corner where the hem or neckband meet the front bands on a cardigan, these edges must be mitred to fit correctly. To do this simply increase one stitch at the joining edge on the 2nd and every following row, work the picot row, then decrease one stitch at the same edge on every row for the completion of the edging, until the original number of cast on stitches remains.

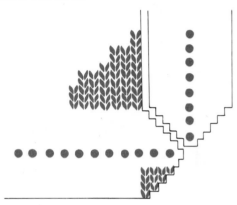

Another alternative is to work turned-under stocking stitch hems or facing in place of ribbing. To do this on a straight hem, work as for the picot edging but end with a knit row, then instead of working the next row as a picot row, knit each stitch through the back of the loop to form the hemline. From this point you can continue in stocking stitch or pattern as required.

To use this method for edges which need to be joined at right angles, you must again mitre the corners where the hem or neckband meet the front band.

As an example, say the original number of cast on stitches for the main section is 54 and an additional 8 stitches are needed for the front band, making a total of 62 stitches for the full width. If you are working a turned-under hem of 9 rows and are increasing one stitch at the front edge for the mitred corner on the 2nd and every following row, you will increase

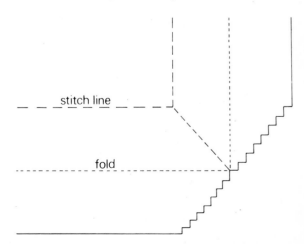

lower front edge

stitch line

fold

8 stitches on this edge and therefore need to cast on 8 stitches less than the total given number, in this case 54 stitches in place of 62 stitches. Work the turned-under hem and the hemline row, increasing as shown, then continue increasing one stitch at the same edge on every row until you have a total of 70 stitches, which will give 8 extra stitches for the turned-under facing. Slip the last stitch of the main fabric on every right side row to form a fold line. When turned in the increased stitches on the hems and front facing will join into a neat mitred corner.

Bust darts

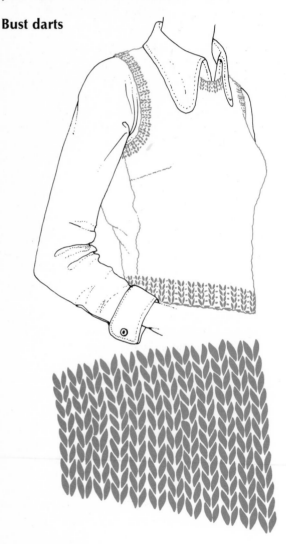

For the fuller figure, slimming bust darts can be incorporated into a plain stocking stitch jersey, to give extra depth across the bust without altering the underarm length of the garment.

Measure the exact underarm position for the darts, which should commence between 4.0cm (1½ inch) and 6.5cm (2½ inch) below the beginning of the armhole shaping. The fuller the figure the greater the number of rows required for shaping the darts and the 12 row example given here is suitable for a 96.5/101.5cm (38/40 inch) bust size. Work the front of the jersey until the position for the bust darts is reached, ending with a knit row, then commence the dart shaping.

1st row P to last 5 sts, turn.
2nd row Sl 1, K to last 5 sts, turn.
3rd row Sl 1, P to last 10 sts, turn.
4th row Sl 1, K to last 10 sts, turn.
5th row Sl 1, P to last 15 sts, turn.
6th row Sl 1, K to last 15 sts, turn.
7th row Sl 1, P to last 20 sts, turn.
8th row Sl 1, K to last 20 sts, turn.
9th row Sl 1, P to last 25 sts, turn.
10th row Sl 1, K to last 25 sts, turn.
11th row Sl 1, P to end of row.
12th row K to end of row, closing holes between groups of 5 sts by picking up loop under the 5th st of each group and K this loop tog with next st on left hand needle.

This completes the dart shaping. Continue until the position for the armhole shaping is reached, remembering to measure on the side seam and not over the bust darts.

Amending proportions of armholes and shoulders

For a narrow shouldered figure it is a simple matter to amend underarm and shoulder shaping. If this is required, first work out the exact number of extra stitches which need to be decreased, based on the tension given. Mark these alterations on the pattern so that you can work the complete armhole and shoulder section without further calculations.

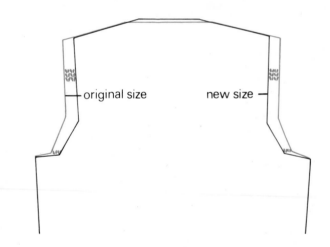

original size   new size

As an example, say you need to lose a further 8 stitches on the back of a jersey, to achieve a narrower fit. Decrease half of this total at the underarm point, casting off 2 extra stitches at each side, then work 2 more decreasing rows to lose the remaining 4 stitches, thus arriving at the required total. At the shoulder line, cast off 3 stitches less than the given number on the last 2 rows and allow for 2 stitches less than the given number in the remaining centre back neck stitches. When working the front remember to make the same adjustments at the underarm and shoulder line and allow for 2 stitches less than the given number in the remaining centre front neck stitches. The top of the sleeve shaping must also be amended to match the underarm shaping.

ADJUSTING LENGTHS

With a little care and patience, horizontal hems can quite easily be lengthened or shortened, to contend with fashion changes or a growing family. Skirt, bodice or cuff lengths can be altered in this way and when making children's garments, it is always useful to buy one or two extra balls of yarn in the same dye lot to put aside for the day when such adjustments can be made quickly and cheaply instead of wasting a whole garment.

When shortening a garment no extra yarn is required – in fact, a quantity of the original yarn will become available. Instead of wasting this, it can be wound into

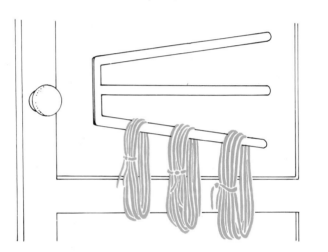

hanks and hand washed, then hung up to dry to remove the kinks. If a design needs to be lengthened, however, extra yarn is needed but it does not necessarily have to be the original yarn. Oddments of the same ply can be used to add a striped hem to a skirt or welt of a jersey and if the neckband is also unpicked and re-knitted in the same stripes, the whole

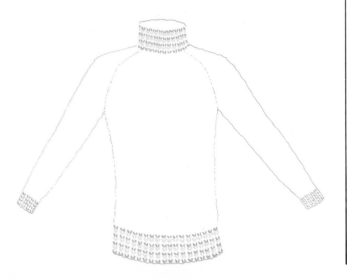

effect will give a completely new look to the garment. Before beginning any adjustment, check the garment to find the best position for the lengthening or shortening. As an example, if the body or sleeves of a jersey need lengthening and it already has a ribbed welt or cuff 5cm (2in) long, then the work must be picked up and re-knitted above the welt or cuff. If a skirt needs shortening and it has a turned under hem, the adjustment must be made above the existing hemline. It is not advisable to attempt these alterations on a fabric which has used a very complicated stitch unless you are quite certain that you will be able to pick up the original number of stitches in their correct sequence but stocking stitch, garter stitch or any simple pattern can be altered quite easily in this way.

Lengthening a garment
Make sure that you have some additional yarn to hand. Check the garment and mark both the position where the garment is to be unpicked and a further point 2·5cm (1in) above this, then count the exact

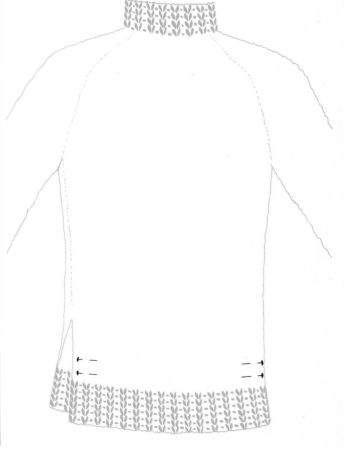

number of rows between each point. Prepare the work by unpicking any hems and side seams to approximately 5cm (2in) above the last marked point, to allow for freedom in manipulating the needles when re-knitting, taking great care not to cut the fabric.

With the right side of the fabric facing and the correct needle size, pick up a loop with a needle at the marked

point above the required adjustment point, and pull this up tightly. Cut through this loop and carefully pull the fabric apart until two sets of stitches are

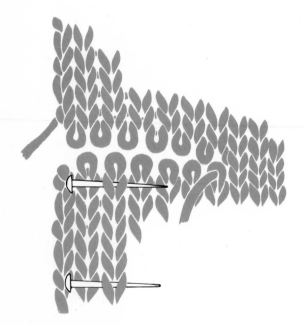

exposed. Pull the cut end of yarn again tightly and cut it, easing the fabric apart. Continue in this way until the fabric is in two separate sections, then pick up the stitches of the main section with a knitting needle, making sure that the original number of stitches are on the needle and that each stitch is lying in the correct direction and has not become twisted.

Unravel the remaining yarn, winding it into a neat ball ready to use for re-knitting. **. Join in the yarn at the beginning of the row and continue knitting for the required number of rows calculated between the two marked points, then continue knitting to give the extra length required. Complete the garment by working the original number of rows in ribbing for a welt or cuff, or by working the exact number of rows used for the original hem on a skirt. Cast off very loosely then work any other sections in the same way. Re-seam any edges or hems and check whether the yarn used can be pressed and proceed accordingly.

Shortening a garment

Check and prepare the garment and work as given for lengthening to **. Join in the yarn at the beginning of the row and continue knitting for the required number of rows calculated between the two marked points. Cast off very loosely and finish the garment as given for lengthening.

Words of warning!

When unpicking seams great care must be taken not to cut the actual fabric but only the yarn used for sewing. Never rush this stage but gently ease the seam apart until you are quite sure which is the exact strand to be cut.

Once the fabric has been divided into two separate sections, check at which end of the work the un-picked yarn finishes, to ascertain whether the next row to be knitted is a right or wrong side row. Only then pick up the stitches with a knitting needle, making sure that each stitch lies in the correct position and that the needle point is facing the correct end, ready to rejoin the yarn. Using a double ended needle can help at this stage. Don't panic if a few of the stitches begin to run! These can quite easily be picked up to the correct depth, using a crochet hook. Because the yarn has already been knitted up once, it will not re-knit to such an even fabric as the original. If the yarn does not require pressing but looks rather uneven, simply wash and dry the garment when it is completed in the recommended way, to even out the fabric.

TUCKS AND TRIMS

The more you know about knitting, the more fascinating it becomes. Once you have mastered the basic techniques, it is the small, finishing touches which make all the difference to any design.

This chapter deals with four ideas which can be applied to almost any basic design – and they are fun to work. Two of these trimmings are worked in with the actual knitting, one is worked as part of the making up and the last can be applied when the garment is completed.

Try incorporating one of these suggestions to lift your knitting from the mundane to the couture class, setting your own individual stamp on any design.

Tucks

Horizontal tucks are easy to work and can be incorporated into the skirt or bodice of almost any plain garment. They look their most effective when worked in stocking stitch with a picot edge – imagine the skirt of a litle girl's dress embellished with two or three layers of tucks, or the yoke of a plain jersey finished with two rows of tucking at underarm level. Remember that these will use extra yarn over and above the quantity stated and allow for one or two more balls before beginning any design.

To work horizontal tucks Mark the position on the pattern where the tucks are to be incorporated and work to this point, ending with a purl row. Mark each end of the last row with a coloured thread. Depending on the depth of tuck required, work a further 5 to 9 rows in stocking stitch, ending with a knit row. On the next row either knit all the stitches through the back of the loops to mark the foldline of the tuck, or work a row of eyelet holes by knitting 2 together, then bringing the yarn forward to make a stitch, all along the row. Beginning with a knit row work a further 4 to 8 rows stocking stitch, ending with a purl row. Using a spare needle, go back to the row marked with coloured thread and pick up the correct number of stitches all along the row on the wrong side of the work, so that the points of the spare needle and the left hand needle holding the stitches are both facing in the same direction. Hold the spare needle behind the left hand needle and knit to the end of the row, working one stitch from the left hand needle together with one stitch from the spare needle. This forms one tuck and can be repeated as required.

To work vertical tucks These can be used to highlight any dart shapings on a design and, again, look their best against a plain stocking stitch background. The continuity of the tucks must be kept throughout the whole length of the design and an additional 2 stitches should be cast on at the beginning for each tuck required. As an example, if the front of a skirt has two dart shapings which begin below hip level, read through the pattern to ascertain the place in the row where these shapings are first worked and allow 2 extra stitches on the right hand side of the first dart and 2 extra stitches on the left hand side of the second dart. Cast on 4 extra stitches at the beginning of the skirt and work as follows:–

1st row K to within 2 sts of the position for the first dart, sl the next 2 sts P-wise keeping the yarn at the back of the work, work the first dart shaping, K to and then work the second dart shaping, sl the next 2 sts P-wise keeping the yarn at the back of the work, K to end.

2nd row P to end.

These 2 rows form the pattern and are repeated throughout, even when the dart shaping has been completed.

Lapped seams

These are worked at the making up stage and are referred to in dressmaking as run and fell seams, such as you would see on a man's shirt. To look most effective they should be worked on a smooth fabric, such as stocking stitch. As an example, a plain raglan sleeved jersey would look highly original where lapped seams are used to join the side, sleeve and raglan seams.

To work lapped seams Depending on the position of the seam and the yarn being used, cast on an additional 2 or 3 stitches for each vertical seam and work a further 3 or 4 rows for each horizontal seam. When the pieces are completed, press as given in the instructions. Now place the two pieces to be joined with right sides together, with the underneath piece extending about 1.5cm ($\frac{1}{2}$in) beyond the edge of the upper piece. Work a firm back stitch seam along this edge. Turn the pieces to the right side and carefully back stitch the loose edge of the seam through both thicknesses of the fabric, about 1.5cm ($\frac{1}{2}$in) from the first seam. Press seam.

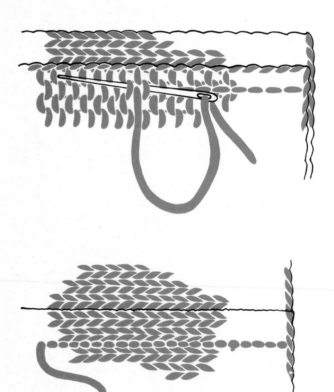

Piping cords

As children, most knitters will have experimented with French knitting, or 'dolly' knitting. The round piping produced by this method can be thick or thin, depending on the yarn used and looks most attractive as a straight length of trimming sewn round the neck of a jersey, or on either side of the front bands of a cardigan. Alternatively, separate lengths can be worked, then wound round and stitched to form flat, circular motifs. These motifs could be stitched at random on the bodice of a child's dress or used in a band above the welt and cuffs on a plain jersey. Any oddments of yarn will do – but think how colourful this piping would look in random yarn. The possibilities are endless and fun to work.

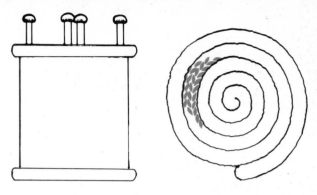

How to work piping cord Either purchase a 'dolly' bobbin or use a wooden cotton reel to make a bobbin, spacing 4 panel pins with heads evenly and firmly round the centre hole at one end of the reel. Thread the yarn to be used through the centre hole of the bobbin or reel, from the opposite end to the panel pins, leaving an end free. Working in a clockwise direction throughout, wind the yarn round each of the 4 pins and work as follows:–

1st round Take the yarn once more round all 4 pins without looping it round the pins and placing the yarn above the first round, using a fine crochet hook lift the first loop over the second strand of yarn from the outside to the centre and over the pin head, repeat on all 4 pins.

Continue repeating this round until the piping is the required length, pulling the cord down through the centre hole of the bobbin or reel as it is formed. When the cord is the required length, break off the yarn leaving an end, thread this end through a blunt ended wool needle, insert needle through loop on pin and lift loop off pin, repeat on all 4 pins, pull up yarn and fasten off securely.

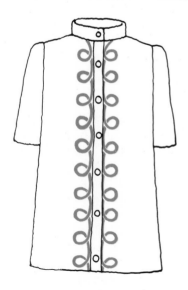

PLEATS

A swirling, pleated skirt is a most useful and adaptable knitted garment, which can form the basis of a mix-and-match wardrobe of skirt, jersey, jacket and hat all worked in toning colours and contrasting patterns or stitch textures.

The method of working the pleats can be a simple, mock version or the inverted type, both of which give such a graceful swing to any skirt. They can be knitted vertically in stripes to form an even more striking variation and this is another ideal way of using up oddments of the same thickness of yarn, to make a warm and practical skirt for a toddler. Use a yarn which will retain its shape without dropping, such as a pure wool crepe, for all versions.

Planning pleats

The mock version is the most economical and is based on the width which is required round the hem of the skirt. Use this measurement and the tension obtained with the yarn chosen to calculate the number of stitches which must be cast on. This number must be divisible by 8, so adjust the total if necessary by adding a few more stitches.

For inverted pleats, work out the required waist measurement and multiply this by three, to arrive at the correct hem measurement. Use this measurement to determine the number of stitches to be cast on at the hem, again based on the tension obtained. This number must be divisible by 12, plus 8, and the total can be adjusted by adding a few more stitches.

For vertical pleats you must measure the length required from waist to hem, plus an allowance of approximately 2.5cm (1in) for a turned under hem. Use this measurement and the tension obtained to arrive at how many stitches must be cast on, having an even number of stitches, and work from side edge to side edge.

Mock pleats

These can be worked on two needles, either in two separate sections to form the back and the front of the skirt with a seam at each side, or in one piece to give the total width, having a centre back seam.
Cast on the required number of stitches.
1st row (RS) *K7, P1, rep from * to end.
2nd row K4, *P1, K7, rep from * to last 4 sts, P1, K3.
These 2 rows form the pattern and are repeated for the required length. Cast off.
To work mock pleats without a seam, use a circular needle and cast on the required number of stitches.
1st round *K7, P1, rep from * to end of round.
2nd round P3, K1, *P7, K1, rep from * to last 4 sts, P4.
These 2 rounds form the pattern and are repeated for

the required length. Cast off.
To complete the skirt, cut a waist length of elastic and

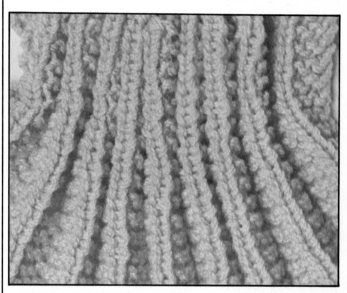

sew inside the waist edge, using casing stitch. As an alternative, cast on the required number of stitches to form a separate waistband, allowing sufficient extra stitches for ease in pulling the skirt on and off, and work 5.5cm (2¼in) st st. Cast off. Sew waistband to waist edge of skirt, fold in half to WS and sl st down. Thread elastic through waistband and fasten off.

Inverted pleats

This method requires a set of 4 needles pointed at both ends to close the pleats. Because of the total number of stitches required, it is easier to work the skirt in two separate sections, having a seam at each side.

Using two of the needles, cast on the required number of stitches.

1st row (RS) *K8, P1, K2, sl 1 P-wise, rep from * to last 8 sts, K8.

2nd row *P11, K1, rep from * to last 8 sts, P8.

These 2 rows form the pattern and are repeated for the required length, less 5cm (*2in*) for the waistband. To close the pleats you will need to use all 4 needles.

Last row (waist edge) K4, *sl next 4 sts on to first extra needle, sl next 4 sts on to 2nd extra needle, place first extra needle behind 2nd extra needle and hold both extra needles behind the left hand needle, (K tog one st from all 3 needles) 4 times, rep from * to last 4 sts, K4.

Cast off.

To complete the skirt join seams, overlapping 4 sts at beg of row over 4 sts at end of row to complete pleating. Make a separate waistband and complete as given for mock pleats.

Vertical pleats

This method is worked on two needles to a length which will give twice the required waist measurement, having one seam at the centre-back. If you are working in stripes, carry the yarn not in use loosely up the side edge until it is required again. For neatness, this edge will become the waist edge, so that the strands of yarn can be sewn inside the waistband when the skirt is completed. Cast on the required number of stitches, allowing approximately 2.5cm (*1in*) extra for the hem.

1st row (RS) K to end.

2nd row P to end.

Rep 1st and 2nd rows 5 times more, then 1st row once more.

14th row P across sts for hem, *yrn, P2 tog, rep from * to end.

Rep 1st and 2nd rows twice more, then 1st row once more.

20th row P across sts for hem, K tbl all sts to end.

These 20 rows form the pattern. Continue until work measures twice the required waist measurement, ending with a 20th row. Cast off.

To complete the skirt, join cast on edge to cast off edge to form centre back seam. Turn hem at lower edge to WS and sl st down. Tack pleats in position along waist edge, folding each pleat at picot row to form inner fold and at knit row to form outer fold. Make separate waistband and complete as given for mock pleats.

Toddler's striped skirt

Size

To fit 51cm (*20in*) waist, adjustable
Length, 25cm (*10in*)

Tension

30 sts and 36 rows to 10cm (*3.9in*) over st st worked on No.10 needles

Materials

4 × 25grm balls of 4 ply Crepe in main shade, A
2 balls of contrast colour, B
One pair No.10 needles
Waist length of elastic

Skirt

Using No.10 needles and A, cast on 76 sts. Keeping 8 sts at lower edge for hem, work as given for vertical pleats, working first 14 patt rows in A and next 6 rows in B throughout, until work measures 101.5cm (*40in*) from beg, or required length. Cast off.

Waistband

Using No.10 needles and A, cast on 180 sts. Work 5cm (*2in*) st st. Cast off.

To make up

Press as directed on ball band. Complete as given for vertical pleats.

DESIGNING
BASIC TECHNIQUES

Designing your own clothes can be the most rewarding of all aspects of hand knitting. Details have already been given in previous chapters of the important part tension plays in any designing, together with the compositions of various yarns and the structure of numerous stitches. These three factors form the basis of all successful hand knitting designs.

Before you can begin any design you need to know the exact measurements of the garment you have in mind. Don't tackle anything too complicated for a first attempt – something as simple as the skirt shown here would be ideal, as it does not entail a great deal of shaping.

Each section must be calculated exactly to the required width and length, based on the tension obtained with any given yarn and needle size. To these measurements you must then add an additional number of stitches which will give sufficient tolerance for ease of movement and also provide multiples of stitches which will work out correctly over the pattern which has been chosen. An overall tolerance of 5cm (2 in) is sufficient for most garments, although something as bulky as a casual jacket which is intended to be worn over another garment will obviously require more tolerance than a sleekly-fitting fine ply jersey.

Measurements

For something as simple as a skirt, five accurate measurements are required.
a The actual waist measurement in width.
b The actual hip measurement in width.
c The actual measurement from waist to hip in depth.
d The actual measurement from hipline to hemline in depth.
e The actual width of hemline at lowest point.

The exact shape of the required skirt must then be determined. It can have almost straight sides, with the hem and hip measurement being almost the same, then gently curving from the hipline into the waist. If a flared hemline is required, this must be shaped into the hips, before shaping from the hips to the waist. Whatever the style of skirt you choose, it can be worked in two separate sections, the back and front being exactly the same. To this actual measurement you must now add the overall tolerance required to give an easy-fitting garment, allowing half this additional measurement for the front and half for the back.

At this stage, decide whether you want a separate waistband or the waist edge knitted in with the main fabric and finished with casing stitch worked over

elastic. If the skirt is to be very slim-fitting you will also need to make provision for a zip fastener on the side seam. Plan the sort of hem you require and take this into your calculations – most skirts hang better with a turned under hem, so you will need to add an additional 2.5cm (1 in) to the length.

Tension

You must now decide on the type of yarn you wish to use and the tension obtained on needles of your choice, which will produce a smooth, even fabric, neither too hard and tight nor too loose and open. Work a sample swatch, using a basic stitch such as stocking stitch to begin with, and measure this accurately. If you do not measure this sample exactly, or feel that half a stitch difference to 2.5cm (1 in) is unimportant, you will not be able to produce the exact shape you require. In printed patterns this procedure has already been overcome, as the yarn is specified and a guide to the needle size has been given. When designing for yourself, however, you are no longer limited to the tension which has been obtained by the original designer but can decide for yourself what tension will produce the effect you require.

Making a diagram

Now that you have established the measurements needed and the tension which will produce the type of fabric you have in mind, you must put all this information down on paper in the form of a diagram.

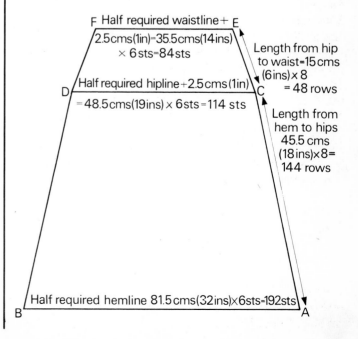

F Half required waistline+ E
2.5cms(1in)=35.5cms(14ins) × 6sts=84sts

Length from hip to waist=15cms (6ins)× 8 = 48 rows

D Half required hipline+2.5cms(1in) C =48.5cms(19ins) × 6sts=114 sts

Length from hem to hips 45.5 cms (18ins)×8= 144 rows

B Half required hemline 81.5cms(32ins)×6sts=192sts A

This does not have to be drawn to scale, as with a dressmaking pattern, but is simply used as a guide.

The diagram shown here has been based on measurements to give a 91.5cm (36 in) hip size and has been calculated on a tension of 6 stitches and 8 rows to 2.5cm (1 in), worked in double knitting yarn on No.8 needles.

Remember that with most knitted stitches the right side of the work is facing you, therefore your first knitted row will be worked from the right hand edge to the left hand edge. Our example has been worked in rice stitch, where the first, or right side row is knitted and the second, or wrong side row is worked in single rib. It has also been worked from the hemline to the waist edge, decreasing as required to give the final waist measurement.

Hemline This is the point marked A−B on the diagram.
Hipline This is the point marked C−D on the diagram.
Waist This is the point marked E−F on the diagram.

Calculating the number of stitches and rows

The measurements shown in the diagram given here now have to be multiplied by the number of stitches and rows to 2.5cm (1 in) which have been obtained in your tension sample. The hemline width is 81.5cm (32 in) and when multiplied by 6 stitches, this gives a total of 192 stitches. Before the hipline point is reached, this width must be decreased to give 45.5cm (18 in) plus 2.5cm (1 in) tolerance, multiplied by 6 stitches to give a total of 114 stitches. Similarly, the depth from the hipline to the waist must be decreased to give 33cm (13 in) plus 2.5cm (1 in) tolerance, multiplied by 6 stitches to give a total of 84 stitches.

If you are working a straight skirt, the required number of stitches can be decreased at the side edges only. A flared skirt, however, has considerably more stitches to begin with and these will need to be decreased as carefully spaced darts as well as at the side edges. Calculate the number of rows which will be worked to give the required length from the hemline to the hipline, then work out how many decrease rows are needed to arrive at the correct number of stitches for the hip measurement, then how many rows are required between each set of decreases to give the correct length.

Skirt
Sizes
To fit 91.5cm (36in) hips
Length, 63.5cm (25in)

Tension
24 sts and 32 rows to 10cm (3.9in) over st st worked on No.8 needles

Materials
18 × 25grm balls of Robin Bernat Klein Shetland No.2
One pair No.8 needles

One pair No.9 needles
Waist length of 2.5cm (1in) wide elastic

Back
Using No.8 needles cast on 192 sts. Beg with a K row work 7 rows st st.
Next row K all sts tbl to form hemline.
Next row K to end.
Next row *K1, P1, rep from * to end.
The last 2 rows form patt. Cont in patt until work measures 15cm (6in) from hemline, ending with a WS row.
Shape darts
Next row Sl 1, K1, psso, K61, sl 1, K2 tog, psso, K60, sl 1, K2 tog, psso, K61, K2 tog. 186 sts.
Work 7 rows patt without shaping.
Next row Sl 1, K1, psso, K59, sl 1, K2 tog, psso, K58, sl 1, K2 tog, psso, K59, K2 tog. 180 sts.
Work 7 rows patt without shaping.
Cont dec in this way on next and every foll 8th row until 114 sts rem, then on every foll 6th row until 84 sts rem. Cont without shaping until work measures 61cm (24in) from hemline, ending with a WS row. Change to No.9 needles. Work 2.5cm (1in) K1, P1 rib. Cast off in rib.

Front
Work as given for back.

To make up
Join side seams. Turn hem at lower edge to WS and sl st down. Sew elastic inside waistband using casing st.

MORE ABOUT DESIGNING

This chapter continues with the necessary know-how required for designing your own clothes. As explained in the previous chapter, you need to know the exact measurements plus tolerance allowance for each section of the garment and the tension obtained with the yarn and needle size of your choice.

To plan the shape of the garment you can either make a diagram of each section and use this as a guide or, if the design you have in mind is rather complicated, you may find it easier to draft the garment out on squared graph paper, where each square represents one stitch and each line of squares shows a complete row of knitting. Most professional designers use the last method as it forms a detailed record of the design which can be checked against the written instructions.

Neither of these methods will be to the exact scale of the completed garment.

The jersey shown here has been worked to the same tension as the skirt featured in the previous chapter, that is, 6 stitches and 8 rows to 2.5cm (1 inch) over stocking stitch worked on No.8 needles. With this knowledge you can make a diagram or knitting chart which will give you the exact measurements you require but if you alter the yarn or needle size, you must first determine the tension you will achieve before you can begin your design.

Basic jersey measurements

The diagrams and charts shown here represent the measurements and details of the shaping required for the body and sleeves of a plain, round-necked jersey.

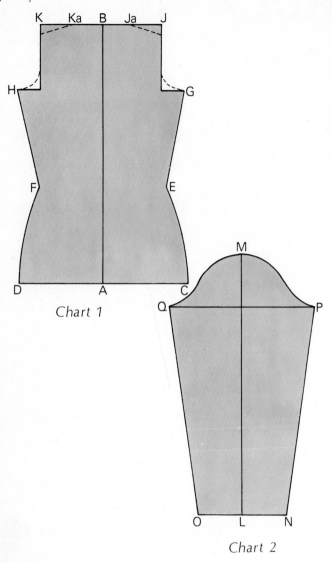

Chart 1

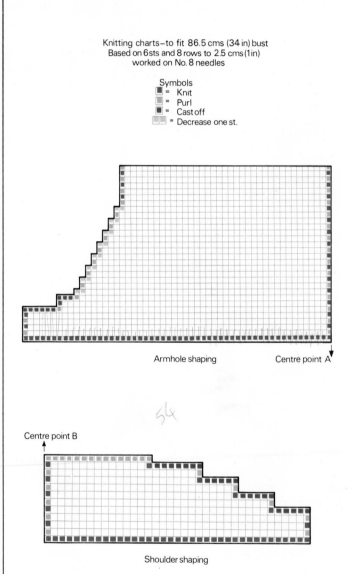

Chart 2

The centre line on Chart 1, from the points marked A−B, represent the total length required from the lower edge to the back neck on the back of the jersey. The points marked C−D give the hemline measurements, E−F the waist measurements, G−H the bust measurement before shaping the armholes and J−K the shoulders and back neck width.

The centre line on Chart 2, from the points marked L−M, show the outside sleeve measurement from the wrist to the shoulder line. The points marked N−O represent the total wrist measurement and P−Q, the underarm sleeve width before shaping the head of the sleeve.

Calculate the number of stitches and rows needed to give these measurements by multiplying the total number of centimetres (*inches*) from point to point by the number of stitches and rows obtained from your tension sample.

Using graph paper

Charts 1 and 2 show the basic measurements needed when planning a jersey design, although the waist

shaping on the body is not always essential and has been omitted on the jersey shown here. However, it is easier to show details of the graduated shaping required for each section on squared graph paper. The symbols used are a form of shorthand and are in standard use throughout all knitting charts.

Armhole shaping Where a set in sleeve is required, the shaping takes place in the first 5/7.5cm (*2/3 inches*)

Knitting charts–to fit 86.5 cms (34 in) bust
Based on 6 sts and 8 rows to 2.5 cms (1 in)
worked on No. 8 needles

Symbols
■ = Knit
□ = Purl
■ = Cast off
▢ = Decrease one st.

Armhole shaping   Centre point A

Centre point B

Shoulder shaping

above the points marked G−H on Chart 1 in a gradual curve, which is more acute at the beginning to give a neat underarm shape. On a raglan sleeve, the same underarm shaping is required but the remaining stitches are then steadily decreased until only the number needed to form the back neck remain.

Shoulder shaping For a set in sleeve, measure the shoulder seam length required from the points marked J−Ja and K−Ka on Chart 1 and commence the shoulder shaping approximately 2.5cm (*1 inch*) below the total length given from points marked A−B

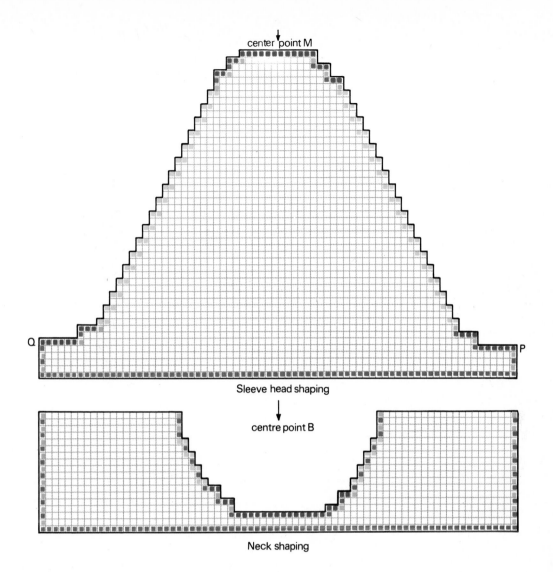

center point M

Sleeve head shaping

centre point B

Neck shaping

on Chart 1. A raglan sleeve does not require shoulder shaping, as the head of the sleeve is continued to form the shoulder line.

Sleeve shaping All sleeves whether long, short, set in or raglan, need to be shaped from the lower edge to the underarm to give a good fit. For a set in sleeve the head must be shaped in a gradual curve, which is again more acute at the beginning to match the underarm shaping on the body. The number of remaining stitches on the last row of the sleeve head should not be less than 7.5cm (3 inches) in width, to fit neatly across the shoulder line, and the final shape will depend on how the stitches are decreased to leave the correct number on the last row. After shaping the underarm, one stitch should be decreased at each end of the next 4–8 rows, depending on the row tension being worked, and then on every alternate row to soften the curve until the sleeve is approximately 2.5cm (1 inch) less than the total length from points marked L–M on Chart 2. The remaining stitches can then be cast off evenly at the beginning of the last few rows until the correct number remain for the final row.

Raglan sleeves should be shaped at the underarm,

then decreased until sufficient stitches remain to form the side neck edge.

Neck shaping For a round neck the back and front body sections are exactly the same, except for the shaping of the front neck. This point should be approximately 5cm (2 inches) lower than the back neck and the stitches need to be divided at this point and each shoulder worked separately. You will have established how many stitches are required to work each shoulder on the back and this total should be deducted from the stitches which remain after the armhole shaping has been completed. The remaining stitches are used to shape the neck in a gradual curve before the shoulder shaping is commenced.

A V-neck will be divided at a lower point, either at the same time as the armhole shaping is commenced or after this section has been completed, depending on the final depth required. Each shoulder is again completed separately, decreasing evenly at the front neck edge until the number of stitches needed to complete the shoulder remain.

The neckband can be completed in a variety of ways, either as a crew neck, polo collar or neat ribbed V-neck.

A BASIC DESIGN PROJECT

The two previous chapters have explained how easy it is to design your own basic garments to a required shape and size. With this knowledge you can begin to combine all the skills and techniques which have been given in this Course, to make the most exciting and original designs – all to your own personal taste. Once you know how to plan a basic shape, you can begin to experiment with different patterns and textures. If you keep to coloured patterns, this need not be an expensive trial run as you can use up all sorts of oddments of the same thickness of yarn in a variety of ways. Keep to a fairly simple shape to begin with but use as many colours and patterns as you like, so that all the interest of the design is in the fabric and not in the shape. Remember to check the multiples of stitches which are required for each pattern and, if necessary, adjust the row beginnings and endings to ensure that each pattern works out correctly over the total number of stitches.

All the stitches, methods and techniques used for the jersey shown here are given throughout the book.

Rainbow jersey
Sizes
To fit 86.5/91.5cm (34/36in) bust
Length to shoulder, 63.5cm (25in)
Sleeve seam, 43cm (17in)

Tension
24 sts and 32 rows to 10cm (3.9in) over st st worked on No. 8 needles

Materials
Total of 30 × 25grm balls of Wendy Double Knitting in 12 contrast colours, or as required
One pair No.8 needles

Note
Colours may be used in any sequence and are not coded

Jersey body
Using No.8 needles and any colour, cast on 112 sts for lower edge. K 9 rows g st.
Work 22 rows Greek key pattern, working one extra st at each end of row (see Mosaic patterns later), K6 rows g st.
Work in stripes of 2 rows, 1 row, 3 rows, 1 row, 4 rows, 1 row, 3 rows, 1 row and 2 rows. K 6 rows g st.

Cast off loosely. Make another section in same way, working same colour sequence.
Using No. 8 needles and any colour, cast on 112 sts for main body. K 6 rows g st.
Work in diagonal stripes of 2 sts in each of 2 colours for 10 rows, see horizontal stripes later. K6 rows g st.
Work in chevron pattern for 20 rows, having multiples of 11 sts plus 2 not 13 stitches plus 2, keeping 3 sts at each side of shaping, see chevron stripes later. K6 rows g stitch.
Work in patchwork pattern across 2nd, 1st, 5th and 3rd patches, or 4 complete patches of 28 sts, for 30 rows, see patchwork later. K6 rows g st.
Work in lattice stitch, omitting 1st row and working one extra st at each end of row for 32 rows, see lattice stitch later.

Shape shoulders
Cont in g st only, cast off at beg of next and every row 10 sts 6 times. K 3 rows g st on rem sts.
Cast off loosely. Make another section in same way, working same colour sequence.

Diamond panel
**Using No.8 needles and any colour, cast on 2 sts. K 1 row. Cont in g st, inc one st at each end of next and every alt row until there are 28 sts. K 3 rows g st. **. Dec one st at each end of next and every alt row until 2 sts rem. K 1 row. Cast off. Make 7 more diamonds in same way, varying colours.
Make 16 half diamonds as given from ** to **, varying colours. Cast off.

Sleeves
Using No.8 needles and any colour, cast on 49 sts. K 9 rows g st, inc one st in every st on last row. 98 sts.
Omitting diamond panel and chevron pattern, work in patterns as given for body, with 6 rows g st between each pattern, ending with 6 rows g st. Cast off loosely.

To make up
Press each section under a damp cloth with a warm iron. Join shoulder seams of main sections and side seams of lower sections. Join side seams of main body leaving 20.5cm (8in) open at top for armholes. Join diamonds and half diamonds as shown in diagram. Sew cast off edge of lower edge of body to lower edge of diamond panel, then sew cast on edge of main body to top edge of diamond panel. Sew in sleeves. Join sleeve seams. Press seams.

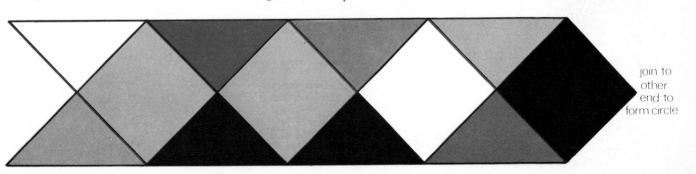

join to other end to form circle

DESIGN DETAILS
FINISHING TOUCHES

Unusual trimmings and finishing touches on a garment are the easiest way of achieving fashion flair and turning a simple, straightforward design into an original which no-one else will have. It may just mean the addition of a belt to a dress or tunic, or your own initials embroidered on the shoulder of a plain jersey. These know-how ideas are invaluable and you will have great fun both in trying them out and applying them.

Twisted cords

These are simple to make and have a variety of uses, depending on their thickness and length. They can be used instead of ribbon on a baby garment – saving additional expense as well as using up any oddments of yarn left over. A thick cord trimmed with tassels makes a most attractive belt and avoids the problem of trying to match colours.

The number of strands of yarn required will vary according to the thickness of the cord needed and the yarn being used. As a guide, try using 4 strands for a baby garment and up to 12 strands for a thick belt. Take the required number of strands and cut them into lengths 3 times the length of the finished cord. As an example, for a cord 51cm (20in) long you will need lengths of 152.5cm (60in). Enlist the aid of another person but if this is not possible, then one end of the strands may be fastened over a convenient hook. Knot each end of the strands together before beginning. If working with another person, each should insert a knitting needle into the knot and twist the strands in a clockwise direction, until they are tightly twisted. Do not let go of the strands but holding them taut, fold them in half at the centre and knot the 2 ends together. Holding the knot, let go of the folded end and give the cord a sharp shake, then smooth it down from the knot to the folded end to even out the twists. Make another knot at the folded end, cut through the folded loops and ease out the ends.

Plaited belt

Here is another idea for a highly original belt. In addition to the yarn you will need 12 small wooden beads. Cut 12 lengths of yarn, preferably double knitting, 228.5cm (90in) long. Take 2 ends together at a time and knot at one end, then slide a bead down to the knot, and make 6 strands in this way. Tie these strands together about 25.5cm (10in) above the beaded ends. Form into 3 strands having 4 lengths in each strand and plait together, taking the left hand strands over the centre strands, then the right hand strands over the centre strands and continuing in this way to within 40.5cm (16in) of the other end. Knot all 12 strands together at this point. Now take 2 ends together and thread a bead on to them, then knot them at the end to hold the bead. Make 5 more strands in this way. Trim ends.

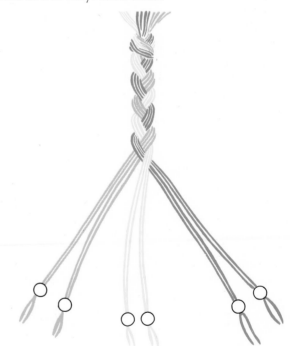

Pompons

These are a most attractive way of trimming a hat, with 2 or more in contrasting colours placed just above the brim, or one enormous loopy pompon placed on the top of a beret.

Round pompon Cut 2 circles of cardboard the size required for the finished pompon, then cut out a circle from the centre of each. Place the 2 pieces of card together and wind the yarn evenly round them and through the centre hole until the hole is nearly filled. Break off the yarn leaving a long end, thread this through a blunt ended wool needle and use this to thread the last turns through the hole until it is completely filled. Cut through the yarn round the outer edge of the circles, working between the 2 pieces of cardboard. Take a double length of yarn and tie very securely round the centre of the pompon, between the 2 pieces of card, leaving an end long enough to sew to the garment. Pull away the card, then tease out the pompon and trim into shape.

Loopy pompon Cut a strip of very thin card about 20.5cm (8in) long by 10cm (4in) wide, depending on the size of pompon required. Leave a short end of yarn free, then wind the yarn very loosely along the length of card for the thickness required. **. Cut the yarn leaving an end about 30.5cm (12in) and thread this into a blunt-ended wool needle. Insert the needle under the loops at one edge of the card, going under 3 or 4 loops at a time, then bring the needle up and back over these loops to form a firm back stitch. Continue along the length of the card until all the loops are secured in this way, then work another row of back stitch if required. Bend the card slightly and remove from the loops, then insert the needle through all the loops at once but do not pull up too tightly. Now bring one end of the secured loops round in a circle to meet the other end and fasten off securely, tying the first short end of yarn to secure and using the remainder of the yarn to sew on the pompon.

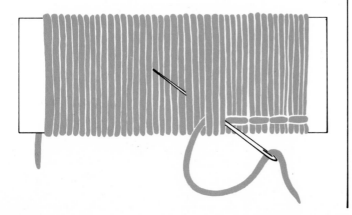

Tassels

Work as given for the loopy pompon to **, then cut the yarn. Using a blunt ended wool needle threaded with yarn, insert the needle at one edge of the card under all the strands and fasten off securely. Cut through the strands of yarn at the other untied edge of the card. Finish the tassel by winding an end of yarn several times round the top, folded ends, about 1.5cm (½in) down and fasten off securely, leaving an end long enough to sew on the tassel.

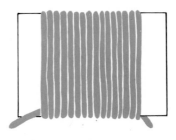

Swiss darning

For this type of embroidery it is advisable to use yarn of the same thickness as the knitted fabric – if the embroidery yarn is too thin the knitting will show through and if it is too thick, it will look clumsy.

Working from the chart, use a blunt ended wool needle threaded with the embroidery yarn and begin at the lower right hand corner of the design to be applied, working from right to left. Bring the needle through from the back to the front at the base of the first stitch to be embroidered and draw yarn through; insert the needle from right to left under the 2 loops of the same stitch one row above and draw yarn through; insert the needle back into the base of this stitch, along the back of the work then into the base of the next stitch to the left from the back to the front and draw the yarn through. Take great care to keep the loops at the same tension as the knitting. Continue along the row in this way. At the end of the row, insert the needle into the base of the last stitch worked, then up in the centre of this same stitch, which will form the base of the same stitch on the next row above. Now insert the needle from left to right under the 2 loops of this stitch on the row above, and continue working as before from left to right.

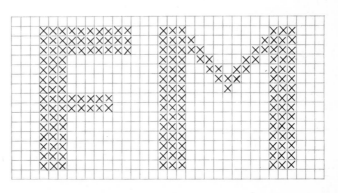

APPLIED EMBROIDERY

Embroidery can quite easily be applied to knitting without the need for charts or transfers. Quite apart from Swiss darning which gives a jacquard effect and is worked from a chart (as described on the previous page), simple embroidery stitches such as cross stitch and chain stitch can be used to highlight a seam or as a border pattern. Because of the amount of give in most knitted fabrics, smocking, either knitted in as part of the main fabric or applied when the garment is completed, is particularly effective.

The following suggestions can be incorporated in a variety of ways but a certain amount of planning is required before beginning any garment. With the exception of smocking, they can all be worked on a plain stocking stitch background but care must be taken in working out the exact position for each stitch. Smocking, worked in one with the fabric or applied, needs a ribbed background and the pattern for any garment using these methods will give detailed instructions for the correct placing. However, if you wish to try some smocking – perhaps on the bodice of a little girl's dress or round the cuffs of a plain jersey – remember to check and make sure that the number of stitches at the required point will allow for the correct multiples of stitches.

Smocking knitted-in

Worked in one with the main fabric over P3, K1 rib. The background colour will be used for the main fabric, coded as A, and a contrast colour in the same quality used to work the smocking, coded as B.

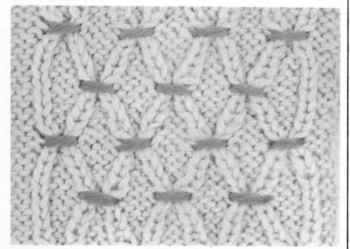

Either cast on or make sure that you have a number of stitches divisible by 8+3. This allows for the knit stitches of the rib to be drawn together with the contrast colour, alternating the position to give the smocked effect.

1st row (RS) Using A, *P3, K1, rep from * to last 3 sts, P3.
2nd row *K3, P1, rep from * to last 3 sts, K3.
Rep 1st and 2nd rows once more.
5th row Using A, P3, *K1, P3, K1, sl these last 5 sts on to a cable needle and hold at front of work, join in B at back of work, pass B in front of sts on cable needle to back of work then round to front and back again in an anti-clockwise direction, leaving B at back sl 5 sts on to right hand needle – called S5 –, P3 A, rep from * to end. Do not break off B.
6th row As 2nd.
Rep 1st and 2nd rows once, then 1st row once more.
10th row Using A, K3, P1, *K3, S5 by P1, K3, P1, holding cable needle at back of work and winding yarn round in a clockwise direction, rep from * to last 7 sts, K3, P1, K3. Do not break off B.
These 10 rows form the pattern.

Smocking applied

Work the background rib as given for knitted-in smocking until the garment or section is completed. Using a blunt ended wool needle threaded with B, *insert needle from back to front of the work after the 2nd knitted st of the 5th row, pass the needle across the front of the knit st, the next 3 purl sts and the next knit st, Insert it from front to back after this knit st and pull yarn through, carry the yarn across the back of the work through to the front and round the 5 sts again through to the back, carry the yarn across the back of the work, miss (P3, K1) twice, rep from * to end. On the 10th row with the WS of the work facing, * work round the 2nd knit st of the first smocked sts, the next 3 purl sts and the first knit st of next smocked sts, then miss (K3, P1) twice, rep from * to the end. Continue in this way for the required depth of smocking.

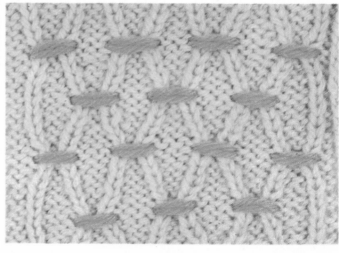

Applied bows

Work the stocking stitch background and mark the positions for the bows on the RS of the work, allowing 5 sts and 5 rows for each bow and a further 5 sts between each bow. Using a blunt ended wool needle threaded with contrast yarn, *insert the needle from back to front at the first marked st of the 1st row and pull yarn through, working from right to left insert the needle under the 3rd st of the 3rd row and pull yarn through, insert the needle from front to back after the 5th st of the 1st row and pull yarn through; carry yarn across back of work, insert needle from back to front at first marked st of 2nd row and pull yarn through, insert needle under same 3rd st of 3rd row and pull yarn through, insert needle from front to back after 5th st of 2nd row and pull yarn through; carry yarn across back, insert needle from back to front at first marked st of 3rd row and pull yarn through, under the same 3rd st of 3rd row and pull yarn through, insert needle from front to back after 5th st of 3rd row and pull yarn through; carry yarn across back, insert needle from back to front at first marked st of 4th row and pull yarn through, under same 3rd st of 3rd row and pull yarn through, insert needle from front to back after 5th st of 4th row and pull yarn through; carry yarn across back, insert needle from back to front at first marked st of 5th row and pull yarn through, under same 3rd st of 3rd row and pull yarn through, insert needle from front to back after 5th st of 5th row and pull yarn through, carry yarn across back to next position and rep from * to end.

The next time the bows are worked on 5 rows above, work them over 5 sts in between each bow of previous row.

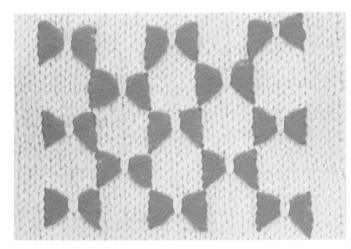

Applied chain stitch

This looks most effective if it is worked in a contrast colour on a stocking stitch background, where wide stripes of the main colour and narrow stripes of the contrast colour have been used, to give a checked effect. Mark the positions for vertical chains depending on the size of check required and allowing one stitch, one above the other, on every row.

Using a blunt ended wool needle threaded with contrast colour, begin at lower edge of first marked position and insert needle from back to front in centre of marked st and pull yarn through, *hold the yarn down with the thumb of the left hand, insert the needle into the same st and up into the next st above pulling the yarn through, rep from * to end and fasten off. Repeat on each marked st as required.

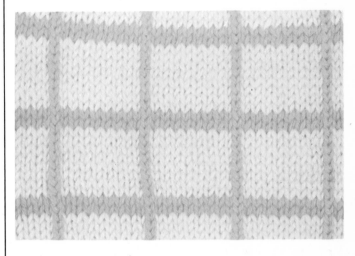

Applied cross stitch

Work the stocking stitch background and mark positions for the cross sts on the RS of work, allowing 3 sts and 4 rows for each cross st, with a further 3 sts between each cross st. Using a blunt ended wool needle threaded with one or two thicknesses of contrast colour begin at lower edge, *insert needle from back to front at side of first marked st and pull yarn through, working from right to left insert needle from front to back after 3rd st on 4th row above and pull yarn through, carry yarn across back of work, insert needle from back to front after first st on 4th row and pull yarn through, insert needle from front to back after 3rd st of 1st row and pull yarn through, carry yarn across back to next position and rep from * to end. The next time the cross sts are worked on 4 rows above, work them over 3 sts in between each cross st of previous row.

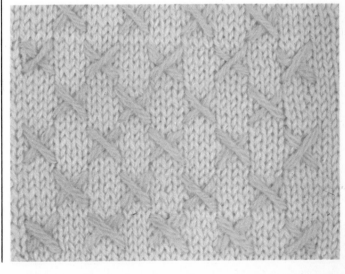

COVERED BUTTONS

Just as untidy buttonholes can mar the effect of an otherwise perfect garment, buttons which do not match exactly or tone in with the yarn used for a design can spoil the whole appearance.

Sometimes it is impossible to find suitable buttons and the cheap and simple answer to this problem is to cover button moulds, such as Trims, with knitting to achieve a perfect match.

Here we give a selection of buttons to suit all garments.

Bouclé yarn button

Using No.14 needles cast on 4 sts. Work in st st, inc one st at each end of every row until there are 12 sts. Work 6 rows without shaping. Dec one st at each end of every row until 4 sts rem. Cast off. Gather over wooden mould.

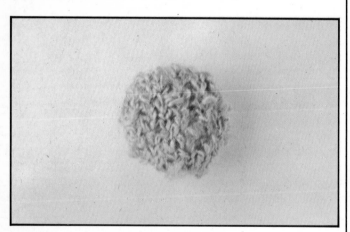

Reversed stocking stitch button

Using No.14 needles and 4 ply, work as given for bouclé yarn button, beg with a P row. Cover 2cm ($\frac{7}{8}$in) Trim.

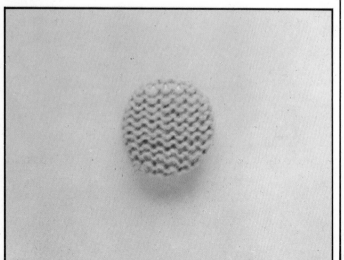

Single rib button

Using No.14 needles and 4 ply, work in K1, P1 rib as given for reversed st st button. Cover 2cm ($\frac{7}{8}$ inch) Trim.

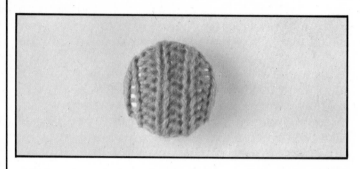

Bobble button

Using No.14 needles and 4 ply, cast on 3 sts. Work in st st, inc one st at each end of every row until there are 11 sts. Work 3 rows without shaping.

Next row K5, K into front and back of next st 5 times, K5.

Next row P5, K5 tog, P5.

Work 2 rows without shaping. Dec one st at each end of every row until 3 sts rem. Cast off. Cover 2cm ($\frac{7}{8}$in) Trim.

Continental stocking stitch button

Using No.14 needles and 4 ply, cast on and work as given for reversed st st button, working in foll patt:

1st row K into back of each st to end.

2nd row P to end.

Cast off. Cover 2cm ($\frac{7}{8}$ in) Trim.

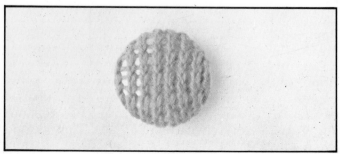

Tweed stitch button

Using No.14 needles and 4 ply, cast on and work as given for reversed st st button, working in foll patt:
1st row *K1, yfwd, sl 1 P-wise, ybk, rep from * to end.
2nd row P to end.
3rd row *Yfwd, sl 1 P-wise, ybk, K1, rep from * to end.
4th row P to end.
Cast off. Cover 2cm ($\frac{7}{8}$in) Trim.

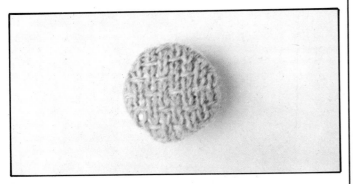

Two-colour button

Using No.14 needles and 4 ply in 2 colours, A and B, cast on and work as given for reversed st st button, working in foll patt:
1st row (WS) Using A, *P1, sl 1 P-wise, rep from * to end.
2nd row Using A, K to end.
3rd row Using B, as 1st.
4th row Using B, as 2nd.
Cast off. Cover 2cm ($\frac{7}{8}$in) Trim.

Embroidered button

Using No.14 needles and 4 ply, cast on 6 sts. Work in st st inc one at each end of every row until there are 16 sts. Work 8 rows without shaping.
Dec one st at each end of every row until 6 sts rem. Cast off. Using 3 colours of stranded embroidery cotton and chain st, work flower motif in centre of button. Gather over wooden mould.

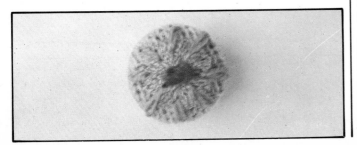

Basket stitch button

Using No.11 needles and double knitting, cast on and work as given for bouclé yarn button, working in foll patt:
1st row *K2, P2, rep from * to end.
2nd row As 1st.
3rd row *P2, K2, rep from * to end.
4th row As 3rd.
Cast off. Gather over wooden mould.

Woven basket stitch button

Using No.11 needles and double knitting, cast on and work as given for Basket stitch button, working in foll patt:
1st row *Pass right hand needle behind first st on left hand needle and K second st, then K first st in usual way, dropping both sts off needle tog, rep from * to end.
2nd row P1, *P second st on left hand needle then P first st and sl both sts off needle tog, rep from * to last st, P1.
Cast off. Gather over wooden mould.

Beret button

Using No.12 needles and double knitting, cast on 11 sts.
1st and every alt row (WS) P to end.
2nd row K1, (K twice into next st, K1) 5 times. 16 sts.
4th row (K2, K twice into next st) 5 times, K1. 21 sts.
6th row (K2, K2 tog) 5 times, K1. 16 sts.
8th row (K1, K2 tog) 5 times, K1. 11 sts.
10th row (K2 tog) 5 times, K1. 5 sts.
Break off yarn, thread through rem sts, insert 3cm ($1\frac{1}{4}$in) wooden mould, draw up and fasten off.

APPLIED EDGINGS

Knitted edgings

Although many beautiful and interesting forms of edgings are given in crochet patterns, reference is seldom made to the equally effective variations of knitted borders. These may be used to trim anything from baby clothes and fashion garments to household linens.

The correct choice of yarn for these borders is very important, depending upon the use to which they will be put. Something as fine as a 2 or 3 ply would produce a delicate edging for a baby dress or shawl, a double knitting quality would give a firm, textured border for a fashion garment, or a crisp cotton would be ideal for household linens. All of the examples shown here are worked separately to the required length, then sewn in place when the item is completed.

Simple lace edging

Cast on a number of stitches divisible by 5 plus 2.
1st row K1, yfwd and over needle to make one st, * K5, turn, lift 2nd, 3rd, 4th and 5th sts over the first st and off the needle, turn, yfwd, rep from * to last st, K1.
2nd row K1, *(P1, yon to make one st, K1 tbl) all into

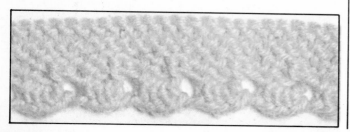

next st, P1, rep from * to end.
3rd row K2, K1 tbl, *K3, K1 tbl, rep from * to last 2 sts, K2.
Work 3 rows g st. Cast off.

Shell edging

Using thumb method, cast on a number of stitches divisible by 11 plus 2.
1st row P to end.
2nd row K2, *K1, sl this st back on to left hand needle and lift the next 8 sts on left hand needle over this st and off the needle, yfwd and round right hand needle twice to make 2 sts, then K first st again, K2, rep from * to end.
3rd row K1, *P2 tog, drop extra loop of 2 made sts on previous row and into this long loop work (K1, K1 tbl) twice, P1, rep from * to last st, K1.
Work 5 rows g st. Cast off.

Leaf edging

Cast on a number of stitches divisible by 13 plus 2.
1st row K1, *K2, sl 1, K1, psso, sl 2, K3 tog, p2sso, K2 tog, K2, rep from * to last st, K1.

2nd row P4, *yrn, P1, yrn, P6, rep from * ending last rep with P4 instead of P6.
3rd row K1, yfwd, *K2, sl 1, K1, psso, K1, K2 tog, K2, yfwd, rep from * to last st, K1.
4th row P2, *yrn, P2, yrn, P3, yrn, P2, yrn, P1, rep from * to last st, P1.
5th row K2, *yfwd, K1, yfwd, sl 1, K1, psso, K1, sl 1, K2 tog, psso, K1, K2 tog, yfwd, K1, yfwd, K1, rep from * to last st, K1.
6th row P to end.
7th row K5, *yfwd, sl 2, K3 tog, p2sso, yfwd, K7, rep from * ending last rep with K5 instead of K7.
Work 4 rows g st. Cast off.

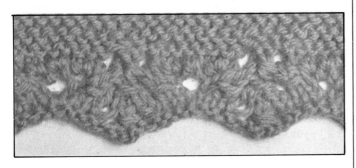

Chain edging
Using 2 needle method and working into each st instead of between sts, cast on a number of stitches divisible by 29.
1st row *K3 tbl, (pick up loop lying between sts and K tbl – called inc 1 –, drop 3 sts off left hand needle, K2 tog tbl) 4 times, inc 1, drop 3 sts off left hand needle, K3, rep from * to end.
2nd row P to end.
3rd row *K2 tbl, (sl 1, K1, psso) twice, sl 1, K2 tog, psso, (K2 tog) twice, K2, rep from * to end.
4th row P to end.
Work 3 rows g st. Cast off.

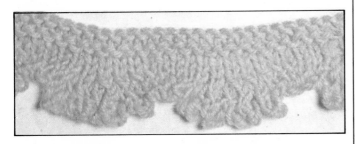

Serrated edging
Cast on 8 sts loosely.
1st row K to last 2 sts, K twice into next st, yfwd and hold at front of work, sl 1 P-wise. 9 sts.
2nd row K1 tbl, K1, (yfwd and over needle – called M1 –, sl 1, K1, psso, K1) twice, yfwd, sl 1 P-wise.
3rd row K1 tbl, K to end, turn and cast on 3 sts.
4th row K1, K twice into next st, K2, (M1, sl 1, K1, psso, K1) twice, M1, K1, yfwd, sl 1 P-wise.
5th row K1 tbl, K to last 2 sts, K twice into next st, yfwd, sl 1 P-wise.
6th row K1 tbl, K twice into next st, K2, (M1, sl 1, K1,

psso, K1) 3 times, K1, yfwd, sl 1 P-wise.
7th row K1 tbl, K to last 2 sts, K2 tog.
8th row Sl 1 P-wise, ybk, K1, psso, sl 1, K1, psso, K4, (M1, sl 1, K1, psso, K1) twice, yfwd, sl 1 P-wise.
9th row K1 tbl, K to last 2 sts, K2 tog.
10th row Cast off 3 sts, K2, M1, sl 1, K1, psso, K1, M1, sl 1, K1, psso, yfwd, sl 1 P-wise. 9 sts.
Rows 3 to 10 inclusive form pattern. Repeat pattern rows until edging is required length. Cast off.

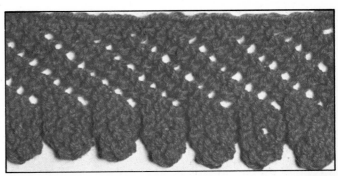

Fan edging
Cast on 13 sts loosely.
1st row (RS) Sl 1, K1, yfwd, K2 tog, K5, yfwd, K2 tog, yfwd, K2.
2nd and every alt row Yrn to inc 1, K2 tog, K to end.
3rd row Sl 1, K1, yfwd, K2 tog, K4, (yfwd, K2 tog) twice, yfwd, K2.
5th row Sl 1, K1, yfwd, K2 tog, K3, (yfwd, K2 tog) 3 times, yfwd, K2.
7th row Sl 1, K1, yfwd, K2 tog, K2, (yfwd, K2 tog) 4 times, yfwd, K2.
9th row Sl 1, K1, yfwd, K2 tog, K1, (yfwd, K2 tog) 5 times, yfwd, K2.
11th row Sl 1, K1, yfwd, K2 tog, K1, K2 tog, (yfwd, K2 tog) 5 times, K1.
13th row Sl 1, K1, yfwd, K2 tog, K2, K2 tog, (yfwd, K2 tog) 4 times, K1.
15th row Sl 1, K1, yfwd, K2 tog, K3, K2 tog, (yfwd, K2 tog) 3 times, K1.
17th row Sl 1, K1, yfwd, K2 tog, K4, K2 tog, (yfwd, K2 tog) twice, K1.
19th row Sl 1, K1, yfwd, K2 tog, K5, K2 tog, yfwd, K2 tog, K1.
20th row Yrn, K2 tog, K11.
These 20 rows form the pattern. Repeat pattern rows until edging is required length. Cast off.

SHAPED EDGINGS

Knitted borders

The last chapter dealt with straight knitted edgings, either worked over multiples of stitches in rows to give the required length, or from side edge to side edge over a set number of stitches for the desired length. Where a border is required to fit a rectangular, square or circular shape, however, provision must be made for working corners or shaping the border so that the outer edge is wider than the inner edge.

The circular border given here is used to trim a baby's shawl, where the centre is knitted in stocking stitch to a circular shape, but if it is worked in a fine cotton yarn, the same border would most effectively trim a circular fabric tablecloth.

The border with corner shaping, used here to trim a fabric traycloth, would also be ideal for trimming pillow cases, tablecloths or a delicate evening stole.

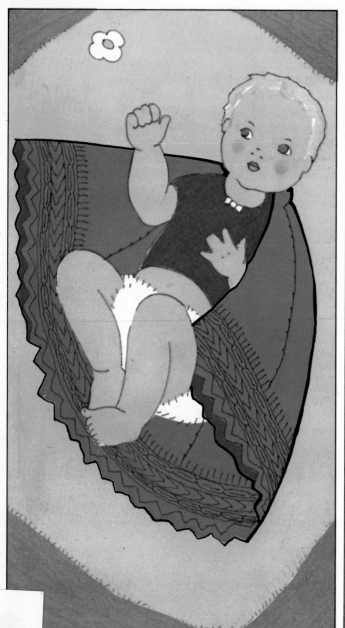

Shawl centre

Using set of 4 needles pointed at both ends, cast on 6 sts.

1st round *K into front then into back of next st, rep from * to end. 12 sts.

2nd round K1, *yfwd to make one, K2, rep from * to last st, yfwd, K1. 18 sts.

3rd round K1, *K into front then into back of yfwd of previous round, K2, rep from * to last 2 sts, K into front then into back of yfwd, K1. 24 sts.

4th round K2, *yfwd, K4, rep from * to last 2 sts, yfwd, K2. 30 sts.

5th round K2, *K into front then into back of yfwd, K4, rep from * to last 3 sts, K into front then into back of yfwd, K2. 36 sts.

6th round K3, *yfwd, K6, rep from * to last 3 sts, yfwd, K3. 42 sts.

7th round K3, *K into front then into back of yfwd, K6, rep from * to last 4 sts, K into front then into back of yfwd, K3.

Cont inc 6 sts on every round in this way until centre is required diameter. Cast off very loosely.

Shawl border

Cast on 52 sts loosely.

1st row K2, (K2 tog, yfwd to make one – called M1 –, K2) 3 times, K2 tog, K11, K2 tog, (K2 tog, M1, K2) 3 times, K2 tog, (M1, K2 tog) 4 times. 49 sts.

2nd row P10, turn and leave 39 sts unworked.

3rd row K2 tog, (M1, K2 tog) 4 times.

4th row P8, (K2 tog, M1, K2) 3 times, P13, (K2 tog, M1, K2) 3 times, K3.

5th row K3, (K2 tog, M1, K2) 3 times, (K2 tog) twice, (M1, K1) 5 times, M1, (K2 tog) twice, (K2 tog, M1, K2) 3 times, K1, (M1, K2 tog) 3 times, M1, K1.

6th row P9, (K2 tog, M1, K2) 3 times, P15, (K2 tog, M1, K2) 3 times, K3.

7th row K3, (K2 tog, M1, K2) 3 times, K2 tog, K11, K2 tog, (K2 tog, M1, K2) 3 times, K2, (M1, K2 tog) 3 times, M1, K1.

8th row P10, (K2 tog, M1, K2) 3 times, P12, turn and leave 16 sts unworked.

9th row K1, K2 tog, (M1, K1) 5 times, M1, (K2 tog) twice, (K2 tog, M1, K2) 3 times, K3, (M1, K2 tog) 3 times, M1, K1.

10th row P11, (K2 tog, M1, K2) 3 times, P14, P2 tog,

(K2 tog, M1, K2) 3 times, K3.

11th row K3, *K2 tog, M1, K1, s1 next 3 sts on to cable needle and hold at back of work, K1, K2 tog from left hand needle, M1, K2 from cable needle, K next st on left hand needle and last st on cable needle tog, M1, K2, *, K2 tog, K11, K2 tog, rep from * to *, K4, (M1, K2 tog) 3 times, M1, K1.

12th row P13, turn and leave 39 sts unworked.

13th row K6, (M1, K2 tog) 3 times, M1, K1.

14th row *P13, (K2 tog, M1, K2) 3 times, rep from * once more, K3.

15th row K3, (K2 tog, M1, K2) 3 times, (K2 tog) twice, (M1, K1) 5 times, M1 (K2 tog) twice, (K2 tog, M1, K2) 3 times, K3, K2 tog, (M1, K2 tog) 4 times.

16th row P12, (K2 tog, M1, K2) 3 times, P15, (K2 tog, M1, K2) 3 times, K3.

17th row K3, (K2 tog, M1, K2) 3 times, K2 tog, K11, K2 tog, (K2 tog, M1, K2) 3 times, K2, K2 tog, (M1, K2 tog) 4 times.

18th row P11, (K2 tog, M1, K2) 3 times, P12, turn and leave 16 sts unworked.

19th row K1, K2 tog, (M1, K1) 5 times, M1, (K2 tog) twice, (K2 tog, M1, K2) 3 times, K1, K2 tog, (M1, K2 tog) 4 times.

20th row P10, (K2 tog, M1, K2) 3 times, P14, P2 tog, (K2 tog, M1, K2) 3 times, K3.

These 20 rows form patt. Cont in patt until inner edge of border fits round outer edge of centre. Sew in place.

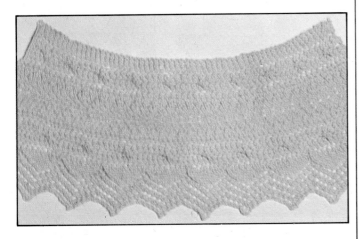

Traycloth

Cut fabric to required size and hem round all edges.

Border

Cast on 9sts. Commence patt.

1st row (RS) K to end.

2nd row K3, K2 tog, yfwd to make one, K2 tog, yfwd, K1, yfwd, K1. 10 sts.

3rd and every alt row K to end.

4th row K2, K2 tog, yfwd, K2 tog, yfwd, K3, yfwd, K1. 11 sts.

6th row K1, K2 tog, yfwd, K2 tog, yfwd, K5, yfwd, K1. 12 sts.

8th row K3, yfwd, K2 tog, yfwd, K2 tog, K1, K2 tog, yfwd, K2 tog. 11 sts.

10th row K4, yfwd, K2 tog, yfwd, K3 tog, yfwd, K2 tog. 10 sts.

12th row K5, yfwd, K3 tog, yfwd, K2 tog. 9 sts.

These 12 rows form patt. Cont in patt until border is required length to first corner, ending with a 6th row.

Shape corner

1st row K10, turn.

2nd row Sl 1 K-wise, yfwd, K2 tog, yfwd, K2 tog, K1, K2 tog, yfwd, K2 tog. 11 sts.

3rd row K8, turn.

4th row Sl 1 K-wise, yfwd, K2 tog, yfwd, K3 tog, yfwd, K2 tog. 10 sts.

5th row K6, turn.

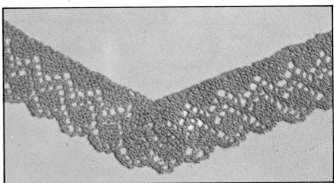

6th row Sl 1 K-wise, yfwd, K3 tog, yfwd, K2 tog. 9 sts.

7th row K6, turn.

8th row K2 tog, yfwd, K2 tog, yfwd, K1, yfwd, K1. 10 sts.

9th row K8, turn.

10th row K2 tog, yfwd, K2 tog, yfwd, K3, yfwd, K1. 11 sts.

11th row K10, turn.

12th row K2 tog, yfwd, K2 tog, yfwd, K5, yfwd, K1. 12 sts.

13th row K to end.

This completes corner shaping. Beg with an 8th patt row, cont in patt to next corner, then rep shaping rows. Cont in this way until border is completed. Sew in place round traycloth.

EDGINGS AND INSERTIONS

Knitted edgings and insertions can be used most effectively as a trim for fabric garments, or household linens. They look their best when worked in a fine cotton, such as No.20, which will also stand up to laundering without losing its shape.

The insertion pattern given here may be used on its own to form a delicate panel on each side of the front of a fabric blouse, or it could be combined with any one of the edgings to form the yoke of a demure nightgown.

Alternatively, the insertion could be applied across the top of a sheet, which could then be finished off with one of the edgings to transform plain household linen into a family heirloom.

7th row K4, P2, K1, P4, K2, (yrn, P2 tog) twice, K1.
8th row K3, (yrn, P2 tog) twice, yon, K1 tbl, K1, K1 tbl, yfwd, sl 1, K2 tog, psso, yfwd, K5.
9th row K5, P7, K2, (yrn, P2 tog) twice, K1.
10th row K3, (yrn, P2 tog) twice, yon, K1 tbl, K3, K1 tbl, yfwd, K7.
11th row Cast off 4 sts, K2, P7, K2, (yrn, P2 tog) twice, K1. The 2nd to 11th rows form the pattern.

Shell edging
Cast on 13 sts.
1st row (WS) P to end.
2nd row Sl 1, K1, yrn, P2 tog, K1, (yfwd, sl1, K1, psso) 3 times, y2rn, K2 tog.

Leaf edging
Cast on 17 sts.
1st row (WS) K to end.
2nd row K3, (yrn, P2 tog) twice, yon, K1 tbl, K2 tog, P1, sl 1, K1, psso, K1 tbl, yfwd, K3.
3rd row K3, P3, K1, P3, K2, (yrn, P2 tog) twice, K1.
4th row As 2nd.
5th row As 3rd.
6th row K3, (yrn, P2 tog) twice, yon, K1 tbl, yfwd, K2 tog, P1, sl 1, K1, psso, yfwd, K4.

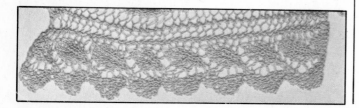

3rd row Yfwd to make 1, K2 tog, P9, yrn, P2 tog, K1, noting that the first K2 tog includes the first loop of

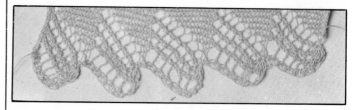

y2rn and the second loop forms the first P st.
4th row Sl 1, K1, yrn, P2 tog, K2, (yfwd, sl 1, K1, psso) 3 times, y2rn, K2 tog.
5th row Yfwd, K2 tog, P10, yrn, P2 tog, K1.
6th row Sl 1, K1, yrn, P2 tog, K3, (yfwd, sl 1, K1, psso) 3 times, y2rn, K2 tog.
7th row Yfwd, K2 tog, P11, yrn, P2 tog, K1.

8th row Sl 1, K1, yrn, P2 tog, K4, (yfwd, sl 1, K1, psso) 3 times, y2rn, K2 tog.

9th row Yfwd, K2 tog, P12, yrn, P2 tog, K1.

10th row Sl 1, K1, yrn, P2 tog, K5, (yfwd, sl 1, K1, psso) 3 times, y2rn, K2 tog.

11th row Yfwd, K2 tog, P13, yrn, P2 tog, K1.

12th row Sl 1, K1, yrn, P2 tog, K6, (yfwd, sl 1, K1, psso) 3 times, y2rn, K2 tog.

13th row Yfwd, K2 tog, P14, yrn, P2 tog, K1.

14th row Sl 1, K1, yrn, P2 tog, K7, (yfwd, sl 1, K1, psso) 3 times, y2rn, K2 tog.

15th row Yfwd, K2 tog, P15, yrn, P2 tog, K1.

16th row Sl 1, K1, yrn, P2 tog, K8, yfwd, K1, return last st to left hand needle and with point of right hand needle lift the next 7 sts one at a time over this st and off needle, then sl st back on to right hand needle.

17th row P2 tog, P9, yrn, P2 tog, K1.

The 2nd to 17th rows form the pattern.

Cockleshell edging

Cast on 16 sts.

1st row K to end.

2nd row Yfwd to make 1, K2 tog, K1, yfwd, K10, yfwd, K2 tog, K1.

3rd row K2, yfwd, K2 tog, K12, P1.

4th row Yfwd, K2 tog, K1, yfwd, K2 tog, yfwd, K9, yfwd, K2 tog, K1.

5th row K2, yfwd, K2 tog, K13, P1.

6th row Yfwd, K2 tog, K1, (yfwd, K2 tog) twice, yfwd, K8, yfwd, K2 tog, K1.

7th row K2, yfwd, K2 tog, K14, P1.

8th row Yfwd, K2 tog, K1, (yfwd, K2 tog) 3 times, yfwd, K7, yfwd, K2 tog, K1.

9th row K2, yfwd, K2 tog, K15, P1.

10th row Yfwd, K2 tog, K1, (yfwd, K2 tog) 4 times, yfwd, K6, yfwd, K2 tog, K1.

11th row K2, yfwd, K2 tog, K16, P1.

12th row Yfwd, K2 tog, K1, (yfwd, K2 tog) 5 times, yfwd, K5, yfwd, K2 tog, K1.

13th row K2, yfwd, K2 tog, K17, P1.

14th row Yfwd, K2 tog, K1, (yfwd, K2 tog) 6 times, yfwd, K4, yfwd, K2 tog, K1.

15th row K2, yfwd, K2 tog, K18, P1.

16th row Yfwd, K2 tog, K1, (yfwd, K2 tog) 7 times, yfwd, K3, yfwd, K2 tog, K1.

17th row K2, yfwd, K2 tog, K19, P1.

18th row Yfwd, (K2 tog) twice, (yfwd, K2 tog) 7 times, K3, yfwd, K2 tog, K1.

19th row As 15th.

20th row Yfwd, (K2 tog) twice, (yfwd, K2 tog) 6 times, K4, yfwd, K2 tog, K1.

21st row As 13th.

22nd row Yfwd, (K2 tog) twice, (yfwd, K2 tog) 5 times, K5, yfwd, K2 tog, K1.

23rd row As 11th.

24th row Yfwd, (K2 tog) twice, (yfwd, K2 tog) 4 times, K6, yfwd, K2 tog, K1.

25th row As 9th.

26th row Yfwd, (K2 tog) twice, (yfwd, K2 tog) 3 times, K7, yfwd, K2 tog, K1.

27th row As 7th.

28th row Yfwd, (K2 tog) twice, (yfwd, K2 tog) twice, K8, yfwd, K2 tog, K1.

29th row As 5th.

30th row Yfwd, (K2 tog) twice, yfwd, K2 tog, K9, yfwd, K2 tog, K1.

31st row As 3rd.

32nd row Yfwd, (K2 tog) twice, K10, yfwd, K2 tog, K1.

33rd row K2, yfwd, K2 tog, K11, P1.

The 2nd to 33rd rows form the pattern.

Diamond insertion panel

Cast on 21 sts.

1st and every alt row (WS) P to end.

2nd row K2, yfwd, sl 1, K1, psso, K1, yfwd, sl 1, K1, psso, K3, K2 tog, yfwd, K1, yfwd, sl 1, K1, psso, K6.

4th row K3, (yfwd, sl 1, K1, psso, K1) twice, K2 tog, yfwd, K3, yfwd, sl 1, K1, psso, K5.

6th row K4, yfwd, sl 1, K1, psso, K1, yfwd, K3 tog, yfwd, K2, yfwd, sl 1, K1, psso, K1, yfwd, sl 1, K1, psso, K4.

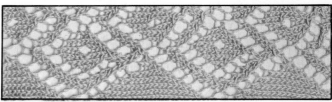

8th row K5, yfwd, sl 1, K1, psso, (K2 tog, yfwd, K1) twice, yfwd, sl 1, K1, psso, K1, yfwd, sl 1, K1, psso, K3.

10th row K6, yfwd, sl 1, K1, psso, K1, K2 tog, yfwd, K3, yfwd, sl 1, K1, psso, K1, yfwd, sl 1, K1, psso, K2.

12th row K7, yfwd, K3 tog, yfwd, K5, (yfwd, sl 1, K1, psso, K1) twice.

14th row K7, K2 tog, yfwd, K3, yfwd, sl 1, K1, psso, K2, yfwd, sl 1, K1, psso, K1, yfwd, sl 1, K1, psso.

16th row K6, K2 tog, yfwd, K1, yfwd, sl 1, K1, psso, K3, K2 tog, yfwd, K1, K2 tog, yfwd, K2.

18th row K5, K2 tog, yfwd, K3, yfwd, sl 1, K1, psso, (K1, K2 tog, yfwd) twice, K3.

20th row K4, K2 tog, yfwd, K1, K2 tog, yfwd, K2, yfwd, sl 1, K2 tog, psso, yfwd, K1, K2 tog, yfwd, K4.

22nd row K3, (K2 tog, yfwd, K1) twice, yfwd, sl 1, K1, psso, K1, yfwd, sl 1, K1, psso, K2 tog, yfwd, K5.

24th row K2, K2 tog, yfwd, K1, K2 tog, yfwd, K3, yfwd, sl 1, K1, psso, K1, K2 tog, yfwd, K6.

26th row (K1, K2 tog, yfwd) twice, K5, yfwd, sl 1, K2 tog, psso, yfwd, K7.

28th row K2 tog, yfwd, K1, K2 tog, yfwd, K2, K2 tog, yfwd, K3, yfwd, sl 1, K1, psso, K7.

These 28 rows form the pattern.

SEQUINS AND BEADS

Beaded and sequinned tops and jackets make glamorous and dazzling garments for evening wear and this technique is very simple to work. The beads or sequins are knitted in with the fabric and they can be used to form an all-over design, or as a most effective trimming.

Most large departmental stores sell packets of beads and sequins which will prove suitable for this type of knitting.

If you are using beads, they should not be too large or heavy, as this will pull the fabric out of shape – small pearl beads are ideal. The hole in the centre of the bead must be large enough to thread over the yarn being used.

Sequins also come in various sizes and shapes and must also have a hole large enough to be threaded over the yarn. This hole should be at the top of the sequin and not in the centre, so that the sequins do not stick out but hang flat against the knitted background.

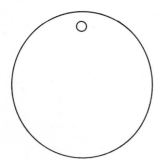

To thread beads or sequins on to a ball of yarn
Cut a 25.5cm (10in) length of ordinary sewing thread and fold this in half. Thread both cut ends through a fine sewing needle, leaving a loop of cotton as shown in diagram 1.

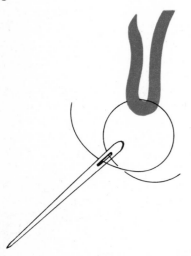

Thread the required number of beads or sequins on to the ball of yarn with which you are going to knit by passing approximately 15cm (6in) of the end of this ball through the loop of sewing cotton. Thread the beads or sequins on to the needle, then slide them down the cotton and on to the ball of yarn, as shown in diagram 2.

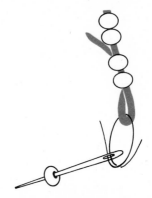

To knit in beads or sequins
Prepare a ball of yarn by threading on the required number of beads or sequins. These should be knitted in on a right side row against a stocking stitch background, although they can be worked in panels and interspersed with a lace pattern, as shown in the evening top given here.

Knit until the position for the bead or sequin is reached, push one bead or sequin up the ball of yarn close to the back of the work, knit the next stitch through the back of the loop in the usual way, pushing the bead or sequin through to the front of the work with the loop of the stitch, taking care not to split the yarn. This allows the bead or sequin to lie flat against the fabric.

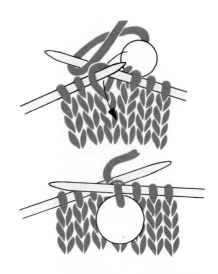

sequins. Commence patt.

1st row (RS) K1, *K2, K2 tog, y2rn, K2 tog tbl, rep from * to last 3 sts, K3.

2nd row *P4, P into front then into back of y2rn, rep from * to last 4 sts, P4.

3rd row K1, *K1, K sequin in with next st tbl – called K1S –, K2 tog, y2rn, K2 tog tbl, rep from * to last 3 sts, K1, K1S, K1.

4th row As 2nd.

5th row As 1st.

6th row As 2nd.

7th row K1, *K1S, K1, K2 tog, y2rn, K2 tog tbl, rep from * to last 3 sts, K1S, K2.

8th row As 2nd.

These 8 rows form patt. Cont in patt until work measures 30.5cm (*12in*) from beg, ending with a WS row.

Shape armholes

Keeping patt correct, cast off 5[6:7:8:9] sts at beg of next 2 rows. Dec one st at each end of next and every alt row 8 times in all, ending with a WS row. 68[72:76:80:84] sts.

Shape neck

Next row Dec one st, patt 20[21:22:23:24] sts, cast off 24[26:28:30:32] sts, patt to last 2 sts, dec one st.
Complete left shoulder first.

Next row Patt to end.

Next row Dec one st, patt to last 2 sts, dec one st.
Rep last 2 rows until 3[2:3:2:3] sts rem. K3[2:3:2:3] tog. Fasten off.
With WS of work facing, rejoin yarn to rem sts and complete right shoulder to match left shoulder.

Front

Work as given for back.

Shoulder straps (make 2)

Using No.10 needles and ball of yarn which has not been threaded with sequins, cast on 11 sts.

1st row K1, *P1, K1, rep from * to end.

2nd row P1, *K1, P1, rep from * to end.

Rep these 2 rows until strap measures 51cm (*20in*) from beg, or required length to fit round armhole to shoulder. Cast off. Join cast on edge to cast off edge. Join side seams. Pin straps in place round armhole.

Neck edging (make 2)

Work as given for shoulder straps until edging fits down side of one shoulder strap, round centre neck edge and up side of other shoulder strap.
Cast off.

To make up

Do not press. Sew shoulder straps in place. Sew neck edging down inner edge of shoulder strap, round neck and along inner edge of other strap, then join shoulder seam. Fold straps and edging in half to WS and sl st down.

Evening top

Sizes

To fit 81.5[86.5:91.5:96.5:101.5]cm (*32[34:36:38:40]in*) bust
Length to centre back, 35.5cm (*14in*)
The figures in brackets [] refer to the 86.5 (*34*), 91.5 (*36*), 96.5 (*38*) and 101.5cm (*40in*) sizes respectively

Tension

24 sts and 36 rows to 10cm (*3.9in*) over patt worked on No.9 needles

Materials

4 x 25grm balls of Jaeger 3 ply Botany wool
Approx 700 sequins with hole at top
One pair No.9 needles
One pair No.10 needles

Note

Thread approx 350 sequins on to each of 2 balls of yarn

Back

Using No.10 needles and ball of yarn which has not been threaded with sequins, cast on 94[100:106:112:118] sts. Work 15cm (*6in*) K1, P1 rib. Break off yarn. Change to No.9 needles. Join in ball threaded with

SIMPLE STRIPES

Striped patterns, using simple stitches and subtle combinations of colours, are the easiest way of achieving a colourful knitted fabric. A plain, basic jersey can be adapted and given a completely new look by working regular or random stripes in three or four colours, and this is a very useful way of using up oddments of yarn in the same thickness.

Twisting yarns to change colour

When working any form of horizontal stripe, there is no problem about joining in a different ball of yarn. As one colour is finished with at the end of a row, the new one is brought in at the beginning of the next row. When each colour has been brought into use it is left until it is required again, then carried loosely up the side of the work and twisted once round the last colour used, before beginning to work with it again. Vertical or diagonal stripes are a little more difficult to work, as the colours must be changed at several points within the same row. When using narrow vertical or diagonal stripes it is best to twist each yarn with the last colour used as it is brought into use, then carry the yarn not in use across the back of the work until it is required again. For wider stripes however it is not advisable to use this method of carrying the yarn across the back of the work as, apart from the waste of yarn, there is a tendency to pull the yarn too tightly, which results in an unsightly bunching of the fabric and loss of tension. It is much better to divide each colour into small separate balls before beginning to work and then use one ball of yarn for each stripe, twisting one colour to the next at the back of the work when a change is made. It is important to remember that stripes worked by twisting the yarn on changing colours give a fabric of normal thickness, while stripes worked by carrying the yarn across the back of the work produce a fabric of double thickness.

Horizontal stripes

These are usually worked in stocking stitch and are achieved by changing colour at the beginning of a knit row. This gives an unbroken line of colour on the right side of the fabric. An even number of rows must be worked, either two, four, six and so on, and the same number of rows can be used for each colour or varied to give a random striped effect.

The purl side of this fabric can also be used as the right side of the work. Where each new colour is brought into use, it gives a broken line of colour on the purl side, which looks most effective.

Ribbed stitches can also be used to produce a striped fabric. Where an unbroken line of colour is required on the right side of the fabric, then the row where a change of colour is made needs to be knitted each time, and the other rows of each stripe worked in ribbing. An interesting fabric is produced by working in ribbing throughout, irrespective of the colour change to give a broken line of colour each time.

Fancy striped rib

Cast on a number of stitches divisible by 10 plus 5.
1st row P5, *K1, yfwd, sl 1, ybk, K1, yfwd, sl 1, ybk, K1, P5, rep from * to end.
2nd row K1, yfwd, sl 1, ybk, K1, yfwd, sl 1, ybk, K1, *P5, K1, yfwd, sl 1, ybk, K1, yfwd, sl 1, ybk, K1, rep from * to end.
These 2 rows form the pattern, changing colours as required.

Chevron stripes

Cast on a number of stitches divisible by 13 plus 2.
1st row *K2, pick up loop lying between needles and place it on the left hand needle then K this loop through the back – called inc 1 –, K4, sl 1 P-wise, K2 tog, psso, K4, inc 1, rep from * to last 2 sts, K2.

2nd row P to end.

These 2 rows form the pattern, changing colours as required on a 1st row.

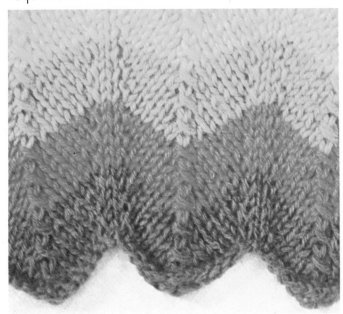

Vertical stripes

To work narrow or wide vertical stripes, the best effect is achieved in stocking stitch with the knit side of the fabric as the right side. The yarn must be carried across or twisted at the back of the fabric.

To work a wide stripe it is necessary to use a separate ball of yarn for each colour. Using two colours, the first colour used would be referred to as A and the second colour as B.

Wide vertical stripe

Cast on 6 stitches with B, 6 with A, 6 with B and 6 with A, making a total of 24 stitches.

1st row *Using A, K6 sts, hold A to the left at the back of the work, take up B and bring it towards the right at the back of the work and under the A thread no longer in use, K6 B, hold B to the left at the back of the work, take up A and bring it towards the right at the back of the work and under the B thread no longer in use, rep from * to end.

2nd row (WS) *Using B, P6 sts, hold B to the left at the front of the work, take up A and bring it towards the right at the front of the work and over the B thread no longer in use, P6 A, hold A to the left at the front of the work, take up B and bring it towards the right at the front of the work and over the A thread no longer in use, rep from * to end.

These 2 rows form the pattern.

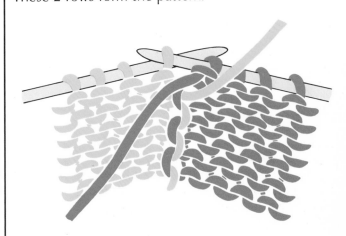

Diagonal stripes

Depending on the width of the stripes, the yarn can either be carried across the back of the work, or separate balls of yarn used for each colour as explained for wide vertical stripes.

Narrow diagonal stripes

Cast on a number of stitches divisible by 5 plus 3, using two colours, A and B.

1st row (RS) K3 A, *pick up B and K2, pick up A and K3, rep from * to end.

2nd row Pick up B and P1, *pick up A and P3, pick up B and P2, rep from * to last 2 sts, pick up A and P2.

3rd row K1 A, *pick up B and K2, pick up A and K3, rep from * to last 2 sts, pick up B and K2.

4th row Pick up A and P1, pick up B and P2, *pick up A and P3, pick up B and P2, rep from * to end.

Continue working in this way, moving the stripes one stitch to the right on K rows and one stitch to the left on P rows.

TWO COLOUR PATTERNS

By combining the working method for horizontal stripes with the clever use of slipped stitches colourful tweed fabrics can be achieved which are quick and easy to work. These stitches can be worked in two or more colours and on each change of colour, the yarn is merely carried up the side of the work and does not have to be carried across the back of the fabric as for the more difficult jacquard and Fair Isle patterns.

Bird's eye stitch

Using 2 colours coded as A and B, cast on multiples of 2 stitches.

1st row Using A, *sl 1 P-wise, K1, rep from * to end.
2nd row Using A, P to end.
3rd row Using B, *K1, sl 1 P-wise, rep from * to end.
4th row Using B, P to end.
These 4 rows form the pattern.

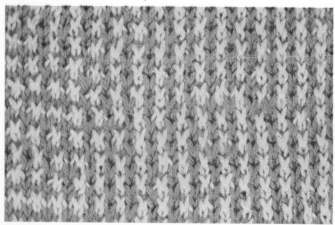

Mock houndstooth stitch

Using 2 colours coded as A and B, cast on multiples of 3 stitches.

1st row Using A, *sl 1 P-wise, K2, rep from * to end.

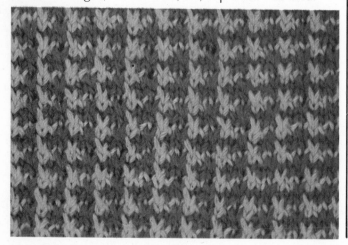

2nd row Using A, P to end.
3rd row Using B, *K2, sl 1 P-wise, rep from * to end.
4th row Using B, P to end.
These 4 rows form the pattern.

Crossed stitch

Using 2 colours coded as A and B, cast on multiples of 2 plus 1.

1st row Using A, K to end.
2nd row Using A, K to end.
3rd row Using B, *K1, sl 1 P-wise, rep from * to last st, K1.
4th row Using B, *K1, yfwd, sl 1 P-wise, ybk, rep from * to last st, K1.
5th row Using A, K to end.
6th row Using A, K to end.
7th row Using B, *sl 1 P-wise, K1, rep from * to last st, sl 1 P-wise.
8th row Using B, *sl 1 P-wise, ybk, K1, yfwd, rep from * to last st, sl 1 P-wise.
These 8 rows form the pattern.

Bee stitch

Using 2 colours coded as A and B, cast on multiples of 2 stitches.

1st row Using A, K to end.
2nd row Using A, K to end.
3rd row Using B, *insert right hand needle into next stitch on the row below and K in usual way – called K1B –, K next st on left hand needle, rep from * to end.
4th row Using B, K to end.
5th row Using A, *K1, K1B, rep from * to end.

6th row Using A, K to end.
Rows 3 to 6 form the pattern.

Two colour fuchsia stitch
Using 2 colours coded as A and B, cast on multiples of 4 stitches.
1st row Using A, K to end.
2nd row Using A, P to end.
Rep 1st and 2nd rows once more.
5th row Using B, *K3, insert right hand needle into next st in first row of A and draw through a loop, K1 and pass the loop over K1, rep from * to end.
6th row Using B, P to end.
7th row Using B, K to end.
8th row Using B, P to end.
9th row Using A, *K1, insert right hand needle into next st in first row of B and draw through a loop, K1 and pass the loop over K1, K2, rep from * to end.
Rows 2 to 9 form the pattern.

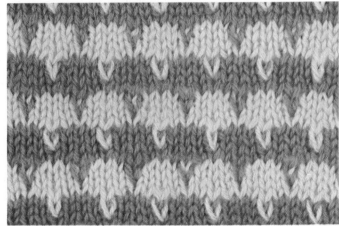

Ladder stitch
Using 2 colours coded as A and B, cast on multiples of 6 stitches plus 5.
1st row Using A, K2, *sl 1 P-wise, K5, rep from * to last 3 sts, sl 1 P-wise, K2.
2nd row Using A, P2, *sl 1 P-wise, P5, rep from * to last 3 sts, sl 1 P-wise, P2.
3rd row Using B, *K5, sl 1 P-wise, rep from * to last 5 sts, K5.

4th row Using B, *K5, yfwd, sl 1 P-wise, ybk, rep from * to last 5 sts, K5.
These 4 rows form the pattern.

Brick stitch
Using 2 colours coded as A and B, cast on multiples of 4 stitches.
1st row Using A, K to end.
2nd row Using A, K to end.
3rd row Using B, *K3, sl 1 P-wise, rep from * to end.
4th row Using B, *sl 1 P-wise, P3, rep from * to end.
5th row As 1st.
6th row As 2nd.
7th row Using B, K2, *sl 1 P-wise, K3, rep from * to last 2 sts, sl 1 P-wise, K1.
8th row Using B, P1, *sl 1 P-wise, P3, rep from * to last 3 sts, sl 1 P-wise, P2.
9th row As 1st.
10th row As 2nd.
11th row Using B, K1, *sl 1 P-wise, K3, rep from * to last 3 sts, sl 1 P-wise, K2.
12th row Using B, P2, *sl 1 P-wise, P3, rep from * to last 2 sts, sl 1 P-wise, P1.
13th row As 1st.
14th row As 2nd.
15th row Using B, *sl 1 P-wise, K3, rep from * to end.
16th row Using B, *P3, sl 1 P-wise, rep from * to end.
These 16 rows form the pattern.

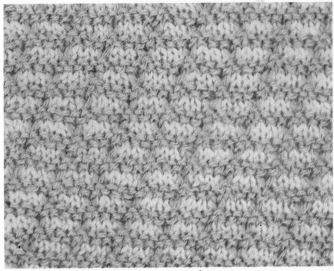

TEXTURED PATTERNS

Unlike patterns which produce a plain knitted fabric with colourful designs, such as Fair Isle (see later), patterns worked in stripes which also combine slipped stitches, form textured fabrics which are further enhanced by contrasting colours. Because these stitches do not need such careful regulation of the tension, they do not necessarily need contrasting yarns of the same thickness. A wool yarn can be combined with many different materials, such as macramé cord, cotton or metallic yarns to give an exciting and colourful effect.

All the stitches illustrated here are produced by working a set number of rows with one or more colours and, however complicated they may appear, the colours are changed at the end of the row just as for more usual striped patterns.

Ridged check stitch

Two colours of the same yarn have been used for this sample, coded as A and B. Cast on a number of stitches divisible by 4 plus 3 in A.

1st row (WS) Using A, P to end.
2nd row Using B, K3, *sl 1 P–wise keeping yarn at back of work – called sl 1B –, K3, rep from * to end.
3rd row Using B, P3, *sl 1 P–wise keeping yarn at front of work – called sl 1F –, P3, rep from * to end.
4th row As 2nd.
5th row Using B, P to end.
6th row Using A, as 2nd.
7th row Using A, as 3rd.
8th row Using A, as 4th.
These 8 rows form the pattern.

1st row (RS) Using A, K to end.
2nd row Using A, P to end.
3rd row Using B, K2, *sl 1 P-wise keeping yarn at back of work – called sl 1B –, K1, rep from * to last st, K1.
4th row Using B, K1, *(K1, sl 1 P-wise keeping yarn at front of work – called sl 1F) twice, P1, sl 1F, rep from * to last 4 sts, K1, sl 1F, K2.
5th row Using A, K5, *sl 1B, K5, rep from * to end.
6th row Using A, P5, *sl 1F, P5, rep from * to end.
7th row As 5th.
8th row As 6th.
9th row Using A, as 1st.
10th row Using A, as 2nd.
11th row Using B, K1, *sl 1B, K1, rep from * to end.
12th row Using B, K1, *sl 1F, P1, (sl 1F, K1) twice, rep from * to last 4 sts, sl 1F, P1, s1 1F, K1.
13th row Using A, K2, *sl 1B, K5, rep from * to last 3 sts, sl 1B, K2.
14th row Using A, P2, *sl 1F, P5, rep from * to last 3 sts, sl 1F, P2.
15th row As 13th.
16th row As 14th.
These 16 rows form the pattern.

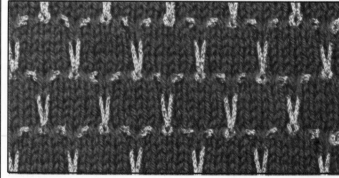

Ribbon stitch

Two colours of contrasting yarn have been used for this sample, a plain yarn coded as A and a macramé cord coded as B. Cast on a number of stitches divisible by 4 plus 3 in A.

1st row (WS) Using A, P to end.
2nd row Using B, K1, *sl 1 P-wise keeping yarn at back of work – called sl 1B –, K3, rep from * to last 2 sts, sl 1B, K1.
3rd row Using B, K1, *sl 1 P-wise keeping yarn at front of work – called sl 1F –, K1, K1 winding yarn 3 times round needle, K1, rep from * to last 2 sts, sl 1F, K1.
4th row Using A, K3, *sl 1B dropping extra loops, K3, rep from * to end.
5th row Using A, P3, *sl 1B, P3, rep from * to end.
6th row Using A, K3, *sl 1B, K3, rep from * to end.

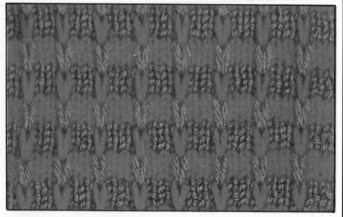

Fancy checked stitch

Two colours of contrasting yarn have been used for this sample, a plain yarn coded as A and a metallic yarn coded as B. Cast on a number of stitches divisible by 6 plus 5 in A.

7th row Using A, as 5th.
8th row Using A, as 6th.
These 8 rows form the pattern.

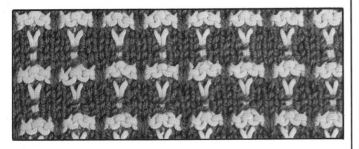

Tapestry stitch

Two colours of the same yarn have been used for this sample, coded as A and B. Cast on a number of stitches divisible by 4 plus 3 in A.

1st row (WS) Using A, P to end.
2nd row Using B, K1, sl 1 P-wise keeping yarn at front of work – called sl 1F –, K1, *sl 1 P-wise keeping yarn at back of work – called sl 1B –, K1, sl 1F, K1, rep from * to end.
3rd row Using B, P3, *sl 1F, P3, rep from * to end.
4th row Using A, K1, *sl 1B, K3, rep from * to last 2 sts, sl 1B, K1.
5th row Using A, P to end.
6th row Using B, K1, sl 1B, K1, *sl 1F, K1, sl 1B, K1, rep from * to end.
7th row Using B, P1, *sl 1F, P3, rep from * to last 2 sts, sl 1F, P1.
8th row Using A, K3, *sl 1B, K3, rep from * to end.
These 8 rows form the pattern.

Lattice stitch

Two colours of contrasting yarn have been used for this sample, a plain yarn coded as A and a metallic yarn coded as B. Cast on a number of stitches divisible by 6 plus 2 in A.

1st row (WS) Using A, K to end.
2nd row Using B, K1, sl 1 P-wise keeping yarn at back of work – called sl 1B –, *K4, sl 2B, rep from * to last 6 sts, K4, sl 1B, K1.
3rd row Using B, P1, sl 1 P-wise keeping yarn at front of work – called sl 1F –, *P4, sl 2F, rep from * to last 6 sts, P4, sl 1F, P1.
4th row Using A, as 2nd.
5th row Using A, K1, sl 1F, *K4, sl 2F, rep from * to last 6 sts, K4, sl 1F, K1.
6th row Using B, K3, *sl 2B, K4, rep from * to last 5 sts, sl 2B, K3.

7th row Using B, P3, *sl 2F, P4, rep from * to last 5 sts, sl 2F, P3.
8th row Using A, as 6th.
9th row Using A, K3, *sl 2F, K4, rep from * to last 5 sts, sl 2F, K3.
Rows 2 – 9 form the pattern.

Cushion

Size

40.5cm (*16in*) wide by 40.5cm (*16in*) deep

Tension

26 sts and 32 rows to 10cm (*3.9in*) over patt worked on No.8 needles

Materials

5 × 25grm balls of Wendy Double Knitting Nylonised in main shade, A
5 balls of contrast colour, B
One pair No.8 needles
40.5cm (*16in*) by 40.5cm (*16in*) cushion pad
1.95 metres (2yd) silk cord, optional
20.5cm (*8in*) zip fastener

Cushion

Using No.8 needles and A, cast on 103 sts. Cont in tapestry st until work measures 40.5cm (*16in*) from beg. Cast off. Make another piece in same way.

To make up

Press each piece under a damp cloth with a warm iron. With RS facing, join 3 sides. Turn RS out. Insert cushion pad. Join rem seam inserting zip in centre. Sew cord round edges, looping at each corner.

MOSAIC PATTERNS

Mosaic patterns are worked in two colours, using the slip-stitch method to form complex and unusual geometric shapes. Although the patterns may appear to be complicated, the working method is very simple and is based on knitting two rows with one colour and two rows with the second colour.

What makes these designs so interesting is that bands of different patterns which require the same multiples of stitches can be worked together to form an overall fabric, using as many different colours as you like. This is another way of using up oddments of yarn which are of the same thickness.

You could use a basic pattern which gives the correct multiples of stitches required for each mosaic pattern to form a colourful and original child's jersey, a cushion or a warm and practical pram or cot cover. Because the yarn is not carried across the back of the work as in Fair Isle knitting, the back of the fabric formed is not untidy and is of a single thickness.

Brick pattern

Two colours are used, coded as A and B. Using A, cast on a number of stitches divisible by 4 plus 3.

1st row (RS) Using A, K to end.
2nd row Using A, P to end.
3rd row Using B, K3, *sl 1, K3, rep from * to end.

4th row Using B, K3, *yfwd, sl 1, ybk, K3, rep from * to end.
5th row Using A, K2, *sl 1, K1, rep from * to last st, K1.
6th row Using A, P2, *sl 1, P1, rep from * to last st, P1.
7th row Using B, K1, *sl 1, K3, rep from * to last 2 sts, sl 1, K1.
8th row Using B, K1, *yfwd, sl 1, ybk, K3, rep from * to last 2 sts, yfwd, sl 1, ybk, K1.
9th and 10th rows As 1st and 2nd.
11th and 12th rows As 7th and 8th.
13th and 14th rows As 5th and 6th.
15th and 16th rows As 3rd and 4th.
These 16 rows form the pattern.

Double brick pattern

Two colours are used, coded as A and B. Using A, cast on a number of stitches divisible by 4 plus 3.
1st row (RS) Using A, K to end.
2nd row Using A, K to end.
3rd row Using B, K3, *sl 1, K3, rep from * to end.
4th row Using B, K3, *yfwd, sl 1, ybk, K3, rep from * to end.
5th row Using A, K1, *sl 1, K3, rep from * to last 2 sts, sl 1, K1.
6th row Using A, K1, *yfwd, sl 1, ybk, K3, rep from * to last 2 sts, yfwd, sl 1, ybk, K1.

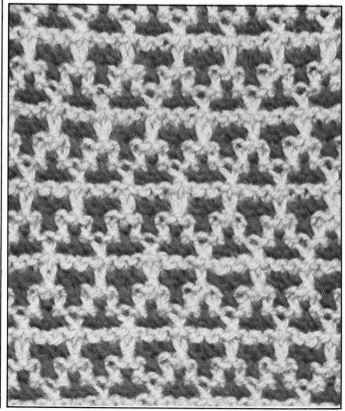

7th row Using B, K2, *sl 1, K1, rep from * to last st, K1.
8th row Using B, K2, *yfwd, sl 1, ybk, K1, rep from * to last st, K1.
9th and 10th rows Using A, as 3rd and 4th.
11th and 12th rows Using B, as 5th and 6th.
13th and 14th rows As 1st and 2nd.
15th and 16th rows As 11th and 12th.
17th and 18th rows As 9th and 10th.
19th and 20th rows As 7th and 8th.
21st and 22nd rows As 5th and 6th.
23rd and 24th rows As 3rd and 4th.
These 24 rows form the pattern.

Vertical chevron pattern

Two colours are used, coded as A and B. Using A, cast on a number of stitches divisible by 6 plus 2.
1st row (RS) Using A, *K5, sl 1, rep from * to last 2 sts, K2.
2nd and every alt row Using same colour as previous row, keep yarn at front of work and P all K sts of previous row and sl all sl sts.
3rd row Using B, K2, * sl 1, K3, sl 1, K1, rep from * to end.
5th row Using A, K3, *sl 1, K5, rep from * to last 5 sts, sl 1, K4.
7th row Using B, K4, *sl 1, K1, sl 1, K3, rep from * to last 4 sts, (sl 1, K1) twice.
9th row Using A, K1, *sl 1, K5, rep from * to last st, K1.
11th row Using B, K2, *sl 1, K1, sl 1, K3, rep from * to end.
13th, 15th, 17th, 19th and 21st rows Rep 1st, 3rd, 5th, 7th and 9th rows.
23rd, 25th, 27th and 29th rows Rep 7th, 5th, 3rd and 1st rows.
31st, 33rd, 35th, 37th and 39th rows Rep 11th, 9th, 7th, 5th and 3rd rows.
40th row As 2nd.
These 40 rows form the pattern.

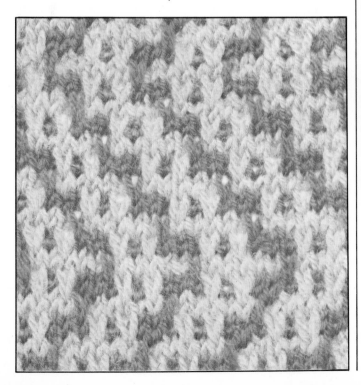

Greek key pattern

Two colours are used, coded as A and B. Using A, cast on a number of stitches divisible by 6 plus 2.
1st row (RS) Using A, K to end.
2nd row Using A, K to end.
3rd row Using B, K1, *sl 1, K5, rep from * to last st, K1.
4th and every alt row Using same colour as previous row, keep the yarn at front of work and K all K sts of previous row and sl all sl sts.
5th row Using A, K2, *sl 1, K3, sl 1, K1, rep from * to end.
7th row Using B, K1, *sl 1, K3, sl 1, K1, rep from * to last st, K1.
9th row Using A, K6, *sl 1, K5, rep from * to last 2 sts, sl 1, K1.
11th and 12th rows Using B, as 1st and 2nd.
13th row Using A, K4, *sl 1, K5, rep from * to last 4 sts, sl 1, K3.
15th row Using B, *K3, sl 1, K1, sl 1, rep from * to last 2 sts, K2.
17th row Using A, K2, *sl 1, K1, sl 1, K3, rep from * to end.
19th row Using B, K3, *sl 1, K5, rep from * to last 5 sts, sl 1, K4.
20th row As 4th.
These 20 rows form the pattern.

Maze pattern

Two colours are used, coded as A and B. Using A, cast on a number of stitches divisible by 12 plus 3.
1st row (RS) Using A, K to end.
2nd row Using A, P to end.
3rd row Using B, K1, *sl 1, K11, rep from * to last 2 sts, sl 1, K1.
4th and every alt row Using same colour as previous row, keep the yarn at front of work and P all K sts of previous row and sl all sl sts.

5th row Using A, K2, *sl 1, K9, sl 1, K1, rep from * to last st, K1.

7th row Using B, (K1, sl 1) twice, *K7, (sl 1, K1) twice, sl 1, rep from * to end omitting sl 1 at end of last rep.

9th row Using A, K2, sl 1, K1, sl 1, *K5, (sl 1, K1) 3 times, sl 1, rep from * to last 10 sts, K5, sl 1, K1, sl 1, K2.

11th row Using B, (K1, sl 1) 3 times, *K3, (sl 1, K1) 4 times, sl 1, rep from * to last 9 sts, K3, (sl 1, K1) 3 times.

13th row Using A, K2, *sl 1, K1, rep from * to last st, K1.

15th, 17th, 19th, 21st, 23rd and 25th rows Rep 11th, 9th, 7th, 5th, 3rd and 1st rows.

27th row Using B, K7, *sl 1, K11, rep from * to last 8 sts, sl 1, K7.

29th row Using A, K6, *sl 1, K1, sl 1, K9, rep from * to last 9 sts, sl 1, K1, sl 1, K6.

31st row Using B, K5, *(sl 1, K1) twice, sl 1, K7, rep from * to last 10 sts, (sl 1, K1) twice, sl 1, K5.

33rd row Using A, K4, *(sl 1, K1) 3 times, sl 1, K5, rep from * to last 11 sts, (sl 1, K1) 3 times, sl 1, K4.

35th row Using B, K3, *(sl 1, K1) 4 times, sl 1, K3, rep from * to end.

37th row As 13th.

39th, 41st, 43rd, 45th and 47th rows Rep 35th, 33rd, 31st, 29th and 27th rows.

48th row As 4th.

These 48 rows form the pattern.

Lattice window pattern

Two colours are used, coded as A and B. Using A, cast on a number of stitches divisible by 12 plus 3. K 1 row.

1st row (RS) Using B, K1, *sl 1, K11, rep from * to last 2 sts, sl 1, K1.

2nd and every alt row Using same colour as previous row, keep the yarn at front of work and K all K sts of previous row and sl all sl sts.

3rd row Using A, K4, *(sl 1, K1) 3 times, sl 1, K5, rep from * to last 11 sts, (sl 1, K1) 3 times, sl 1, K4.

5th row Using B, K3, *sl 1, K7, sl 1, K3, rep from * to end.

7th row Using A, K2, *sl 1, K3, sl 1, K1, rep from * to last st, K1.

9th row Using B, K5, *sl 1, K3, sl 1, K7, rep from * to last 10 sts, sl 1, K3, sl 1, K5.

11th row Using A, K2, *sl 1, K1, sl 1, K5, (sl 1, K1) twice, rep from * to last st, K1.

13th row Using B, K7, *sl 1, K11, rep from * to last 8 sts, sl 1, K7.

15th and 16th rows As 11th and 12th.

17th and 18th rows As 9th and 10th.

19th and 20th rows As 7th and 8th.

21st and 22nd rows As 5th and 6th.

23rd and 24th rows As 3rd and 4th.

These 24 rows form the pattern.

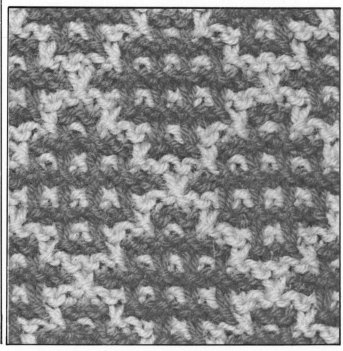

MOCK FAIR ISLE

Although they look rather complicated, Fair Isle patterns are quite simple to work as they rarely use more than two colours in one row at a time. The beautiful, multi-coloured effects are achieved by varying the two combinations of colours.

A form of 'mock' Fair Isle, however, is even simpler to work as this only requires two colours throughout – a plain background colour and a random yarn used for the contrast colour. As the random yarn is worked, it changes its colour sequence to give a most striking effect.

Unlike striped patterns, where the colour is changed at the end of a row, two yarns will be in use during the course of a row. As only a few stitches are worked in one colour, the yarn not in use can be carried loosely across the back off the work until it is required, then twisted round the last colour before it is brought into use again (see colour in knitting).

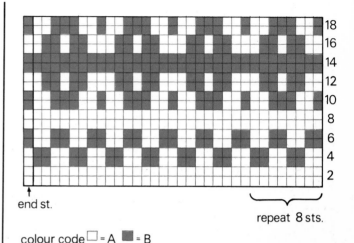

↑ end st.

repeat 8 sts.

colour code ☐ = A ◼ = B

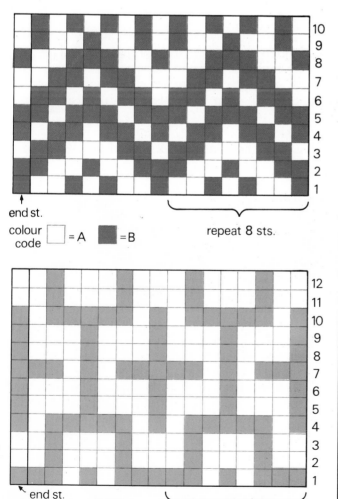

↑ end st.

colour code ☐ = A ◼ = B

repeat 8 sts.

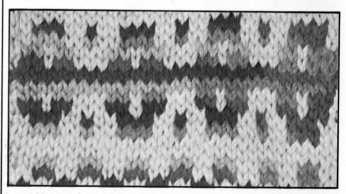

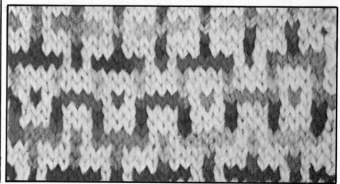

Three 'mock' Fair Isle patterns

We give three samples and charts here, any one of which can be used for the short sleeved jersey, as each pattern requires multiples of 8 stitches plus one.

Mock Fair Isle jersey

Sizes

To fit 86.5[91.5:96.5:101.5]cm (34[36:38:40]in) bust
Length to shoulder, 61[62:66:67.5]cm (24[24½:26:26½]in)
Sleeve seam, 10cm (4in)
The figures in brackets [] refer to the 91.5 (36), 96.5 (38) and 101.5cm (40in) sizes respectively

Tension

26 sts and 32 rows to 10cm (3.9in) over patt worked on No.9 needles

Materials

7[7:8:8] × 40grm balls of Wendy Marina Double Crepe in main shade, A
6[7:8:9] × 20grm balls of Wendy Random Courtelle Double Crepe in contrast colour, B
One pair No.9 needles
One pair No.11 needles

Back

Using No.11 needles and A, cast on 113[121:129:137] sts.
1st row K1, *P1, K1, rep from * to end.
2nd row P1, *K1, P1, rep from * to end.
Rep these 2 rows 11 times more. Change to No.9 needles. Beg with a K row cont in st st, working in any patt from chart, until work measures 43[43:45.5:45.5]cm (17[17:18:18]in) from beg, ending with a WS row.

Shape armholes

Keeping patt correct, cast off 6[7:8:9] sts at beg of next 2 rows. Dec one st at each end of next 8[9:10:11] rows. 85[89:93:97] sts. Cont in patt without shaping until armholes measure 18[19:20.5:21.5]cm (7[7½:8:8½]in) from beg, ending with a WS row.

Shape shoulders

Cast off at beg of next and every row 8[8:9:9] sts twice, 8[9:9:9] sts twice and 9[9:9:10] sts twice. Leave rem 35[37:39:41] sts on holder for back neck.

Front

Work as given for back until armhole shaping has been completed. 85[89:93:97] sts. Cont without shaping until armholes measure 14[15:16.5:18]cm (5½[6:6½:7]in) from beg, ending with a WS row.

Shape neck

Next row Patt 32[33:34:35], turn and leave rem sts on holder.
Complete this side first. Dec one st at neck edge on next and every row 7 times in all. 25[26:27:28] sts. Cont without shaping until front matches back to shoulder, ending at armhole edge.

Shape shoulder

Cast off at beg of next and every alt row 8[8:9:9] sts once, 8[9:9:9] sts once and 9[9:9:10] sts once.
With RS of work facing, sl first 21[23:25:27] sts on holder for front neck, rejoin yarn to rem sts and patt to end. Complete to match first side, reversing shaping.

Short sleeves

Using No.11 needles and A, cast on 81[89:89:97] sts. Work 12 rows rib as given for back. Change to No.9 needles. Beg with a K row cont in st st, working in any patt from chart and inc one st at each end of 3rd and every foll 6th row, until there are 87[95:95:103] sts. Cont without shaping until sleeve measures 10cm (4in) from beg, ending with a WS row.

Shape top

Cast off 6[7:8:9] sts at beg of next 2 rows. Dec one st at each end of next and every foll alt row until 47[55:47:49] sts rem. Patt one row. Cast off 2 sts at beg of next 16[18:14:14] rows. Cast off rem 15[17:19:21] sts.

Neckband

Join right shoulder seam. Using No.11 needles, A and with RS of work facing, K up 18 sts down left front neck, K across front neck sts on holder, K up 19 sts up right front neck and K across back neck sts on holder. 87[91:95:99] sts. Work 12 rows rib as given for back. Cast off loosely in rib.

To make up

Press under a dry cloth with a warm iron. Join left shoulder and neckband seam. Set in sleeves. Join side and sleeve seams. Press seams.

Toddler's dressing gown

The mock Fair Isle technique has been used for this trendy cardigan dressing gown for a toddler. An even more interesting pattern has been achieved, however, by using a plain background with a contrasting random yarn for the first pattern repeat, then reversing the pattern by using a second random yarn as the background and a second plain colour for the contrast for the next repeat.

Dressing gown
Sizes
To fit 56[61]cm (22[24]in) chest
Length to shoulder, 56[61]cm (22[24]in)

Sleeve seam, 16.5[20.5]cm (6½[8]in)
The figures in brackets [] refer to the 61cm (24in) size only

Tension
28 sts and 36 rows to 10cm (3.9in) over patt worked on No.10 needles

Materials
3[4] × 20grm balls of Sirdar Wash'n'wear 4 ply Crepe in 1st contrast, A
3[3] × 25grm balls of Sirdar Multi 4 ply in 2nd contrast, B
2[2] × 20grm balls of Sirdar Wash'n'Wear 4 ply Crepe in 3rd contrast, G

2[3] × 25grm balls of Sirdar Multi 4 ply in 4th contrast, D
One pair No.10 needles
One pair No.12 needles
8 buttons

Back and fronts

Using No.12 needles and A, cast on 162[175] sts and work in one piece to underarm. Beg with a K row work 9 rows st st.

Next row K all sts tbl to form hemline.

Change to No.10 needles. Beg with a K row cont in st st, join in B and work **22 rows from chart using A and B. Break off A and B. Join in C and D and work 22 rows from chart, using C for A and D for B. **. Cont in patt from ** to ** until work measures 43[47.5] cm (17[18¾]in) from hemline, ending with a WS row.

Divide for armholes

Next row Patt 37[39] sts, cast off 6[8] sts, patt 76[81] sts, cast off 6[8] sts, patt 37[39] sts.

Complete left front first. Keeping patt correct, dec one st at armhole edge on every row until 31[32] sts rem. Cont without shaping until armhole measures 9[9.5]cm (3½[3¾]in) from beg, ending at neck edge.

Shape neck

Cast off 5 sts at beg of next row. Dec one st at neck edge on every row until 20[20] sts rem. Cont without shaping until armhole measures 11.5[12]cm (4½[4¾]in) from beg, ending at armhole edge.

Shape shoulder

Cast off at beg of next and foll alt row 10 sts twice.

With WS of work facing, rejoin yarn to sts for back. Keeping patt correct, dec one st at each end of every row until 64[67] sts rem. Cont without shaping until armholes measure same as left front to shoulder, ending with a WS row.

Shape shoulders

Cast off at beg of next and every row 10 sts 4 times and 24[27] sts once.

With WS of work facing, rejoin yarn to rem sts and complete right front to match left front, reversing shaping.

Sleeves

Using No.12 needles and A, cast on 44[48] sts. Work 10 rows K1, P1 rib, inc 19[15] sts evenly across last row. 63[63] sts. Change to No.10 needles. Cont in patt as given for back until sleeve measures 16.5[20.5]cm (6½[8]in) from beg, taking care to beg with a patt row and colour which will enable sleeve seam to be completed on same row as back and fronts at underarm, ending with a WS row.

Shape top

Cast off 3[4] sts at beg of next 2 rows. Dec one st at each end of next and every alt row until 39[41] sts rem, then at each end of every row until 27 sts rem. Dec 2 sts at each end of every row until 11 sts rem. Cast off.

Button band

Using No.12 needles and A, cast on 12 sts. Work in

K1, P1 rib until band is long enough, when slightly stretched, to fit from hemline to beg of neck shaping. Leave sts on holder. St button band in place on left front for a girl and right front for a boy from hemline to neck. Mark positions for 8 buttons on button band, the first to come in neckband with 7 more evenly spaced at 5cm (2in) intervals, measured from base of previous buttonhole.

Buttonhole band

Work as given for button band, making buttonholes as markers are reached, as foll:

1st row (buttonhole row) Rib 5 sts, cast off 2, rib to end.
2nd row Rib to end, casting on 2 sts above those cast off in previous row.

Leave sts on holder.

Neckband

Join shoulder seams. St buttonhole band in place. Using No.12 needles, A and with RS of work facing, sl 12 sts of band on to needle, K up 59[63] sts evenly round neck then rib across rem sts on holder. Work 1 row K1, P1 rib. Make buttonhole as before on next 2 rows. Work 3 more rows rib. Cast off in rib.

To make up

Press each piece under a damp cloth with a warm iron. Join sleeve seams. Set in sleeves. Press seams. Turn hem to WS at lower edge and sl down. Sew on buttons.

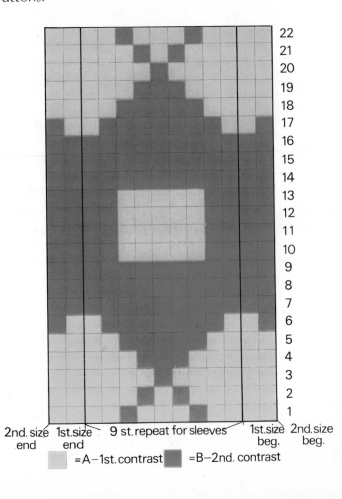

2nd. size end   1st.size end   9 st. repeat for sleeves   1st.size beg.   2nd.size beg.

=A–1st.contrast   =B–2nd. contrast

TRADITIONAL FAIR ISLE
Simple patterns

Traditional Fair Isle patterns produce beautiful designs and fabrics, which are world-renowned for their subtle colour combinations. Ideally, they should be worked in the authentic, softly shaded yarn but they look just as effective when worked in bright, contrasting colours.

These patterns may be used to form an all-over fabric or as a border to highlight the welt and sleeves of a basic jersey or cardigan. When the pattern is small and is repeated as an all-over design, it is a fairly simple matter to work from a chart, where each colour in the pattern is shown as a separate symbol. Some knitters, however, experience difficulty in working from a chart when the pattern is large and fairly complex, particularly where shaping is required. In this event, it is preferable to work from a pattern which gives row-by-row instructions, where each separate colour is coded with a letter, such as A, B or C. To help you decide which method you wish to follow, the patterns here have been given with row by row instructions.

Fair Isle pattern No. 1
Cast on multiples of 12 stitches plus 6.
1st row *K3 A, 1 B, 5 A, 1 B, 2 A, rep from * to last 6 sts, 3 A, 1 B, 2 A.
2nd row *(P1 A, 1 B) twice, 2 A, rep from * to end.
3rd row *K1 A, 1 B, 3 A, 1 B, rep from * to end.
4th row As 2nd.
5th row *K1 B, 2 A, rep from * to end.
6th row *(P1 B, 1 A) twice, 2 B, rep from * to end.
7th row *K2 B, (1 A, 1 B) twice, rep from * to end.
Rep 6th and 7th rows once more.
10th row *P2 A, 1 B, rep from * to end.
11th row *K2 A, (1 B, 1 A) twice, rep from * to end.

12th row *P1 B, 3 A, 1 B, 1 A, rep from * to end.
13th row As 11th.
14th row *P2 A, 1 B, 5 A, 1 B, 3 A, rep from * to last 6 sts, 2 A, 1 B, 3 A.
15th row *K1 B, 5 A, rep from * to end.
16th row *P1 B, 3 A, 1 B, 1 A, rep from * to end.
17th row *K2 A, (1 B, 1 A) twice, rep from * to end.
18th row As 16th.
19th row *K1 B, 2 A, rep from * to end.
20th row *P1 A, 3 B, 1 A, 1 B, rep from * to end.
21st row *K1 B, 1 A, 3 B, 1 A, rep from * to end. Rep 20th and 21st rows once more.
24th row *P2 A, 1 B, rep from * to end.
25th row *K1 A, 1 B, 3 A, 1 B, rep from * to end.
26th row *(P1 A, 1 B) twice, 2 A, rep from * to end.
27th row As 25th.
28th row *P5 A, 1 B, rep from * to end.
These 28 rows form the pattern.

Fair Isle pattern No. 2
Cast on multiples of 18 stitches plus 1.
1st row *K1 B, 1 A, rep from * to last st, 1 B.
2nd row Using A, P to end.
3rd row Using A, K to end.
4th row *P1 C, 1 A, 1 C, 6 A, 1 C, 6 A, 1 C, 1 A, rep from * to last st, 1 C.
5th row *K2 C, 1 A, 1 C, 4 A, 3 C, 4 A, 1 C, 1 A, 1 C, rep from * to last st, 1 C.
6th row *P1 C, 3 A, 1 C, 2 A, 2 C, 1 A, 2 C, 2 A, 1 C, 3 A, rep from * to last st, 1 C.
7th row *K1 C, 4 A, 1 C, 1 A, 5 C, 1 A, 1 C, 4 A, rep from * to last st, 1 C.
8th row *P1 A, 1 C, 4 A, 3 C, 1 A, 3 C, 4 A, 1 C, rep from * to last st, 1 A.
9th row *K1 B, 3 A, 3 B, 2 A, 1 B, 2 A, 3 B, 3 A, rep from

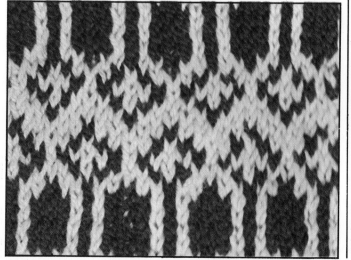

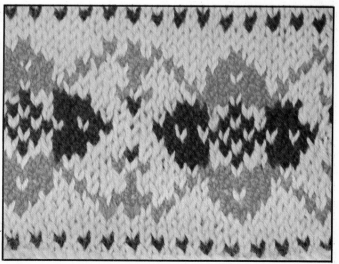

* to last st, 1 B.
10th row *P3 A, 4 B, (1 A, 1 B) twice, 1 A, 4 B, 2 A, rep from * to last st, 1 A.
11th row *K2 A, 2 B, (1 A, 1 B) 5 times, 1 A, 2 B, 1 A, rep from * to last st, 1 A.
Rep 10th to 1st rows. These 21 rows form border pattern, working 22nd row for all-over pattern.

Fair Isle pattern No. 3

Cast on multiples of 18 stitches plus 1.
1st row *K1 B, 1 A, rep from * to last st, 1 B.
2nd row *P1 A, 1 B, rep from * to last st, 1 A.
3rd row Using A, K to end.
4th row Using A, P to end.
5th row As 3rd.
6th row *P3 A, 1 C, 5 A, 1 C, 5 A, 1 C, 2 A, rep from * to last st, 1 A.
7th row *K2 A, 2 C, 4 A, 3 C, 4 A, 2 C, 1 A, rep from * to last st, 1 A.
8th row *P1 A, 3 C, 5 A, 1 C, 5 A, 3 C, rep from * to last st, 1 A.
9th row *K1 D, 2 C, 2 D, 3 C, 3 D, 3 C, 2 D, 2 C, rep from * to last st, 1 D.
10th row *P1 D, 1 C, 2 D, 3 C, 5 D, 3 C, 2 D, 1 C, rep from * to last st, 1 D.
11th row *K1 B, 2 E, 3 B, 3 E, 1 B, 3 E, 3 B, 2 E, rep from * to last st, 1 B.
12th row *P1 F, 2 B, 5 F, 3 B, 5 F, 2 B, rep from * to last st, 1 F.
Rep 11th to 3rd rows.
22nd row *P1 B, 1 A, rep from * to last st, 1 B.
23rd row *K1 A, 1 B, rep from * to last st, 1 A.
These 23 rows form border pattern, repeating 22 rows only for all-over pattern.

Fair Isle pattern No. 4

Cast on multiples of 28 stitches plus 1.
1st row *K2 B, 1 A, 1 B, rep from * to last st, 1 B.
2nd row *P1 B, 3 A, rep from * to last st, 1 B.
3rd row Using A, K to end.
4th row *P1 A, 2 C, 2 A, 2 C, 2 A, 2 C, 3 A, 1 C, 3 A, 2 C, 2 A, 2 C, 2 A, 2 C, rep from * to last st, 1 A.
5th row *K1 A, 1 C, (2 A, 2 C) twice, 3 A, 1 C, 1 A, 1 C, 3 A, (2 C, 2 A) twice, 1 C, rep from * to last st, 1 A.
6th row *P1 A, 1 C, 1 A, 2 C, 2 A, 2 C, 3 A, (1 C, 1 A) twice, 1 C, 3 A, 2 C, 2 A, 2 C, 1 A, 1 C, rep from * to last st, 1 A.
7th row *K1 A, 3 C, 2 A, 2 C, 3 A, 1 C, 1 A, 3 C, 1 A, 1 C, 3 A, 2 C, 2 A, 3 C, rep from * to last st, 1 A.
8th row *P1 A, 2 C, 2 A, 2 C, 3 A, 1 C, 2 A, 3 C, 2 A, 1 C, 3 A, 2 C, 2 A, 2 C, rep from * to last st, 1 A.
9th row *K1 A, 1 D, 2 A, 2 D, 3 A, 3 D, 2 A, 1 D, 2 A, 3 D, 3 A, 2 D, 2 A, 1 D, rep from * to last st, 1 A.
10th row *P1 A, 1 D, 1 A, 2 D, 3 A, 1 D, 2 A, 2 D, 1 A, 1 D, 1 A, 2 D, 2 A, 1 D, 3 A, 2 D, 1 A, 1 D, rep from *to last st, 1 A.
11th row *K1 A, 3 D, 3 A, 2 D, 3 A, 5 D, 3 A, 2 D, 3 A, 3 D, rep from * to last st, 1 A.
12th row *P1 A, 2 D, 3 A, 1 D, 1 A, 2 D, 3 A, 3 D, 3 A, 2 D, 1 A, 1 D, 3 A, 2 D, rep from * to last st, 1 A.
13th row *K1 A, 1 D, 3 A, 1 D, 3 A, 2 D, 3 A, 1 D, 3 A, 2 D, 3 A, 1 D, 3 A, 1 D, rep from * to last st, 1 A.
14th row *P1 A, 1 D, 2 A, 1 D, 1 A, 2 D, 2 A, 2 D, (1 A, 1 D) twice, 1 A, 2 D, 2 A, 2 D, 1 A, 1 D, 2 A, 1 D, rep from * to last st, 1 A.
15th row *K1 A, (1 B, 1 A) twice, 8 B, 1 A, 1 B, 1 A, 8 B, (1 A, 1 B) twice, rep from * to last st, 1 A.
Rep from 14th to 1st rows. These 29 rows form border pattern, working 30th row for all-over pattern.

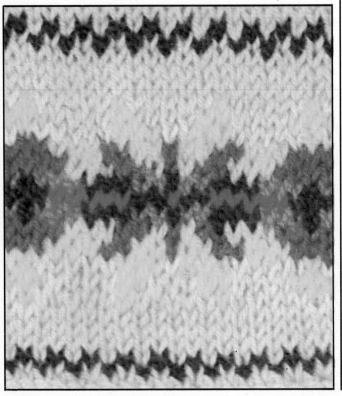

Snowflake patterns

The Scandinavian countries provide an endless source of what are loosely termed 'Fair Isle' designs, particularly variations of the delightful snowflake pattern. They are worked in the same way as the traditional Shetland designs but the patterns are usually bolder and the choice of colour is more distinctive.

From the middle European countries and further east, more intricate and colourful designs are introduced, often involving the use of three or more colours at a time. These beautiful fabrics, often based upon traditional carpet designs, feature floral or symmetrical patterns in rich, jewel colours.

To look most effective, the samples given here should not be used as over-all patterns but as borders, pockets, or cuff motifs.

Border pattern

This can either be worked as a horizontal or vertical

border. For a horizontal border cast on multiples of 20 stitches plus 7 and work the 7 pattern rows from the chart. To work the border vertically, turn the chart sideways and work over 7 stitches for 20 rows.

Star pattern

Another motif which can be used singly or as a horizontal border pattern.

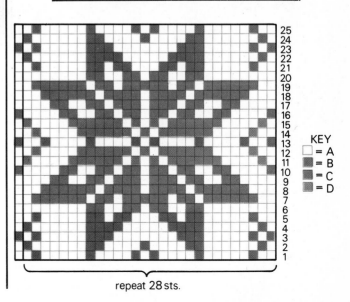

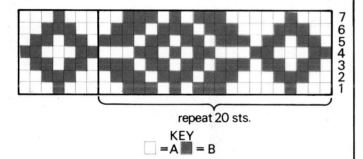

repeat 20 sts.

KEY
□ = A ■ = B

KEY
□ = A
■ = B
■ = C
■ = D

repeat 28 sts.

JACQUARD KNITTING

Whereas traditional Fair Isle knitting normally uses only two colours in any one row, jacquard, collage and patchwork knitting are all forms of the same technique, where more than two colours are used at a time in any one pattern row. These designs are best worked in stocking stitch against a stocking stitch background, although collage knitting may also combine many different stitches to great effect.

Unlike Fair Isle knitting, this means that this method is very clumsy and untidy to work, when more than one strand has to be carried across the back of the work until required again. It is possible to work a small repeating jacquard design in this way, carrying the yarn not in use loosely across the back of the work but this does, inevitably, mean a variance in tension against the main fabric. When working in this way, it is therefore advisable to change to one size larger needles to work the jacquard pattern, reverting to the correct needle size to work the main pattern.

The correct method of working all large, multi-coloured patterns, motifs, wide vertical stripes and patchwork designs, is to use small, separate balls of yarn for each colour. In this way a fabric of single thickness is formed, without any strands of yarn across the back of the work. These patterns are usually worked from a chart, just as in Fair Isle knitting, with each different colour coded with a symbol.

Use of bobbins

Before beginning to knit, wind all the colours which are required into small, separate balls round a bobbin. These are easy to handle and hang at the back of the work, keeping each colour free from tangles.

To make a bobbin Use a stiff piece of cardboard and cut to shape as shown in the diagram, having a slit at the top of each bobbin. Wind the yarn round the centre of the bobbin with the working end passing through the slit as illustrated.

Joining in each new colour

The next important point to remember is that knitting patterns of a geometric or random shape, such as diamonds or flower motifs, as opposed to straight vertical stripes, require the colour to be changed by means of looping the two yarns round each other, on a right side row, to avoid gaps in the knitting. On the return purl row it is not so essential to loop the yarns round each other, as the purl stitch will probably encroach into the pattern sequence and the yarns will automatically be looped. Vertical bands of colour, however, must be looped on every row, as there will be no encroaching stitch to form a natural link in either direction.

To loop yarns on a knit row Keep each ball of yarn at the back of the work until it is required, knit the last stitch in the first colour, then take this end of yarn over the next colour to be used and drop it, pick up the next colour under this strand of yarn, take it over the strand ready to knit the next stitch.

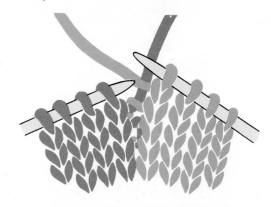

To loop yarns on a purl row Keep each ball of yarn at the front of the work until it is required, purl the last stitch in the first colour, then take this end of yarn over the next colour to be used and drop it, pick up the next colour under this strand of yarn, take it over the strand ready to purl the next stitch.

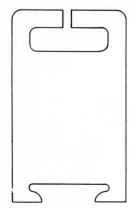
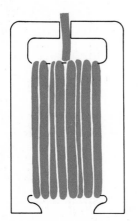

Jacquard borders

Begin by working something as simple as an all-over jacquard border pattern in three colours, stranding each colour across the back of the work until it is required again.

In these charts, the background, or main colour, is coded as A and shown as a blank square; the first contrast colour is coded as B and the 2nd contrast colour coded as C.

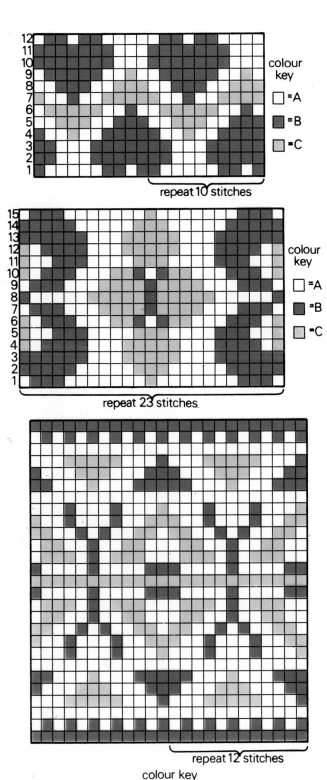

repeat 10 stitches

colour key

☐ = A

■ = B

☐ = C

repeat 23 stitches.

colour key

☐ = A

■ = B

☐ = C

repeat 12 stitches

colour key

☐ = A   ■ = B   ☐ = C

MOTIFS AND COLLAGE

As explained in the previous Chapter, jacquard and collage knitting provide tremendous scope for interesting all-over patterned fabrics, or as a single motif incorporated into an otherwise plain background.

The examples shown here should be worked with small, separate balls of yarn, twisting the yarns at the back of the work when changing colours.

Motifs

Almost any shape or design can be used as a separate jacquard motif, but if you are working out your own pattern it must be charted out on graph paper first, allowing one square for each stitch and one line of squares for each row. Code each different colour with a symbol and make a colour key of these symbols.

If you do not want to make up your own design, use an embroidery chart, such as given for cross stitch embroidery, and adapt this to suit your own colour scheme, again coding each different colour with a symbol.

Butterfly motif

This motif is worked in five contrasting colours against a plain background, making six colours in all. Each motif requires a total of 28 stitches and 34 rows to complete.

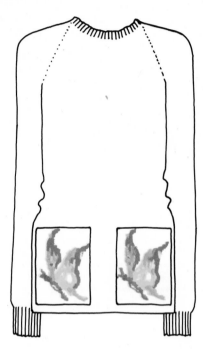

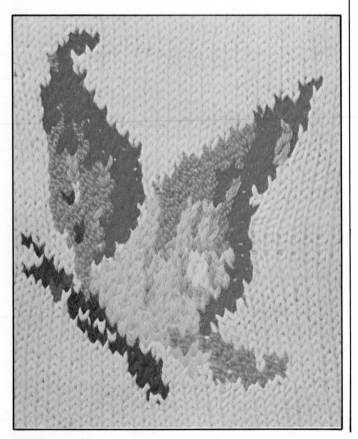

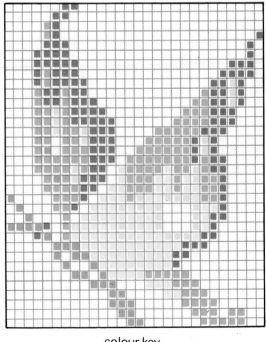

colour key

☐=B ▦=C ☐=D ▩=E ☐=F

Heart motif

Here again, five contrasting colours have been used against a plain background, making a total of six. Each motif requires a total of 35 stitches and 32 rows to complete.

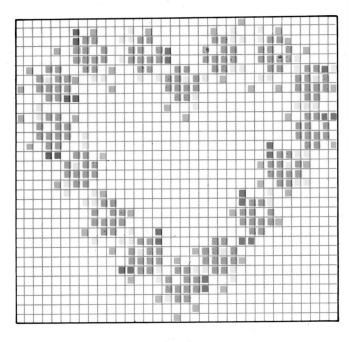

colour key

☐ =B ☐ =C ☐ =D ☐ =E ☐ =F

Multi-coloured collage pattern

This design can be worked with as many colours as you require, varying the sequence to ensure that you

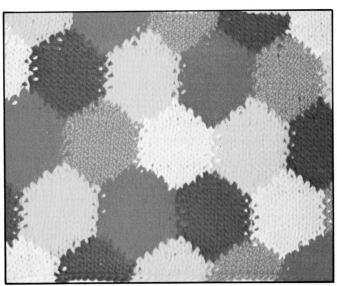

do not use the same colours next to each other.
Cast on a number of stitches divisible by 10, using the main colour. The sample shown here has been worked over 50 stitches with five colours.

1st row (RS) K10 sts in each of 5 colours.
2nd row Using same colours, P10 sts in each of 5 colours.
Rep 1st and 2nd rows once more.
5th row Varying colour sequence as required, K1 with contrast colour, K8 with original colour, *K2 with next contrast colour, K8 with original colour, rep from * to last st, K1 with last contrast colour.
6th row P2 with same contrast colour, *P6 with original colour, P4 with same contrast colour, rep from * to last 8 sts, P6 with original colour, P2 with same contrast colour.
7th row K3 with same contrast colour, *K4 with original colour, K6 with same contrast colour, rep from * to last 7 sts, K4 with original colour, K3 with same contrast colour.
8th row P4 with same contrast colour, *P2 with original colour, break off original colour, P8 with same contrast colour, rep from * to last 6 sts, P2 with original colour, break off original colour, P4 with same contrast colour.
9th row K5 with same contrast colour, keeping colour sequence correct as now set, K10 sts with each colour to last 5 sts, K5 sts with same colour.
10th row P as 9th row.
Rep 9th and 10th rows 3 times more.
17th row K4 sts with original colour as now set, *K2 sts with next contrast colour, K8 sts with original colour as now set, rep from * to last 6 sts, K2 sts with next contrast colour, K4 sts with original colour as now set.
18th row P3 sts with original colour, *P4 with same contrast colour, P6 with original colour, rep from * to last 7 sts, P4 with same contrast colour, P3 with

101

original colour.

19th row K2 with original colour, *K6 with same contrast colour, K4 with original colour, rep from * to last 8 sts, K6 with same contrast colour, K2 with original colour.

20th row P1 with original colour, break off original colour, *P8 with same contrast colour, P2 with original colour, break off original colour, rep from * to last 9 sts, P8 with same contrast colour, P1 with original colour, break off original colour.

21st row Keeping colour sequence correct as now set, work as given for 1st row.

22nd row As 2nd

23rd row As 1st.

24th row As 2nd.

These 24 rows form the pattern.

Collage pram cover

Size

56cm (*22in*) wide by 81.5cm (*32in*) long

Tension

18 sts and 22 rows to 10cm (*3.9in*) over st st worked on No.6 needles

Materials

5 × 50grm balls of Sirdar Pullman in main shade, A

1 ball each of 7 contrast colours, B, C, D, E, F, G and H
One pair No.6 needles

Pram cover centre

Using No.6 needles and A, cast on 80 sts. Work in multi-coloured collage pattern until work measures 71cm (*28in*) from beg, ending with a 12th patt row. Cast off.

Border

Using No.6 needles and A, cast on 100 sts. K 16 rows g st.

Next row K10 sts, cast off 80 sts, K10 sts.

Complete this side first. Cont in g st until band fits along side edge of cover, ending at inside edge. Break off yarn. Leave sts on holder.

With WS of work facing, rejoin yarn to rem 10 sts and complete to match first side, ending at outside edge. Do not break off yarn.

Next row K across first 10 sts, turn and cast on 80 sts, K across rem 10 sts on holder. 100 sts.

K16 rows g st. Cast off loosely.

To make up

Press centre only under a damp cloth with a warm iron. With RS facing, sew border round outer edge of centre. Press seams.

PATCHWORK KNITTING

Completely random patchwork fabrics are worked in the same way as collage patterns, using separate balls of yarn for each colour.

Each patch can be worked over any even number of stitches, or as many number of rows as required, and as each patch is completed it is not necessary to cast off, as you simply carry on with the next patch and colour sequence. The exciting part of this technique comes in arranging the sequence of patches, as no two knitters will work either the same colour or patch in identical order, so each sample has a completely original appearance.

The required number of stitches may be cast on to work two, three, or more patches side by side to give an overall fabric, or single patches can be worked in separate strips to the required length and then sewn together. The latter method means that shaping can be achieved on each side of the strips, to achieve a well-fitting skirt or the delightful patchwork dungarees shown here.

Patchwork samples
In all the examples given here the first, or main colour, is coded as A, the next colour as B, the next as C, and so on and a total of six colours have been used. Once you have decided which colours you would like to use, make a note of the sequence in which you are going to work them so that when you have to pick up contrast colour E you will know immediately to which colour this refers.

These samples have been worked over 28 stitches, allowing 30 rows for each patch. Cast on with A.

1st patch
1st row Using A, K to end.
2nd row Using A, P to end.
Rep these 2 rows 14 times more, using each colour in turn to form stripes. 30 rows.

2nd patch
1st row K14 B, 14 C.
2nd row P14 C, 14 B.
Rep these 2 rows 6 times more.
15th row Using D, K to end.
16th row Using D, P to end.
17th row K14 E, 14 F.
18th row P14 F, 14 E.
Rep last 2 rows 6 times more. 30 rows.

3rd patch
1st row Using A, K to end.
2nd row Using A, P to end.
Rep these 2 rows 4 times more.
11th row K10 B, 8 C, 10 D.
12th row P10 D, 8 C, 10 B.
Rep last 2 rows 9 times more. 30 rows.

4th patch
1st row Using E, K to end.
2nd row Using E, P to end.
Rep these 2 rows 14 times more. 30 rows.
Each time you work a repeat of this patch, use a different colour.

5th patch
1st row K12 F, 4 A, 12 B.
2nd row P12 B, 4 A, 12 F.
Rep these 2 rows 5 times more.
13th row Using C, K to end.
14th row Using C, P to end.
Rep last 2 rows twice more.
19th row K12 D, 4 E, 12 F.
20th row P12 F, 4 E, 12 D.
Rep last 2 rows 5 times more. 30 rows.

Dungarees
Size
Length to back waist, 45.5cm (*18in*)
Inside leg, 25.5cm (*10 in*)

Tension
30 sts and 38 rows to 10cm (*3.9in*) over st st worked on No.10 needles

Materials
2 × 25grm balls of Emu Scotch Superwash 4 ply in main shade, A
1 ball each of 5 contrast colours, B, C, D, E and F
One pair No.10 needles
2 buttons
Waist length of elastic

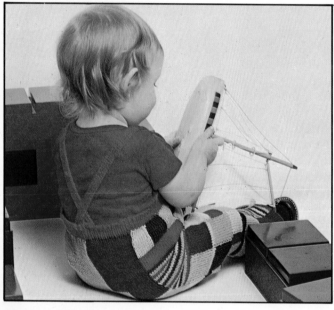

Right front leg
**Using No.10 needles and A, cast on 28 sts. Beg with a K row work 7 rows st st.
Next row Using A, K all sts tbl to form hemline. Work 1st, 2nd, 3rd, 4th and 5th patches, dec one st at beg of 9th and every foll 4th row 4 times in all, noting that less sts will be worked in first block of colour. 24 sts. Cont in patt without shaping until 60th patt row has been completed. **. Keeping patt correct, inc one st at beg of next and every foll 4th row 6 times in all, noting that extra sts will be worked in first block of colour. 30 sts. Cont without shaping until 82nd patt row has been completed.
Shape crotch
Cast off 2 sts at beg of next row. Work 1 row. Dec one st at beg of next and foll alt rows 4 times in all. 24 sts. Cont without shaping until 142nd patt row has been completed. Using A, work 8 rows K1, P1 rib. Cast off loosely in rib.
Right side leg
Using No.10 needles and A, cast on 32 sts. Work hem as given for right front leg. Work 4th, 5th, 2nd, 1st and 3rd patches, shaping dart on 9th row as foll:—

1st dec row Patt 14 sts, K2 tog, sl 1, K1, psso, patt 14 sts. Work 3 rows without shaping.
2nd dec row Patt 13 sts, K2 tog, sl 1, K1, psso, patt 13 sts. Work 3 rows without shaping. Cont dec in this way twice more. 24 sts. Cont in patt without shaping until 143rd row has been completed, ending with a K row.
Shape back
***Next 2 rows** Patt to last 8 sts, turn, patt to end.
Next 2 rows Patt to last 16 sts, turn, patt to end.
Next row Patt across all sts.
Using A, work 8 rows K1, P1 rib. Cast off loosely in rib.
***

Right back leg
Work as given for right front leg from ** to ** reversing shaping and working 3rd, 1st, 5th, 2nd and 4th patches. Inc one st at end of next and every alt row 10 times in all, noting that extra sts will be worked in last block of colour. 34 sts. Cont in patt without shaping until 83rd row has been completed, ending with a K row.
Shape crotch
Cast off 2 sts at beg of next row. Work 1 row. Dec one st at beg of next and every alt row 8 times in all. 24 sts. Cont in patt until 149th row has been completed, ending with a K row.
Shape back
Work as given for side from *** to ***, continuing 4th patch.

Left leg
Work 3 sections as given for right leg, reversing all shaping and sequence of patches, as required.

Bib
Using No.10 needles and A, cast on 44 sts.
1st row Using A, (K1, P1) 4 times, patt 28 sts as 1st row of 5th patch, using separate ball of A, (P1, K1) 4 times.
2nd row Using A, (P1, K1) 4 times, patt 28 sts as given for 2nd row of 5th patch, using A, (K1, P1) 4 times.
Cont in this way until 30th row of patch has been completed. Using A, work 8 rows K1, P1 rib across all sts.
Next row Rib 8, cast off 28 sts, rib to end.
Cont in rib on each set of 8 sts until strap is long enough to reach centre back of dungarees, making a buttonhole 2.5cm (*1 in*) before casting off as foll:—
Next row (buttonhole row) Rib 3 sts, yfwd to make 1, work 2 tog, rib 3 sts.

To make up
Press each part under a damp cloth with a warm iron. Join 3 right leg sections tog including hem and waistband. Join left leg in same way. Press seams. Join front, back and inner leg seams. Turn hems to WS at lower edge and sl st down. St bib in centre of front at top of waist ribbing. Sew elastic inside waistband from each side of bib using casing st. Sew on buttons inside back waist.

ADVANCED STITCHES
SIX STITCH PATTERNS

All patterns given here are made up of multiples of six stitches plus two edge stitches. Using the basic pattern which follows, which gives a tension of 24 stitches and 32 rows to 10cm (3.9in), you can use any of these stitches providing you make sure you achieve the correct tension over stocking stitch.

Cane basket stitch
Cast on a number of stitches divisible by 6 + 2.
1st row K2, *P4, K2, rep from * to end.
2nd row P2, *K4, P2, rep from * to end.
Rep these 2 rows once more.
5th row P3, *K2, P4, rep from * to last 5 sts, K2, P3.
6th row K3, *P2, K4, rep from * to last 5 sts, P2, K3.
Rep last 2 rows once more. These 8 rows form the pattern.

5th row P1, *sl next 2 sts on to cable needle and hold at back of work, K1 then P2 from cable needle – called C3B –, sl next st on to cable needle and hold at front of work, P2 then K1 from cable needle – called C3F –, rep from * to last st, P1.
6th row K1, P1, *K4, P2, rep from * to last 6 sts, K4, P1, K1.
7th row P1, K1, *K4, P2, rep from * to last 6 sts, P4, K1, P1.
Rep 6th and 7th rows once more, then 6th row once.
11th row P1, *C3F, C3B, rep from * to last st, P1.
12th row As 2nd.
These 12 rows form the pattern.

Trellis stitch
Cast on a number of stitches divisible by 6 + 2.
1st row P3, *K2, P4, rep from * to last 5 sts, K2, P3.
2nd row K3, *P2, K4, rep from * to last 5 sts, P2, K3.
Rep these 2 rows once more.

Stepped stitch
Cast on a number of stitches divisible by 6 + 2.
1st row P2, *K4, P2, rep from * to end.
2nd row K2, *P4, K2, rep from * to end.
Rep these 2 rows once more.
5th row P3, *K2, P4, rep from * to last 5 sts, K2, P3.
6th row K3, *P2, K4, rep from * to last 5 sts, P2, K3.
Rep last 2 rows once more.
9th row P to end.
10th row K to end.
These 10 rows form the pattern.

Stepped stitch

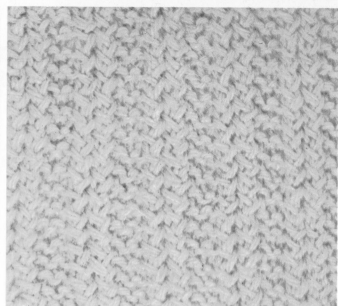

Corded rib

Spiral rib

Cast on a number of stitches divisible by 6 + 2.
1st row P2, *K4, P2, rep from * to end.
2nd and every alt row K2, *P4, K2, rep from * to end.
3rd row P2, *K 2nd st on left hand needle then first st and sl them both off needle tog – called Tw2 –, Tw2, P2, rep from * to end.
5th row P2, *K1, Tw2, K1, P2, rep from * to end.
6th row As 2nd.
The 3rd to 6th rows form the pattern.

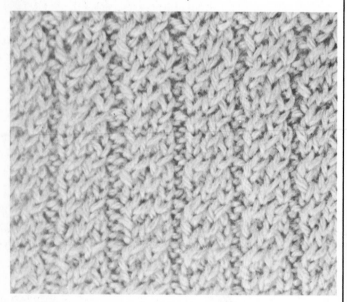

Corded rib

Cast on a number of stitches divisible by 6 + 2.
1st row P2, *K4, P2, rep from * to end.
2nd row P to end.
3rd row P2, *(sl 1, K1, yfwd, pass slip st over K1 and yfwd) twice, P2, rep from * to end.
4th row As 2nd.
The 3rd and 4th rows form the pattern.

Bobble rib

Cast on a number of stitches divisible by 6 + 2.
1st row P2, *K1, P2, rep from * to end.
2nd row K2, *P1, K2, rep from * to end.
3rd row P2, *K1, P2, (P1, K1, P1, K1) all into next st – called K4 from 1 –, P2, rep from * to end.
4th row K2, *P4, K2, P1, K2, rep from * to end.
5th row P2, *K1, P2, P4, turn and K4, turn and P4, P2, rep from * to end.
6th row K2, *P4 tog, K2, P1, K2, rep from * to end.
Rep 1st and 2nd rows once more.
9th row P2, *K4, from 1, P2, K1, P2, rep from * to end.
10th row K2, *P1, K2, P4, K2, rep from * to end.
11th row P2, *P4, turn and K4, turn and P4, P2, K1, P2, rep from * to end.
12th row K2, *P1, K2, P4 tog, K2, rep from * to end.
These 12 rows form the pattern.

A short sleeved sweater

This pretty bobble rib sweater (see opposite), illustrates the versatility of knitting. It can be made from any of the stitches shown on the previous two pages, providing that you can correctly gauge the tension before starting.

Sizes

To fit 86.5[91.5:96.5]cm (34[36:38]in) bust
Length to shoulder 56[57:58.5]cm (22[22½:23]in), adjustable
Sleeve seam, 10cm (4in)
The figures in brackets [] refer to the 91.5cm (36in) and 96.5cm (38in) sizes respectively

Tension

24 sts and 32 rows to 10cm (3.9in) over st st worked on No.9 needles

Materials

16[17:18] × 25grm balls of Lee Target Motoravia Double Knitting
One pair of No.9 needles
One pair of No.11 needles
Set of 4 No.11 needles pointed at both ends

Back

Using No. 11 needles, cast on 109[115:121]sts.
1st row K1, *P1, K1, rep from * to end.
    2nd row P1, *K1, P1, rep from * to end.
Rep these 2 rows for 4cm (1½in) ending with a 2nd row and inc one st in centre of last row. 110[116:122]sts. Change to No.9 needles. Work in patt as required from any of st patts in the previous chapter until work measures 37cm (14½in) from beg or required length to underarm, ending with a WS row.

Shape armholes

Cast off at beg of next and every row 4 sts twice and 2 sts twice. Dec one st at each end of next and foll 5[6:7] alt rows. 86[90:94]sts. Cont without shaping until armholes measure 19[20.5:21.5]cm (7½[8:8½]in) from beg, ending with a WS row.

Shape neck and shoulders

Next row Cast off 6[7:7]sts, patt 25[25:26]sts, turn and leave rem sts on holder.
Next row Cast off 2 sts, patt to end.
Next row Cast off 6[7:7]sts, patt to end.
Rep last 2 rows once more then first of them again. Cast off rem 7[5:6]sts.
With RS of work facing, sl first 24[26:28]sts onto holder, rejoin yarn to rem sts and patt to end.
Complete to match first side, reversing shaping.

Front

Work as given for back until armhole shaping is completed. Cont without shaping until armholes measure 14[15:16]cm (5½[6:6½]in) from beg, ending with a WS row.

Shape neck

Next row patt 35[36:37]sts, turn and leave rem sts on holder.
Cast off 2 sts at beg of next and foll 2 alt rows, then dec one st at neck edge on foll 4 alt rows.
Cont without shaping until armhole measures same as back shoulder, ending at armhole edge.

Shape shoulder

Cast off at beg of next and every alt row 6[7:7]sts 3 times and 7[5:6]sts once. With RS of work facing, sl first 16[18:20]sts on to holder, rejoin yarn to rem sts and patt to end. Complete to match first side, reversing shaping.

Sleeves

Using No.11 needles cast on 73[73:79]sts. Work 2.5cm (1in) rib as given for back, ending with a 2nd row and inc one st in centre of last row. 74[74:80]sts. Change to No.9 needles. Cont in patt as for back, inc one st at each end of 3rd and every foll 8th[6th:6th] row until there are 78[82:86]sts. Cont without shaping until sleeve measures 10cm (4in) from beg, ending with a WS row.

Shape top

Cast off 4 sts at beg of next 2 rows. Dec one st at each end of next and foll 11[12:13] alt rows, ending with a WS row. Cast off at beg of next and every row 2 sts 8[8:10] times, 3 sts 4 times, 4 sts twice and 10[12:10] sts once.

Neckband

Join shoulder seams. Using set of 4 No.11 needles and with RS of work facing, K up 8 sts down right back neck, K across back neck sts inc one st in centre, K up 8 sts up left back neck and 24 sts down left front neck, K across front neck sts inc one st in centre and K up 24 sts up right front neck. 106[110:114]sts. Cont in rounds of K1, P1 rib for 6.5cm (2½in). Cast off loosely in rib.

To make up

Press each piece under a damp cloth with a warm iron. Set in sleeves. Join side and sleeve seams. Press seams. Fold neckband in half to WS and sl st down.

TEXTURED PATTERNS

These fabric stitches are more complicated than the examples given in the previous chapter and use larger multiples of stitches and rows to form the pattern repeat. Each pattern is formed either by stitches which travel from one position to another in a row or by decreased stitches which are then compensated for by means of a made stitch without giving a lacy effect.

Pyramid pattern
Cast on a number of stitches divisible by 15 + 1.
1st row K to end.
2nd row P4, *K8, P7, rep from * to last 12 sts, K8, P4.
3rd row K1, *K up 1, K2, sl 1, K1, psso, P6, K2 tog, K2, K up 1, K1, rep from * to end.
4th row P5, *K6, P9, rep from * to last 11 sts, K6, P5.
5th row K2, *K up 1, K2, sl 1, K1, psso, P4, K2 tog, K2, K up 1, K3, rep from * to last 14 sts, K up 1, K2, sl 1, K1, psso, P4, K2 tog, K2, K up 1, K2.
6th row P6, *K4, P11, rep from * to last 10 sts, K4, P6.
7th row K3, *K up 1, K2, sl 1, K1, psso, P2, K2 tog, K2, K up 1, K5, rep from * to last 13 sts, K up 1, K2, sl 1, K1, psso, P4, K2 tog, K2, K up 1, K2.
8th row P7, *K2, P13, rep from * to last 9 sts, K2, P7.
9th row K4, *K up 1, K2, sl 1, K1, psso, K2 tog, K2, K up 1, K7, rep from * to last 12 sts, K up 1, K2, sl 1, K1, psso, K2 tog, K2, K up 1, K4.
10th row P to end.
These 10 rows form the pattern.

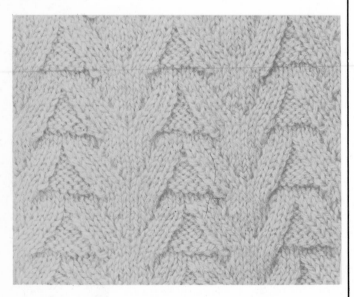

Leaf pattern
Cast on a number of stitches divisible by 24 + 1.
1st row K1, *K up 1, sl 1, K1, psso, K4, K2 tog, K3, K up 1, K1, K up 1, K3, sl 1, K1, psso, K4, K2 tog, K up 1, K1, rep from * to end.

2nd and every alt row P to end.
3rd row K1, *K up 1, K1, sl 1, K1, psso, K2, K2 tog, K4, K up 1, K1, K up 1, K4, sl 1, K1, psso, K2, K2 tog, K1, K up 1, K1, rep from * to end.
5th row K1, *K up 1, K2, sl 1, K1, psso, K2 tog, K5, K up 1, K1, K up 1, K5, sl 1, K1, psso, K2 tog, K2, K up 1, K1, rep from * to end.
7th row K1, *K up 1, K3, sl 1, K1, psso, K4, K2 tog, K up 1, K1, K up 1, sl 1, K1, psso, K4, K2 tog, K3, K up 1, K1, rep from * to end.
9th row K1, *K up 1, K4, sl 1, K1, psso, K2, K2 tog, K1, K up 1, K1, K up 1, K1, sl 1, K1, psso, K2, K2 tog, K4, K up 1, K1, rep from * to end.
11th row K1, *K up 1, K5, sl 1, K1, psso, K2 tog, K2, K up 1, K1, K up 1, K2, sl 1, K1, psso, K2 tog, K5, K up 1, K1, rep from * to end.
12th row P to end.
These 12 rows form the pattern.

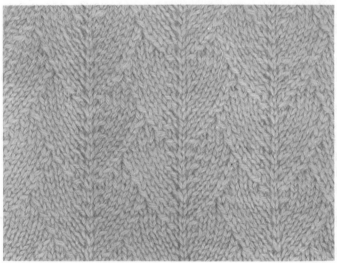

Seeded chevron pattern
Cast on a number of stitches divisible by 14 + 2.
1st row K14, *K second st on left hand needle then K first st and sl both sts off needle tog – called TwR –, K12, rep from * to last 2 sts, K2.
2nd row P1, *sl 1, P12, sl 1, rep from * to last st, P1.
3rd row K1, *put needle behind first st on left hand needle and K into back of second st then K first st and sl both sts off needle tog – called TwL –, K10, TwR, rep from * to last st K1.
4th row P1, K1, *sl 1, P10, sl 1, P1, K1, rep from * to end.
5th row K1, P1, *TwL, K8, TwR, K1, P1, rep from * to end.
6th row P1, K1, *P1, sl 1, P8, sl 1, K1, P1, K1, rep from * to end.
7th row K1, P1, *K1, TwL, K6, TwR, P1, K1, P1, rep from * to end.

8th row *(P1, K1) twice, sl 1, P6, sl 1, P1, K1, rep from * to last 2 sts, P1, K1.

9th row *(K1, P1) twice, TwL, K4, TwR, K1, P1, rep from * to last 2 sts, K1, P1.

10th row P1, *(K1, P1) twice, sl 1, P4, sl 1, (K1, P1) twice, rep from * to last st, K1.

11th row K1, *(P1, K1) twice, TwL, K2, TwR, (P1, K1) twice, rep from * to last st, P1.

12th row *(P1, K1) 3 times, sl 1, P2, sl 1, (P1, K1) twice, rep from * to last 2 sts, P1, K1.

13th row (K1, P1) 3 times, *TwL, TwR, (K1, P1) twice, TwR, (K1, P1) twice, rep from * to last 10 sts, TwL, TwR, (K1, P1) 3 times.

14th row P1, sl 1, *(P1, K1) 3 times, sl 1, K1, (P1, K1) twice, sl 2, rep from * to last 14 sts, (P1, K1) 3 times, sl 1, K1, (P1, K1) twice, sl 1, P1.

15th row K1, *TwL, (P1, K1) twice, TwL, (P1, K1) twice, TwR, rep from * to last st, K1.

16th row P2, *sl 1, (K1, P1) 5 times, sl 1, P2, rep from * to end.

17th row K2, *TwL, (K1, P1) 4 times, TwR, K2, rep from * to end.

18th row P3, *sl 1, (P1, K1) 4 times, sl 1, P4, rep from * to last 13 sts, sl 1, (P1, K1) 4 times, sl 1, P3.

19th row K3, *TwL, (P1, K1) 3 times, TwR, K4, rep from * to last 13 sts, TwL, (P1, K1) 3 times, TwR, K3.

20th row P4, *sl 1, (K1, P1) 3 times, sl 1, P6, rep from * to last 12 sts, sl 1, (K1, P1) 3 times, sl 1, P4.

21st row K4, *TwL, (K1, P1) twice, TwR, K6, rep from * to last 12 sts, TwL, (K1, P1) twice, TwR, K4.

22nd row P5, *sl 1, (P1, K1) twice, sl 1, P8, rep from * to last 11 sts, sl 1, (P1, K1) twice, sl 1, P5.

23rd row K5, *TwL, P1, K1, TwR, K8, rep from * to last 11 sts, TwL, P1, K1, TwR, K5.

24th row P6, *sl 1, K1, P1, sl 1, P10, rep from * to last 10 sts, sl 1, K1, P1, sl 1, P6.

25th row K6, *TwL, TwR, K10, rep from * to last 10 sts, TwL, TwR, K6.

26th row P8, *sl 1, P13, rep from * to last 8 sts, sl 1, P7.

27th row K7, *TwL, K12, rep from * to last 9 sts, TwL, K7.

28th row P to end.

These 28 rows form the pattern.

Travelling rib pattern

Cast on a number of stitches divisible by 12 + 2.

1st row P6, *K7, P5, rep from * to last 8 sts, K7, P1.

2nd row K1, *P7, K5, rep from * to last st, K1.

3rd row P5, *K second st on left hand needle then K first st and sl both sts off needle tog – called TwR –, K4, TwR, P4, rep from * to last 9 sts, TwR, K4, TwR, P1.

4th row K2, *P7, K5, rep from * to end.

5th row P4, *TwR, K4, TwR, P4, rep from * to last 10 sts, TwR, K4, TwR, P2.

6th row K3, *P7, K5, rep from * to last 11 sts, P7, K4.

7th row P3, *TwR, K4, TwR, P4, rep from * to last 11 sts, TwR, K4, TwR, P3.

8th row K4, *P7, K5, rep from * to last 10 sts, P7, K3.

9th row P2, *TwR, K4, TwR, P4, rep from * to end.

10th row K5, *P7, K5, rep from * to last 9 sts, P7, K2.

11th row P1, *TwR, K4, TwR, P4, rep from * to last st, P1.

12th row K6, *P7, K5, rep from * to last 8 sts, P7, K1.

13th row P1, *put needle behind first st on left hand needle and K into back of second st then K first st and sl both sts off needle tog – called TwL –, K4, TwL, P4, rep from * to last st, P1.

14th row As 10th.

15th row P2, *TwL, K4, TwL, P4, rep from * to end.

16th row As 8th.

17th row P3, *TwL, K4, TwL, P4, rep from * to last 11 sts, TwL, K4, TwL, P3.

18th row As 6th.

19th row P4, *TwL, K4, TwL, P4, rep from * to last 10 sts, TwL, K4, TwL, P2.

20th row As 4th.

21st row P5, *TwL, K4, TwL, P4, rep from * to last 9 sts, TwL, K4, TwL, P1.

22nd row As 2nd.

The 3rd to 22nd rows form the pattern.

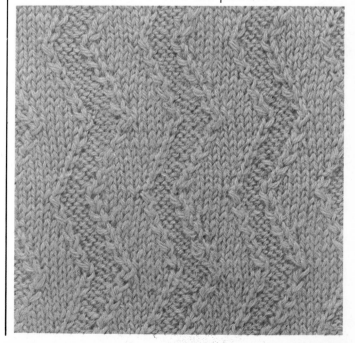

WOVEN FABRIC STITCHES

Just as the yarn can be carried over the needle in a pattern sequence to form additional stitches, or carried across the back of the work to form stripes or multi-coloured patterns, it can also be held in front of a sequence of stitches to form a woven fabric. In many instances, this fabric as with Fair Isle and Jacquard patterns, is double the thickness of ordinary knitting and may be used in a variety of ways.

If you use a very fine yarn and any of the all-over stitches given in this Chapter you will produce a very warm but light fabric, suitable for baby garments, bedjackets or lingerie, where extra warmth may be required but not extra weight. Using a double knitting quality yarn, the fabric will be firm and virtually windproof and most suitable for heavy outdoor garments, such as windcheaters, ski anoraks or chunky jackets.

All these stitches are simple to work as the patterns merely require a given sequence of stitches to be slipped from one needle to the other, carrying the yarn in front of these stitches ready to knit the next stitch. They do not have to be worked to produce an all-over fabric but can be worked at given intervals, as with cluster stitch and woven butterfly stitch, to add texture to an otherwise plain fabric. To keep the sides of the patterns neat and to avoid any 'fluting' effect, it is advisable to knit the first and last stitch on every row to form a firm, garter stitch edge.

Diagonal woven stitch
Cast on a number of stitches divisible by 4+2.
1st row K2, *yfwd, sl 2 P-wise, ybk, K2, rep from * to end.
2nd and every alt row K1, P to last st, K1.
3rd row Yfwd, sl 1 P-wise, ybk, *K2, yfwd, sl 2 P-wise, ybk, rep from * to last st, K1.

5th row Yfwd, sl 2 P-wise, ybk, *K2, yfwd, sl 2 P-wise, ybk, rep from * to end.
7th row K1, yfwd, sl 2 P-wise, ybk, *K2, yfwd, sl 2 P-wise, ybk, rep from * to last 3 sts, K2, yfwd, sl 1 P-wise, ybk.
8th row As 2nd.
These 8 rows form the pattern.

Woven bar stitch
Cast on a number of stitches divisible by 3+1.
1st row (RS) K to end.
2nd row *K1, keeping yarn at back of work sl 2 P-wise, rep from * to last st, K1.
These 2 rows form the pattern.

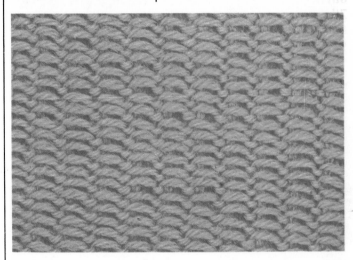

Woven ladder stitch
Cast on a number of stitches divisible by 8+1.
1st row *K5, yfwd, sl 3 P-wise, ybk, rep from * to last st, K1.

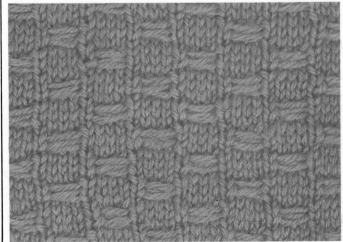

2nd row K1, *ybk, sl 3 P-wise, yfwd, P5, rep from * to end, ending last rep with K1.
3rd row As 1st.
4th row K1, P to last st, K1.
5th row K1, *yfwd, sl 3 P-wise, ybk, K5, rep from * to end.
6th row K1, *P4, ybk, sl 3 P-wise, yfwd, P1, rep from * to end, ending last rep K1.
7th row As 5th.
8th row As 4th.
These 8 rows form the pattern.

Woven chevron stitch
Cast on a number of stitches divisible by 10.
1st row *K1, yfwd, sl 3 P-wise, ybk, K2, yfwd, sl 3 P-wise, ybk, K1, rep from * to end.
2nd row *Ybk, sl 3 P-wise, yfwd, P2, rep from * to end, ending last rep K1.
3rd row Yfwd, *sl 1 P-wise, ybk, K2, yfwd, sl 3 P-wise, ybk, K2, yfwd, sl 2 P-wise, rep from * to end.
4th row Yfwd, *sl 1 P-wise, yfwd, P2, ybk, sl 3 P-wise, yfwd, P2, ybk, sl 2 P-wise, rep from * to end.
5th row *Yfwd, sl 3 P-wise, ybk, K2, rep from * to end.
6th row *P1, ybk, sl 3 P-wise, yfwd, P1, rep from * to end.
7th row As 5th.
8th row As 4th.
9th row As 3rd.

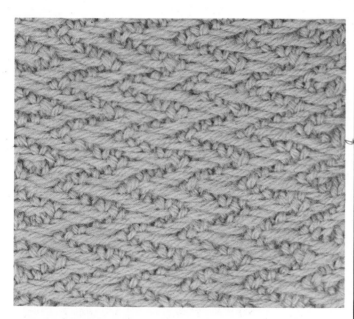

10th row As 2nd. These 10 rows form the pattern.

Cluster stitch
Cast on a number of stitches divisible by 8 + 5.
1st row K to end.
2nd row P to end.
3rd row *K5, sl next 3 sts on to cable needle and hold at front of work, pass the yarn across the back of these stitches and right round them 6 times in an anti-clockwise direction then K3 sts from cable needle – called 1CL, –, rep from * to last 5 sts, K5.
4th row P to end.
Rep 1st and 2nd rows once more.

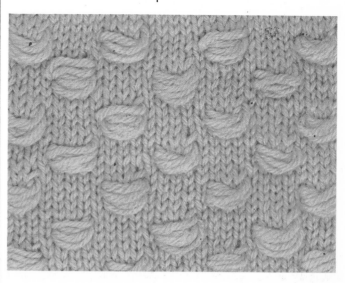

7th row *K1, 1CL, K4, rep from * to last 5 sts, **K1, 1CL, K1.**
8th row P to end.
These 8 rows form the pattern.

Woven butterfly stitch
Cast on a number of stitches divisible by 10 + 7.
1st row K6, *yfwd, sl 5 P-wise, ybk, K5, rep from * to last st, K1.
2nd row P to end.
Rep 1st and 2nd rows 3 times more.
9th row K8, *insert right hand needle under the 4 long loops, yarn round the needle and draw through a stitch, keeping this st on right hand needle K the next st on the left hand needle then pass the first st over the K1 – called B1 –, K9, rep from * to last 9 sts, B1, K8.
10th row As 2nd.
11th row K1, yfwd, sl 5 P-wise, ybk, *K5, yfwd, sl 5 P-wise, ybk, rep from * to last st, K1.
12th row As 2nd.
Rep 11th and 12th rows 3 times more.
19th row K3, B1, *K9, B1, rep from * to last 3 sts, K3.
20th row As 2nd.
These 20 rows form the pattern.

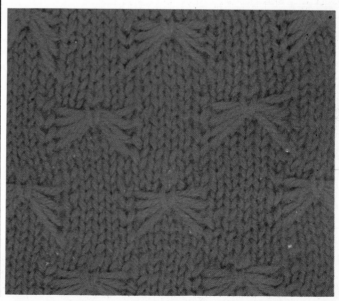

RAISED STITCHES

Bobble and cluster stitches

Although the overall heading refers to a cluster of raised stitches, which can be arranged to give an interesting and highly textured fabric, the size of a bobble or cluster can vary considerably.

There are various ways of working bobbles but the basic principle is always the same – working more than once into the stitch where the bobble is required and then decreasing again to the original stitch, either in the same row or several rows later.

Cluster stitches also are worked on this principle but they are not intended to be as dense as bobble stitches and once the cluster is formed, it is decreased more gradually over a number of rows until only the original stitch remains.

Both bobble and cluster stitches may be used most effectively to form an all-over pattern but, combined with other stitches such as cables, they produce some of the most beautiful variations of Aran patterns, which are renowned throughout the world.

Bobble patterns

The simplest forms of bobble stitches are small and easy to work. The working methods of the two samples given here differ slightly but both produce a small, berry type of stitch. Trinity stitch, which is used in Aran patterns, derives its name from the method of working 'three into one and one into three'.

Blackberry stitch

Cast on a number of stitches divisible by 4.
1st row *(K1, yfwd to make one st, K1) all into next st, P3, rep from * to end.
2nd row *P3 tog, K3, rep from * to end.
3rd row *P3, (K1, yfwd to make one st, K1) all into next st, rep from * to end.
4th row *K3, P3 tog, rep from * to end.
These 4 rows form the pattern.

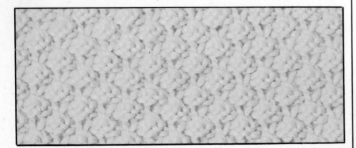

Trinity stitch

Cast on a number of stitches divisible by 4.
1st row *(K1, P1, K1) all into next st, P3 tog, rep from * to end.

2nd row P to end.
3rd row *P3 tog, (K1, P1, K1) all into next st, rep from * to end.
4th row As 2nd.
These 4 rows form the pattern.

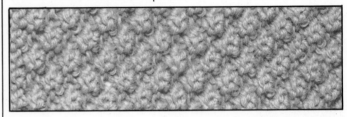

Small bobble stitch

Cast on a number of stitches divisible by 6 plus 5.
1st row (WS) P to end.
2nd row K2, (K1, P1, K1, P1, K1) all into next st then using point of left hand needle lift 2nd, 3rd, 4th and 5th sts over first st and off right hand needle – called B1 –, *K5, B1, rep from * to last 2 sts, K2.
3rd row P to end.
4th row *K5, B1, rep from * to last 5 sts, K5.
These 4 rows form the pattern.

Popcorn stitch

Cast on a number of stitches divisible by 6 plus 5.
1st row (WS) P to end.
2nd row K2, (K1, P1, K1, P1, K1) all into next st, turn and K these 5 sts, turn and P5 then using point of left hand needle lift 2nd, 3rd, 4th and 5th sts over first st and off right hand needle – called B1 –, *K5, B1, rep from * to last 2 sts, K2.
3rd row P to end.
4th row *K5, B1, rep from * to last 5 sts, K5.
These 4 rows form the pattern.

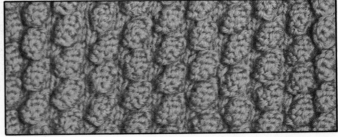

Currant stitch

Cast on a number of stitches divisible by 2 plus 1.
1st row (RS) K to end.
2nd row K1, *(P1, yrn to make one st, P1, yrn, P1) all into next st, K1, rep from * to end.
3rd row P to end.
4th row K1, *sl 2 P-wise keeping yarn at front of work – called sl 2F –, P3 tog, p2sso, K1, rep from * to end.
5th row K to end.
6th row K2, *(P1, yrn, P1, yrn, P1) all into next st, K1, rep from * to last st, K1.
7th row P to end.
8th row K2, *sl 2F, P3 tog, p2sso, K1, rep from * to last st, K1.
These 8 rows form the pattern.

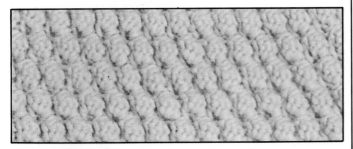

Long bobble stitch

Cast on a number of stitches divisible by 6 plus 3.
1st row (WS) P to end.
2nd row K1, *K3, (K1, yfwd to make one st, K1) all into next st, K1, (turn and P5, turn and K5) twice, K1, rep from * to last 2 sts, K2.
3rd row P1, *P2, P2 tog, P1, P2 tog tbl, P1, rep from * to last 2 sts, P2.
4th row K3, *K4, (K1, yfwd, K1) all into next st, K1, (turn and P5, turn and K5) twice, rep from * to last 6 sts, K6.
5th row P3, *P3, P2 tog, P1, P2 tog tbl, rep from * to last 6 sts, P6.
Rows 2–5 form the pattern.

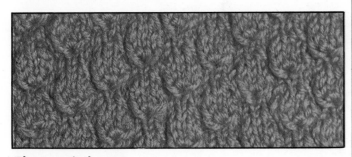

Cluster stitches

These patterns may be worked in two ways – either by increasing and shaping the cluster and working the stitches on either side row by row at the same time, or by working the cluster separately and then continuing to knit the background fabric until it has reached the same height as the cluster.

Bell cluster

Cast on a number of stitches divisible by 4 plus 4.
1st row (WS) K to end.

2nd row P4, *turn and cast on 8 sts – called C1 –, P4, rep from * to end.
3rd row *K4, P8, rep from * to last 4 sts, K4.
4th row P4, *K8, P4, rep from * to end.
5th row As 3rd.
6th row P4, *sl 1, K1, psso, K4, K2 tog, P4, rep from * to end.
7th row *K4, P6, rep from * to last 4 sts, K4.
8th row P4, *sl 1, K1, psso, K2, K2 tog, P4, rep from * to end.
9th row *K4, P4, rep from * to last 4 sts, K4.
10th row P4, *sl 1, K1, psso, K2 tog, P4, rep from * to end.
11th row *K4, P2, rep from * to last 4 sts, K4.
12th row P4, *K2 tog, P4, rep from * to end.
13th row *K4, P1, rep from * to last 4 sts, K4.
14th row P4, *K2 tog, P3, rep from * to end.
These 14 rows form the pattern.

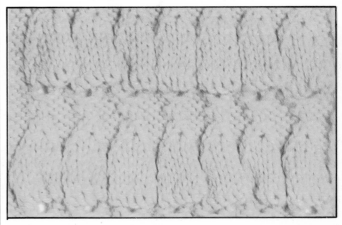

Detached cluster

Cast on a number of stitches divisible by 6 plus 5.
1st row (RS) P to end.
2nd row K to end.
3rd row *P5, (yfwd to make one st, K into next st) 3 times into same st to make 6 out of one, turn and P these 6 sts, turn and sl 1, K5, turn and sl 1, P5, turn and sl 1, K5, turn and (P2 tog) 3 times, turn and sl 1, K2 tog, psso – called C1 –, rep from * to last 5 sts, P5.
4th row K to end.
5th row P to end.
6th row K to end.
7th row P2, *C1, P5, rep from * to last 3 sts, C1, P2.
8th row K to end.
These 8 rows form the pattern.

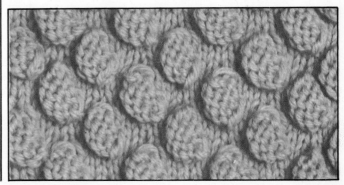

FUR FABRICS

Knitting patterns which have the appearance of fur fabrics are achieved by means of loops of yarn which are worked as the row is knitted on to the main background.

The usual method is to loop the yarn round the fingers or a strip of card for the required number of times, then to secure these loops to the knitted stitch so that they do not unravel. The fabric produced is warm and light and is most suitable for outer garments, trimmings such as collars and cuffs, pram and cot covers, or household items such as bath mats.

Another method given here combines a knitted background with lengths of crochet chains forming the fur effect, which gives a close, astrakan texture to the fabric. The loops achieved by this method will not catch or break as easily as the first method and this pattern is therefore most suitable for babies and childrens garments, where frequent washing, or rough-and-tumble use is required. Although it is not as quick or simple to work as the usual method, its appearance is so attractive that it is well worth a little time and trouble spent in practising this stitch.

Looped patterns

The density of these patterns may be varied as required, either by the number of times the yarn is looped round, or by the position of each loop on the background fabric. The samples given here have been worked in a double knitting yarn, alternating the position of the loops on every 4th row.

Single loop stitch

Here the loops are formed on a right side row when the work is facing you. Cast on a number of stitches divisible by 2 plus 1.

1st row (RS) K to end.
2nd row P to end.
3rd row *K1, K next st without letting it drop off left hand needle, yfwd, pass yarn over left thumb to make a loop approximately 4cm (1½in) long, ybk and K st rem on left hand needle letting it drop from the needle, return the 2 sts just worked to the left hand needle and K them tog tbl – called L1 –, rep from * to last st, K1.
4th row P to end.
Rep 1st and 2nd rows once more.
7th row K1, *K1, L1, rep from * to last 2 sts, K2.
8th row P to end.
These 8 rows form the pattern.

Double loop stitch

Here the loops are formed on the right side of the fabric when the wrong side of the work is facing you. Cast on a number of stitches divisible by 2 plus 1.

1st row (RS) K to end.
Rep 1st row twice more.
4th row (WS) K1, *insert right hand needle into next st on left hand needle as if to knit it, wind yarn over right hand needle point and round first and 2nd fingers of left hand twice, then over and round right hand needle point once more, draw all 3 loops through st and sl on to left hand needle, insert right hand needle through back of these 3 loops and through the original st and K tog tbl – called L1 –, K1, rep from * to end.
5th 6th and 7th rows K to end.

8th row K1, *K1, L1, rep from * to last 2 sts, K2. These 8 rows form the pattern.

Chain loop stitch

Here again, the density of the pattern can be altered by the position of each chain loop on the background fabric and by the number of rows worked between each pattern row. To work the sample given here you will require double knitting yarn, a pair of No.8 needles and a No.4.00 (ISR) crochet hook. Cast on a number of stitches divisible by 2 plus 1.

1st row (RS) K to end.
2nd row P to end.

3rd row K1, *K next st without letting it drop off left hand needle, insert crochet hook from front to back through loop on left hand needle, draw a loop through and leave on hook then drop st from left hand needle, wind yarn round left hand and make 12ch in the usual way, keeping ch at front of work and yarn at back of work sl loop on to right hand needle and remove hook, then lift last K st over loop – called L1 –, K1, rep from * to end.
4th row P to end.
Rep 1st and 2nd rows once more.
7th row K1, *K1, L1, rep from * to last 2 sts, K2.
8th row P to end.
These 8 rows form the pattern.

Cravat
Size
18cm (*7in*) wide at lower edge by 101.5cm (*40in*) long

Tension
22 sts and 30 rows to 10cm (*3.9in*) over st st worked on No.8 needles

Materials
4 × 50grm balls of Patons Bracken Tweed Double Knitting
One pair No.8 needles

Cravat

Using No.8 needles cast on 45 sts. K 3 rows g st. Commence patt.
1st row (RS) K2, work in any loop patt over next 41 sts, K2.
2nd row K2, patt 41 sts, K2.
Cont in patt, keeping 2 sts at each end in g st throughout, until work measures 12.5cm (*5in*) from beg, ending with a WS row.
Next row K2, sl 1, K1, psso, patt to last 4 sts, K2 tog, K2. Work 3 rows patt without shaping. Rep last 4 rows 8 times more. 27 sts. Cont without shaping until work measures 73.5cm (*29in*) from beg, ending with a WS row.
Next row K2, pick up loop lying between sts and K tbl – called inc 1 –, patt to last 2 sts, inc 1, K2. Work 3 rows patt without shaping. Rep last 4 rows 8 times more. 45 sts. Cont without shaping until work measures 101cm (*39¾in*) from beg. K 3 rows g st. Cast off.

Loop fastening
Using No.8 needles cast on 6 sts. Work 10cm (*4in*) g st. Cast off.

To make up
Do not press. St loop fastening across back of one end approximately 18cm (*7in*) above lower end.
Slot other end through loop to secure.

FISHERMAN KNITTING

Fisherman knitting is the name given to seamless jerseys, knitted in a very closely woven fabric similar to a patterned brocade. Because of the fineness of the needles used for this type of knitting, sometimes on as fine a gauge as No.17, the textured patterns do not stand out in relief as with Aran stitches. The whole purpose is to make a fabric which is virtually wind-proof and a jersey which will stand up to the constant wear-and-tear of a fisherman's life.

As with many of the folk crafts which have been handed down to us through countless generations, these jerseys were often knitted by the fishermen themselves but were more often lovingly knitted by their womenfolk, in traditional patterns which varied from region to region.

The very name, 'jersey', originates from the island of that name. Another name in regular use is a 'guernsey', or 'gansey' as it became known, from the sister island in the same group.

Each port around the coastline of the British Isles has developed its own regional style of fisherman knitting. Some have patterned yokes, others have vertical panels of patterns, some have horizontal bands of patterns, but the original guernseys, which were made purely as hard-wearing working garments, were nearly always made in stocking stitch with very little decoration and always in the traditional colour, navy blue. The more elaborate examples which evolved were kept for Sunday best and in Cornwall they were often referred to as bridal shirts and were knitted by the young women for their betrothed.

A traditional guernsey is knitted entirely without seams, often worked on sets of 5, 6, or even more double pointed needles. The body is knitted in rounds to the armholes, then instead of dividing the work for the back and front at this point, the work is continued in rounds with the position of the armholes separated from the main sections of the guernsey by a series of loops wound round the needle on every round. These loops are dropped from the needle on the following round and the process is repeated until the guernsey is the required length. When this section is completed, a series of what look like the rungs of a ladder mark each armhole. These loops are cut in the middle and the ends carefully darned into the main fabric, then the sleeve stitches are picked up round the armholes and the sleeve is knitted in rounds down to the cuff. The shoulder stitches are grafted together to finish the garment without one sewn seam.

The shape of these garments is as distinctive as the patterns. They all feature a dropped shoulder line and crew neckline, with little, if any, shaping. Sometimes buttons and buttonholes would be added to one shoulder for ease in dressing and undressing, a gusset made before the armhole division and carried on into the top of the sleeve, or the neck would be continued to form a small collar but the simplicity of the basic design has never been bettered, to give the utmost warmth, freedom of movement and protection to the wearer.

Traditional guernsey
Sizes
To fit 96.5[101.5:106.5:112]cm (38[40:42:44]in) chest
Length to shoulder, 58.5[59.5:61:62]cm (23[23½:24: 24½]in)
Sleeve seam, 45.5cm (18in), adjustable
The figures in brackets [] refer to the 101.5 (40), 106.5 (42) and 112cm (44in) sizes respectively

Tension
28 sts and 36 rows to 10cm (3.9in) over st st worked on No.10 needles

Materials
14[15:16:17] × 50grm balls of Double Knitting
Set of 4 No.10 needles pointed at both ends or No.10 circular Twin Pin
Set of 4 No.12 needles pointed at both ends or No.12 circular Twin Pin

Guernsey body
Using set of 4 No.12 needles cast on 264[276:288:300] sts. Mark beg of round with coloured thread. Cont in rounds of K1, P1 rib for 7.5cm (3in). Change to set of 4 No.10 needles. Cont in rounds of st st until work measures 33cm (13in) from beg. Commence yoke patt.
**1st round P to end.
2nd round K to end.
Rep these 2 rounds twice more, then 1st round once more. **.
***Work 5 rounds st st.
Divide for armholes
1st round *K132[138:144:150] sts ,wind yarn 10 times round right hand needle – called loop 10 –, rep from * once more.
Rep last round once more, dropping extra loops from needle before loop 10.
3rd round *K6[9:0:3], (K6, P1, K11, P1, K5) 5[5:6:6]

times, K6[9:0:3], drop extra loops, loop 10, rep from * once more.
4th round *K6[9:0:3], (K4, P1, K1, P1, K9, P1, K1, P1, K5) 5[5:6:6] times, K6[9:0:3], drop extra loops, loop 10, rep from * once more.
5th round *K6[9:0:3], (K4, P1, K3, P1, K7, P1, (K1, P1) twice, K3) 5[5:6:6] times, K6[9:0:3], drop extra loops, loop 10, rep from * once more.
6th round *K6[9:0:3], (K2, P1, (K1, P1) 3 times, (K5, P1) twice, K3) 5[5:6:6] times, K6[9:0:3], drop extra loops, loop 10, rep from * once more.
7th round *K6[9:0:3], (K2, P1, K7, P1, K3, P1, (K1, P1) 4 times, K1) 5[5:6:6] times, K6[9:0:3], drop extra loops, loop 10, rep from * once more.
8th round *K6[9:0:3], (P1, (K1, P1) 6 times, K9, P1, K1) 5 [5:6:6] times, K6[9:0:3], drop extra loops, loop 10, rep from * once more.
9th round *K6[9:0:3], (P1, K11, P12) 5[5:6:6] times, K6[9:0:3], drop extra loops, loop 10, rep from * once more.
10th round *K6[9:0:3], (P11, K1, P1, K9, P1, K1) 5[5:6:6] times, K6[9:0:3], drop extra loops, loop 10, rep from * once more.
11th round *K6[9:0:3], (K2, P1, K7, P1, K13) 5[5:6:6] times, K6[9:0:3], drop extra loops, loop 10, rep from * once more.
12th round *K6[9:0:3], (K14, P1, K5, P1, K3) 5[5:6:6] times, K6[9:0:3], drop extra loops, loop 10, rep from * once more.
13th round *K6[9:0:3], (K4, P1, K3, P1, K15) 5[5:6:6] times, K6[9:0:3], drop extra loops, loop 10, rep from * once more.
14th round *K6[9:0:3], (K16, P1, K1, P1, K5) 5[5:6:6] times, K6[9:0:3], drop extra loops, loop 10, rep from * once more.
15th and 16th rounds As 1st, dropping extra loops.
Keeping armhole loops correct, work 5 rounds st st, then rep from ** to ** once. ***. Rep from *** to *** once more. Beg with a 2nd row, cont working in patt from ** to ** until work measures 21.5[23:25:25.5]cm (8½[9:9½:10]in) from beg of loops, omitting loop 10 at end of last round. Break off yarn.
Divide for shoulders
Keeping patt correct, sl first and last 35[37:39:41] sts of back and front sections on to holders, knit across each set of 62[64:66:68] sts of neck separately for 6 rows. Cast off loosely. Graft shoulder sts from holders.

Sleeves
Cut loops of armholes and darn in ends. Using set of 4 No.10 needles and with RS of work facing, K up 110[114:118:122] sts round armhole. K 5 rounds st st, then rep from ** to ** as given for body.
Cont in rounds of st st, dec one st at beg and end of next and every foll 6th round until 74[80:84:88] sts rem. Cont without shaping until sleeve measures 40.5cm (16in) from beg, or required length less 5cm (2in). Change to set of 4 No.12 needles. Work 5cm (2in) K1, P1 rib. Cast off in rib.

MAXI KNITTING

Working a fabric on very large knitting needles can be both speedy and fun, as even the most basic stitches take on a completely different appearance. This particular type of knitting is often referred to as 'maxi-knitting' and needles of a special gauge are available in varying sizes.

The most popular needles are made from a special lightweight wood and are graded upwards from the smallest size 0, on to 00, 000, to the largest size 0000. Hollow jumbo sized needles are also available, to overcome the weight problem, and these are made from a plastic material and graded as sizes No.1 and No.2.

Great care must be taken in selecting a suitable yarn for this type of knitting, as two or more ends are used at the same time, which can produce a very heavy fabric. Any lightweight yarn, such as mohair, is ideal as this gives sufficient bulk to the fabric without being too heavy.

The stitch chosen also plays an important part, as the texture must be firm enough to avoid the knitting dropping but not so dense that it produces a thick, harsh fabric. Stocking stitch does not work too well with this method as it is very difficult to keep the smooth, even tension which is the main characteristic of this stitch. On the other hand, garter stitch, moss stitch and small, repeating lace or fabric patterns, such as given here, do produce interesting textures which will hold their shape.

When casting on and off, the stitches must be worked very loosely to avoid pulling the fabric out of shape.

Indian pillar stitch

Use two or more ends of yarn, depending upon the size of needle chosen. Cast on a number of stitches divisible by 4 plus 2.

1st row P1, *insert needle purlwise into next 3 sts as if to purl them tog but instead (P1, K1, P1) into these 3 sts, K1, rep from * to last st, P1.
2nd row P to end.
These 2 rows form the pattern.

Waffle stitch

Use two or more ends of yarn and cast on a number of stitches divisible by 2.
1st row *K1 tbl, P1, rep from * to end.
2nd row *P1 tbl, K1, rep from * to end.
These 2 rows form the pattern.

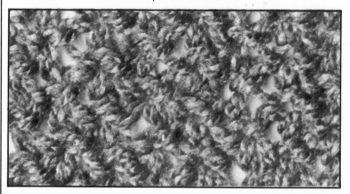

Grecian plait stitch

This stitch requires one small and one large needle, the large needle being twice the size of the small needle. Use two ends of yarn and cast on an even number of stitches with the large needle.
1st row Using the small needle, K to end.
2nd row Using the large needle, P to end.
3rd row Using the small needle, lift the 2nd st over the first st and K it then K the first st, lift the 4th st over the 3rd st and K it then K the 3rd st, cont in this way all along the row.
4th row Using the large needle, P to end.
These 4 rows form the pattern.

Maxi-knit scarf

Size
Approx 23cm (9in) wide by 167.5cm (66in) long, excluding fringe

Tension
10 sts to 7.5cm (3in) over Indian pillar st worked on No.0000 needles

Materials
10 × 25grm balls of Hayfield DuBarry Double Knitting in each of 2 contrast colours, A and B
One pair No.0000 Milwards disc needles, or as required

Scarf
Using No.0000 needles if working in Indian pillar st or waffle st, or one No.0 and one No.0000 needle if working in Grecian plait st, and one strand each of A and B, cast on 30 sts loosely. Work in patt as required until scarf measures 167.5cm (66in) from beg. Cast off very loosely.

To make up
Do not press. Using 2 ends of A and B tog, make a fringe along each short end, knotting fringe into every alt st.
Trim fringe.

TRAVELLING STITCHES

Crossed stitches, which have a twisted appearance, are used extensively in Aran patterns and the same methods may be used to create effective miniature and mock cable patterns. Because only two, or at most three, stitches are crossed at any one time, it is not necessary to use a cable needle, so these patterns are simple to work.

Crossed stitches should be knitted against a purl background to show to their best advantage, but to produce an even tighter twist on the stitches, it is also necessary to know how to twist them on the wrong side, or on a purl row against a knitted background.

Knitted crossed stitches with back twist

The crossed stitches are worked over two knitted stitches and the twist lies to the left. Pass the right hand needle behind the first stitch on the left hand needle, knit into the back of the next stitch on the left hand needle then knit into the front of the first missed stitch and slip both stitches off the left hand needle together. The abbreviation for this is 'T2B'.

Mock cable

Cast on a number of stitches divisible by 5 + 3.
1st row P3, *K2, P3, rep from * to end.

2nd row K3, *P2, K3, rep from * to end.
Rep 1st and 2nd rows once more.
5th row P3, *T2B, P3, rep from * to end.
6th row As 2nd.
These 6 rows form the pattern.

Twisted rib

Cast on a number of stitches divisible by 14 + 2.
1st row P2, *T2B, P2, K4, P2, T2B, P2, rep from * to end.
2nd row K2, *P2, K2, P4, K2, P2, K2, rep from * to end.
Rep 1st and 2nd rows once more.
5th row P2, *T2B, P2, into 4th and 3rd sts on left hand needle work T2B leaving sts on needle then work T2B into 2nd and 1st sts and sl all 4 sts off needle tog, P2, T2B, P2, rep from * to end.
6th row As 2nd.
These 6 rows form the pattern.

Knitted crossed stitches with front twist

The crossed stitches are worked over two knitted stitches and the twist lies to the right. Pass the right hand needle in front of the first stitch on the left hand needle, knit into the front of the next stitch on the left hand needle then knit into the front of the first missed stitch and slip both stitches off the needle together. The abbreviation for this is 'T2F'.

Three stitches can be crossed in the same way by working into the 3rd stitch, then into the 2nd and then into the first, slipping all 3 stitches off the left hand needle together. The abbreviation for this is 'T3F'.

Twisted panels
Cast on a number of stitches divisible by 8 + 2.
1st row P2, *(T2F) 3 times, P2, rep from * to end.
2nd row K2, *P6, K2, rep from * to end.
3rd row P2, *(T3F) twice, P2, rep from * to end.
4th row As 2nd.
These 4 rows form the pattern.

Purled crossed stitches with front twist
The crossed stitches are worked over two purled stitches and form a crossed thread lying to the right on the knitted side of the work. Pass the right hand needle in front of the first stitch on the left hand needle and purl the next stitch on the left hand needle, purl the first missed stitch and slip both stitches off the left hand needle together. The abbreviation for this is 'T2PF'.

Purled crossed stitches with back twist
The crossed stitches are worked over two purled stitches and form a crossed thread lying to the left on the knitted side of the work. Pass the right hand

needle behind the first stitch on the left hand needle and purl the next stitch on the left hand needle through the back of the loop, purl the first missed stitch and slip both stitches off the left hand needle together. The abbreviation for this is 'T2PB'.

Crossing two knitted stitches to the right
Pass the right hand needle in front of the first stitch on the left hand needle and knit into the next stitch on the left hand needle, lift this stitch over the first missed stitch and off the needle then knit the first missed stitch. The abbreviation for this is 'C2R'.

Crossing two knitted stitches to the left
Slip the first stitch on to the right hand needle without knitting it, knit the next stitch on the left hand needle and slip it on to the right hand needle, using the left hand needle point pass the first slipped stitch over the knitted stitch, knitting into the slipped stitch at the same time. The abbreviation for this is 'C2L'.

Crossed cable
Cast on a number of stitches divisible by 7 + 3.
1st row P3, *K4, P3, rep from * to end.
2nd row K3, *P4, K3, rep from * to end.
3rd row P3, *C2R, C2L, P3, rep from * to end.
4th row As 2nd.
These 4 rows form the pattern.

CABLES
Basic stitches

Cable patterns, using variations of stitches, are among the most popular in knitting, since they are easy to work and give an interesting fabric with many uses – they can be thick and chunky for a sports sweater, or fine and lacy for baby garments. Twisting the cables in opposite directions can produce an all-over fabric, or simple panels of cables against the purl side of stocking stitch can give a special look to the most basic garment. All cable patterns are based on the method of moving a sequence of stitches from one position to another in a row, giving the effect of the twists you see in a rope – the more stitches moved, the thicker the rope.

The previous chapter dealt with the method of crossing two or three stitches to give a twisted effect but when altering the position of more than two stitches, it is easier to do so by means of a third needle, which is used to hold the stitches being moved until they are ready to be worked. For this purpose a special cable needle is the best, although any short, double pointed needle will do. Cable needles are very short and manoeuvrable and are made in the same sizes as knitting needles. If the cable needle is not the same thickness as the needles being used for the garment, then it should be finer and not thicker. A thicker needle is more difficult to use and, apart from this, it will stretch the stitches and spoil the appearance of the finished work.

Cable abbreviations

Although working instructions and abbreviations will usually be found in detail in any cable pattern, before beginning to knit it would be as well to study these, as they do vary considerably. As a general guide, the letter 'C' stands for the word 'cable', followed by the number of stitches to be cabled, then the letter 'B' for back, or 'F' for front, indicating the direction in which the stitches are to be moved. In this way a cable twist from right to left over 6 stitches is abbreviated as 'C6F' and a cable twist from left to right over 6 stitches is abbreviated as 'C6B'.

Cable twist from right to left

A simple cable worked over 6 knitted stitches against a purl background. To work this sample cast on 24 stitches.

1st row (RS) P9, K6, P9.
2nd row K9, P6, K9.
Rep 1st and 2nd rows twice more.
7th row P9, sl next 3 sts on to cable needle and hold at front of work, K next 3 sts from left hand needle then K3 sts from cable needle – called C6F –, P9.

8th row As 2nd.
These 8 rows form the pattern. Repeat pattern rows twice more. Cast off.

This sample produces a rope-like pattern in the centre, consisting of 6 knitted stitches twisted 3 times. Each twist lies in the same direction from the right to the left.

Cable twist from left to right

Cast on and work the first 6 rows as given for cable twist from right to left.

122

7th row P9, sl next 3 sts on to cable needle and hold at back of work, K next 3 sts from left hand needle then K3 sts from cable needle – called C6B –, P9.
8th row As 2nd.
These 8 rows form the pattern. Repeat pattern rows twice more. Cast off.
This sample will be similar to the first, but each twist will lie in the opposite direction from the left to the right.

Cable twist from right to left with row variations
The appearance of each cable twist is altered considerably by the number of rows worked between each twist. Cast on and work the first 4 rows as given for cable twist from right to left.
5th row P9, C6F, P9.
6th row As 2nd.
Rep 1st and 2nd rows twice more, then 5th and 6th rows once more.
Rep 1st and 2nd rows 4 times more, then 5th and 6th rows once more.
Rep 1st and 2nd rows 6 times more, then 5th and 6th rows once more.
Rep 1st and 2nd rows once more. Cast off.

This sample shows that the cable twist on every 4th row gives a very close, tight, rope look, whereas twisting on every 8th or 12th row gives a much softer look.

Alternating cables
This combines both the cable twist from right to left and cable twist from left to right, to produce a fabric with a completely different look although the methods used are exactly the same. Cast on and work the first 8 rows as given for cable twist from right to left.
9th row As 1st.
10th row As 2nd.
Rep 9th and 10th rows twice more.
15th row P9, C6B, P9.
16th row As 10th.
Rep 9th and 10th rows twice more. Cast off.
This sample shows the same 3 stitches being moved on each twist.

Panels of cable twist from right to left
This pattern is made up of panels of 4 knitted stitches, with one purl stitch between each panel, twisted from right to left on different rows to give a diagonal appearance. Cast on 31 stitches.
1st row P1, *K4, P1, rep from * to end.
2nd row K1, *P4, K1, rep from * to end.
3rd row P1, *K4, P1, sl next 2 sts on to cable needle and hold at front of work, K next 2 sts from left hand needle then K2 sts from cable needle – called C4F –, P1, rep from * to end.
4th row As 2nd.
Rep 1st and 2nd rows once more.
7th row P1, *C4F, P1, K4, P1, rep from * to end.
8th row As 2nd.
These 8 rows form the pattern. Repeat pattern rows 3 times more. Cast off.

More cable stitches

Based on combinations of the simple cable twists given in the previous chapter, the patterns which can be produced are numerous. All of the variations given here can be worked as all-over patterns or as separate panels against a purl background.

Try incorporating single plaited cable as an all-over pattern on a plain jersey design, or use a panel of link cables to highlight the front and centre of the sleeves on a basic cardigan. Another simple alternative would be to work two samples of honeycomb cable and use these as patch pockets on a stocking stitch cardigan, using the reverse side, or purl side as the right side of the cardigan fabric.

Link cable

The cable pattern is worked over 12 knitted stitches against a purl background. For this sample cast on 24 stitches.

1st row P6, K12, P6.
2nd row K6, P12, K6.
Rep 1st and 2nd rows twice more.
7th row P6, sl next 3 sts on to cable needle and hold at back of work, K next 3 sts from left hand needle then K3 sts from cable needle – called C6B –, sl next 3 sts on to cable needle and hold at front of work, K next 3 sts from left hand needle then K3 sts from cable needle – called C6F –, P6.
8th row As 2nd.
These 8 rows form the pattern. Repeat pattern rows twice more. Cast off.
This pattern gives the appearance of chain links, each link coming upwards out of the one below.

Inverted link cable

Cast on and work the first 6 rows as given for link cable.

7th row P6, C6F, C6B, P6.
8th row As 2nd.
These 8 rows form the pattern. Repeat pattern rows twice more. Cast off.
This pattern has the reverse appearance of link cables with each link joining and passing under the link above.

Honeycomb cable

This pattern combines the working methods of link cable and inverted link cable. For this sample cast on 24 stitches.
1st row P6, K12, P6.
2nd row K6, P12, K6.
Rep 1st and 2nd rows once more.

5th row P6, C6B, C6F, P6.
6th row As 2nd.
Rep 1st and 2nd rows twice more.
11th row P6, C6F, C6B, P6.
12th row As 2nd.
These 12 rows form the pattern. Repeat pattern rows twice more. Cast off.
This pattern forms a cable which appears to be superimposed on the fabric beneath.

Single plaited cable

This pattern is achieved by dividing the groups of stitches which are to be cabled into three sections instead of two and cabling each group alternately. For this sample cast on 30 stitches.
1st row P3, *K6, P3, rep from * to end.
2nd row K3, *P6, K3, rep from * to end.
3rd row P3, *sl next 2 sts on to cable needle and hold at back of work, K next 2 sts from left hand needle then K2 from cable needle – called C4B –, K2, P3, rep from * to end.
4th row As 2nd.
5th row P3, *K2, sl next 2 sts on to cable needle and hold at front of work, K next 2 sts from left hand needle then K2 from cable needle – called C4F –, P3, rep from * to end.
6th row As 2nd.
The 3rd to 6th rows form the pattern. Repeat pattern rows 6 times more. Cast off.

Double plaited cable

This pattern is even more textured than single plaited cable and is worked over 18 knitted stitches against a purl background. For this sample cast on 30 stitches.
1st row P6, K18, P6.
2nd row K6, P18, K6.
3rd row P6, (C6B) 3 times, P6.
4th row As 2nd.
Rep 1st and 2nd rows once more.

7th row P6, K3, (C6F) twice, K3, P6.
8th row As 2nd.
These 8 rows form the pattern. Repeat pattern rows twice more. Cast off.

Cable waves

Cable patterns have a completely different appearance when the stitches being moved are worked in knitting against a knitted background, instead of a purl fabric. For this sample cast on 24 stitches.
1st row K to end.
2nd and every alt row P to end.
3rd row *C6F, K6, rep from * to end.
5th row K to end.
7th row *K6, C6B, rep from * to end.
9th row K to end.
10th row As 2nd.
Rows 3 to 10 form the pattern. Repeat pattern rows twice more. Cast off.

Cables in rounds

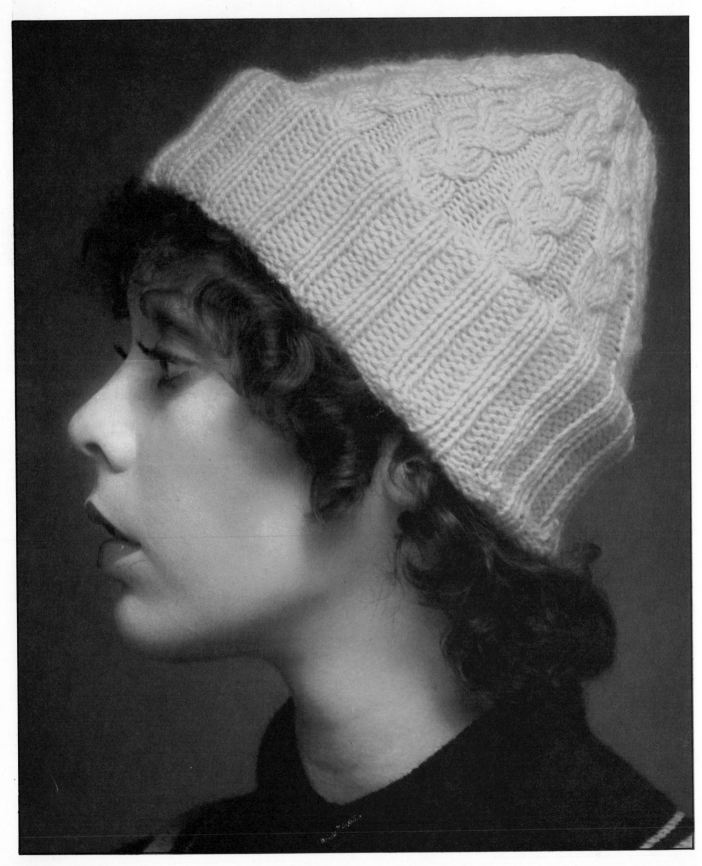

Cable patterns are just as easy to work in rounds as in rows. Unless otherwise stated in a pattern, the cable twists are worked on the right side of the fabric and as the right side of the work is always facing you when knitting in rounds, it is quite a simple matter to combine both of these techniques.

This jaunty little hat has been specially designed so that the cable panels can be worked in any one of three variations. This will help you master the method of working cable stitches – at the same time resulting in a snug, warm, fashion extra!

Size
To fit an average head

Tension
22 sts and 30 rows to 10cm (3.9in) over st st worked on No.7 needles

Materials
3 × 25 grm balls of any Double Knitting quality
Set of 4 No.6 needles pointed at both ends
Set of 4 No. 7 needles pointed at both ends
Cable needle

Hat
Using set of 4 No.6 needles cast on 96 sts and arrange on 3 needles.

1st round *P2, K2, rep from * to end.

Rep this round for 10cm (4in), to form turned back brim. Change to set of 4 No.7 needles. Commence patt.

Cable patt 1
1st round *P2, K6, rep from * to end.
2nd round As 1st.
3rd round As 1st.
4th round *P2, sl next 3 sts on to cable needle and hold at front of work, K next 3 sts from left hand needle then K3 from cable needle – called C6F –, rep from * to end.
These 4 rounds form the patt.

Cable patt 2
1st round *P2, K6, rep from * to end.
2nd round As 1st.
3rd round As 1st.
4th round *P2, sl next 3 sts on to cable needle and hold at front of work, K next 3 sts from left hand needle then K3 from cable needle – called C6F –, rep from * to end.
5th round As 1st.
6th round As 1st.
7th round As 1st.
8th round *P2, sl next 3 sts on to cable needle and hold at back of work, K next 3 sts from left hand needle then K3 from cable needle – called C6B –, rep from * to end.
These 8 rounds form the patt.

Cable patt 3
1st round *P2, K6, rep from * to end.

2nd round As 1st.
3rd round As 1st.
4th round *P2, sl next 2 sts on to cable needle and hold at back of work, K next 2 sts from left hand needle then K2 from cable needle – called C4B –, K2, rep from * to end.
5th round As 1st.
6th round As 1st.
7th round As 1st.
8th round *P2, K2, sl next 2 sts on to cable needle and hold at front of work, K next 2 sts from left hand needle then K2 from cable needle – called C4F –, rep from * to end.
These 8 rounds form the patt.

Cont in patt as required until work measures 20cm (8in) from beg of patt, ending with a 4th or 8th patt round.

Shape top
Next round (dec round) *P2, sl 1, K1, psso, K2, K2 tog, rep from * to end. 72 sts.
Next round *P2, K4, rep from * to end.
Next round *P2, sl1, K1, psso, K2 tog, rep from * to end. 48 sts.
Next round *P2, K2, rep from * to end.
Next round *P2 tog, K2 tog, rep from * to end. 24 sts.
Next round *P1, K1, rep from * to end.
Next round *Sl 1, K1, psso, rep from * to end. 12 sts.
Break off yarn, thread through rem sts, draw up and fasten off.

To make up
Pressing on WS is required, omitting ribbing and taking care not to flatten patt. Turn RS out. Fold brim in half to outside then fold back again to form a double brim.

Cable panels

Panels of cable stitches are a most effective way of highlighting even a most basic jersey or cardigan design. They can be incorporated as separate bands spaced between panels of purl background stitches to form an all-over jersey fabric, or a single panel of cable stitches can be used as a border inside the ribbed front bands of a cardigan. Worked lengthways, they can be used as separate bands which can be sewn on to the lower edge or sleeves of a jersey, or as a headband on a snug little cap, as shown here.

Seeded cable
Cast on 12 stitches.
1st row (WS) K4, P4, K4.
2nd row P4, K4, P4.
3rd row K4, P1, sl next 2 sts keeping yarn at front of work, P1, K4.
4th row P2, sl next 3 sts on to cable needle and hold at back of work, K1 then K1, P1, K1 from cable needle, sl next st on to cable needle and hold at front of work, K1, P1, K1 then K1 from cable needle, P2.
5th row K2, (P1, K1) 3 times, P2, K2.
6th row P2, (K1, P1) 3 times, K2, P2.
Rep 5th and 6th rows twice more.
11th row K2, yfwd, sl 1 keeping yarn at front of work, ybk, (K1, P1) 3 times, sl 1 keeping yarn at front of work, ybk, K2.
12th row P2, sl next st on to cable needle and hold at front of work, P2, K1 then K1 from cable needle, sl next 3 sts on to cable needle and hold at back of work, K1 then K1, P2 from cable needle, P2.
Rep 1st and 2nd rows twice more. These 16 rows form the pattern.

Round linked cable
Cast on 12 sts.
1st row (WS) K2, yfwd, sl 1 keeping yarn at front of work, P6, sl 1 keeping yarn at front of work, ybk, K2.
2nd row P2, sl next st on to cable needle and hold at front of work, P3 then K1 from cable needle, sl next 3 sts on to cable needle and hold at back of work, K1 then P3 from cable needle, P2.

3rd row K5, P2, K5.
4th row P2, sl next 3 sts on to cable needle and hold at back of work, K1 then K3 from cable needle, sl next st on to cable needle and hold at front of work, K3 then K1 from cable needle, P2.
5th row K2, P8, K2.
6th row P2, K8, P2.
Rep 5th and 6th rows twice more. These 10 rows form the pattern.

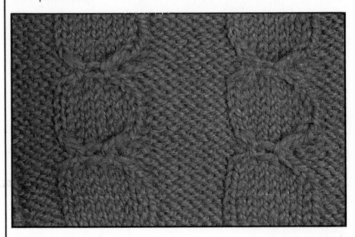

Wishbone cable
Cast on 12 sts.
1st row (RS) P2, sl next 3 sts on to cable needle and hold at back of work, K1 then P1, K1, P1 from cable needle, sl next st on to cable needle and hold at front of work, K1, P1, K1 then K1 from cable needle, P2.
2nd row K2, (P1, K1) 3 times, P2, K2.
3rd row P2, (K1, P1) 3 times, K2, P2.
Rep 2nd and 3rd rows once more.
6th row As 2nd.
7th row P2, K1, P1, K3, P1, K2, P2.
8th row K2, P1, K1, P3, K1, P2, K2.
These 8 rows form the pattern.

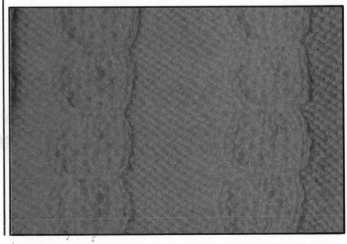

Cross cable

Cast on 12 sts.
1st row (RS) P3, K6, P3.
2nd row K3, P6, K3.
Rep 1st and 2nd rows twice more.
7th row P3, sl next 3 sts on to cable needle and hold at back of work, K3 then K3 from cable needle, P3.
8th row As 2nd.
9th row As 1st.
Rep 8th and 9th rows once more, then 8th row once more.
13th row P5, K2, P5.
14th row K5, P2, K5.
Rep 13th and 14th rows 3 times more. These 20 rows form the pattern.

Diagonal link cable

Cast on 12 sts.
1st and every alt row (WS) K2, P8, K2.
2nd row P2, K2, sl next 2 sts on to cable needle and hold at front of work, K2 then K2 from cable needle, K2, P2.
4th row P2, K8, P2.
6th row As 2nd.
8th row As 4th.
10th row As 6th.
12th row P2, K2, K2 tog, sl 1, K1, psso, K2, P2.
13th row (WS) K2, P6, K2.
14th row P2, K1, sl1, K1, psso, K2 tog, K1, P2.
15th row K2, P4, K2.
16th row P2, sl next 2 sts on to cable needle and hold at back of work, K2 then K2 from cable needle, P2.
17th row As 15th.
18th row P2, K1, pick up loop lying between needles and K tbl – called M1 –, K2, M1, K1, P2.
19th row As 13th.
20th row P2, (K2, M1) twice, K2, P2.
These 20 rows form the pattern.

Pull-on cap

Size
To fit an average adult head

Tension
24 sts and 32 rows to 10cm (3.9*in*) over st st worked on No.8 needles

Materials
3 × 25 grm balls of any Double Knitting quality
One pair No.8 needles
Cable needle

Cap
Using No.8 needles cast on 96 sts. Beg with a P row cont in reversed st st until work measures 11.5cm (4$\frac{1}{2}$*in*) from beg, ending with a P row.
Shape top
Next row *K2 tog, K6, rep from * to end. 84 sts.
Next row P to end.
Next row *K2 tog, K5, rep from * to end. 72 sts.
Next row P to end.
Cont dec 12 sts in this way on next and every alt row until 12 sts rem. Break off yarn, thread through rem sts, draw up and fasten off.

Headband
Using No.8 needles cast on 24 sts. Work any cable patt as required.
1st row Patt 12 sts, K12.
2nd row P12, patt 12 sts.
Rep last 2 rows until band fits round lower edge of cap. Cast off.

To make up
Press as required. With RS tog, sew patt edge of headband to lower edge of cap. Join centre back seam. Fold st st edge of headband in half to WS and sl st down.

129

Experiments with cable stitch

More about cable patterns! There are so many variations of cable stitches and the fabric formed is so effective that it is well worth experimenting to see how best they can be included as for instance part of a basic jersey or cardigan design.

As already suggested in the preceding chapters, the cable patterns do not need to be worked as an all-over fabric, but panels can be incorporated in many interesting ways. The patterns shown here require a given number of stitches to form one panel, but if you wish to work more than one panel side by side, intersperse each panel with a few extra stitches, to give definition to each pattern.

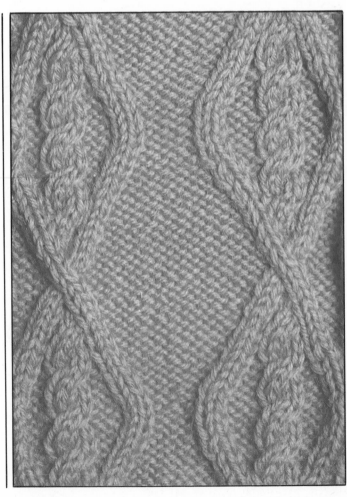

Diamond rope cable
This panel is worked over 18 stitches.
1st row (WS) K7, P4, K7.
2nd row P6, sl next st on to cable needle and hold at back of work, K2 then K1 from cable needle – called Cb3 –, sl next 2 sts on to cable needle and hold at front of work, K1 then K2 from cable needle – called Cf3 –, P6.
3rd and every alt row K all K sts and P all P sts.
4th row P5, Cb3, K2, Cf3, P5.
6th row P4, sl next st on to cable needle and hold at back of work, K2 then P1 from cable needle – called Bc3 –, sl next 2 sts on to cable needle and hold at back of work, K2 then K2 from cable needle – called Cb4 –, sl next 2 sts on to cable needle and hold at front of work, P1 then K2 from cable needle – called Fc3 –, P4.

8th row P3, Bc3, P1, K4, P1, Fc3, P3.
10th row P2, Bc3, P2, Cb4, P2, Fc3, P2.
12th row P1, Bc3, P3, K4, P3, Fc3, P1.
14th row P1, K2, P4, Cb4, P4, K2, P1.
16th row P1, Fc3, P3, K4, P3, Bc3, P1.
18th row P2, Fc3, P2, Cb4, P2, Bc3, P2.
20th row P3, Fc3, P1, K4, P1, Bc3, P3.
22nd row P4, Fc3, Cb4, Bc3, P4.
24th row P5, Fc3, K2, Bc3, P5.
26th row P6, Fc3, Bc3, P6.
28th row P7, sl next 2 sts on to cable needle and hold at front of work, K2 then K2 from cable needle, P7.
These 28 rows form the pattern.

Plaited braid cable
This panel is worked over 16 stitches.

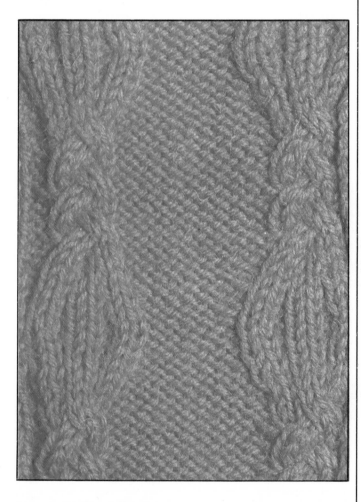

1st row (WS) K5, P6, K5.
2nd row P5, K2, sl next 2 sts on to cable needle and hold at back of work, K2 then K2 from cable needle – called Cb4 –, P5.
3rd and every alt row K all K sts and P all P sts.
4th row P5, sl next 2 sts on to cable needle and hold at front of work, K2 then K2 from cable needle – called Cf4 –, K2, P5.
6th row As 2nd.
8th row As 4th.
10th row As 2nd.
12th row As 4th.

14th row P4, sl next st on to cable needle and hold at back of work, K2 then P1 from cable needle – called Bc3 –, K2, sl next 2 sts on to cable needle and hold at front of work, P1 then K2 from cable needle – called Fc3 –, P4.
16th row P3, Bc3, P1, K2, P1, Fc3, P3.
18th row P2, Bc3, P2, K2, P2, Fc3, P2.
20th row P2, Fc3, P2, K2, P2, Bc3, P2.
22nd row P3, Fc3, P1, K2, P1, Bc3, P3.
24th row P4, Fc3, K2, Bc3, P4.
These 24 rows form the pattern.

Outlined cable
This panel is worked over 18 stitches.

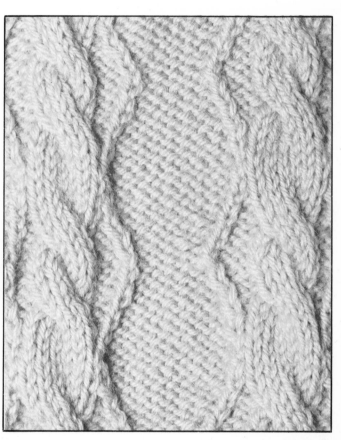

1st row (WS) K5, P8, K5.
2nd row P4, sl next st on to cable needle and hold at back of work, K1 tbl then P1 from cable needle – called Cb2 –, K6, sl next st on to cable needle and hold at front of work, P1 then K1 tbl from cable needle – called Cf2 –, P4.
3rd and every alt row K all K sts and P all P sts.
4th row P3, Cb2, P1, K6, P1, Cf2, P3.
6th row P2, Cb2, P2, sl next 3 sts on to cable needle and hold at front of work, K3 then K3 from cable needle – called Cf6 –, P2, Cf2, P2.
8th row P1, Cb2, P3, K6, P3, Cf2, P1.
10th row P1, Cf2, P3, K6, P3, Cb2, P1.
12th row P2, Cf2, P2, Cf6, P2, Cb2, P2.
14th row P3, Cf2, P1, K6, P1, Cb2, P3.
16th row P4, Cf2, K6, Cb2, P4.
These 16 rows form the pattern.

ARAN KNITTING
Basic stitches

The skilful and imaginative use of such patterns as cables, bobbles and crossed stitches, form the basis for a range of intricate and densely textured fabrics referred to as 'Aran' patterns. Most of the traditional stitches, with their highly evocative names, were originated in the remote Aran islands and derived their inspiration from the daily life of the islanders. The rocks are depicted by chunky bobble stitches, the cliff paths by zig-zag patterns, whilst the fishermen's ropes inspire a vast number of cable variations. The wealth of the sea around the islands, religious symbols and the ups and downs of married life all play a part in the formation of a rich tapestry of patterns, unique in knitting.

The Irish name for the thick, homespun yarn used for Aran knitting is 'bainin', which literally means 'natural'. These traditional stitches show to their best advantage in this light-coloured yarn but many vivid colours are now used with these stitches, to make fashion garments.

Practise the samples given here, using a Double Knitting yarn and No.8 needles, to form separate squares or panels, which can then be joined together to form cushions, afghans or even bedspreads.

Ladder of life

This simple design depicts man's eternal desire to climb upwards, the purl ridges forming the rungs of the ladder. Cast on a number of stitches divisible by 6 plus 1.

1st row (RS) P1, *K5, P1, rep from * to end.
2nd row K1, *P5, K1, rep from * to end.
3rd row P to end.
4th row As 2nd.
These 4 rows form the pattern.

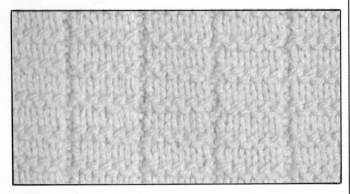

Lobster claw stitch

This represents the bounty of the sea. Cast on a number of stitches divisible by 9.

1st row (RS) *P1, K7, P1, rep from * to end.
2nd row *K1, P7, K1, rep from * to end.
3rd row *P1, sl next 2 sts on to cable needle and hold at back of work, K1 from left hand needle then K2 from cable needle, K1 from left hand needle, sl next st on to cable needle and hold at front of work, K2 from left hand needle then K1 from cable needle, P1, rep from * to end.
4th row As 2nd.
These 4 rows form the pattern.

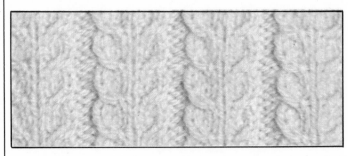

Tree of life

Narrow lines of travelling stitches branching out from a central stem form the basis for this traditional pattern. Cast on a number of stitches divisible by 15.

1st row (RS) *P7, K1, P7, rep from * to end.
2nd row *K7, P1, K7, rep from * to end.
3rd row *P5, sl next st on to cable needle and hold at back of work, K1 from left hand needle then P1 from cable needle – called C2B –, K1 from left hand needle, sl next st on to cable needle and hold at front of work, P1 from left hand needle then K1 from cable needle – called C2F –, P5, rep from * to end.
4th row *K5, sl 1 P-wise keeping yarn at front of work, K1, P1, K1, sl 1, K5, rep from * to end.
5th row *P4, C2B, P1, K1, P1, C2F, P4, rep from * to end.
6th row *K4, sl 1, K2, P1, K2, sl 1, K4, rep from * to end.
7th row *P3, C2B, P2, K1, P2, C2F, P3, rep from * to end.
8th row *K3, sl 1, K3, P1, K3, sl 1, K3, rep from * to end.

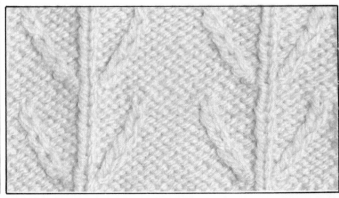

9th row *P2, C2B, P3, K1, P3, C2F, P2, rep from * to end.
10th row *K2, sl 1, K4, P1, K4, sl 1, K2, rep from * to end.
These 10 rows form the pattern.

Aran plaited cable
This simple cable depicts the interweaving of family life. Cast on a number of stitches divisible by 12.
1st row (WS) *K2, P8, K2, rep from * to end.
2nd row *P2, (sl next 2 sts on to cable needle and hold at back of work, K2 from left hand needle then K2 from cable needle) twice, P2, rep from * to end.
3rd row As 1st.
4th row *P2, K2, sl next 2 sts on to cable needle and hold at front of work, K2 from left hand needle then K2 from cable needle, K2, P2, rep from * to end.
These 4 rows form the pattern.

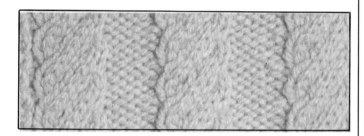

Aran diamond and bobble cable
The small diamond outlined with knitted stitches represents the small, walled fields of Ireland and the bobble depicts the stony nature of the ground. Cast on a number of stitches divisible by 17.
1st row (WS) *K6, P2, K1, P2, K6, rep from * to end.
2nd row *P6, sl next 3 sts on to cable needle and hold at back of work, K2 from left hand needle, sl P1 from end of cable needle back on to left hand needle and P1 then K2 from cable needle, P6, rep from * to end.
3rd row As 1st.
4th row *P5, sl next st on to cable needle and hold at back of work, K2 from left hand needle then P1 from cable needle – called C3B –, K1, sl next 2 sts on to cable needle and hold at front of work, P1 from left hand needle then K2 from cable needle – called C3F –, P5, rep from * to end.
5th and every alt row K all K sts and P all P sts.
6th row *P4, C3B, K1, P1, K1, C3F, P4, rep from * to end.

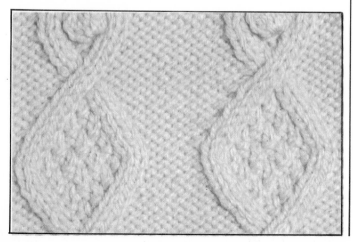

8th row *P3 C3B, (K1, P1) twice, K1, C3F, P3, rep from * to end.
10th row *P2, C3B, (K1, P1) 3 times, K1, C3F, P2, rep from * to end.
12th row *P2, C3F, (P1, K1) 3 times, P1, C3B, P2, rep from * to end.
14th row *P3, C3F, (P1, K1) twice, P1, C3B, P3, rep from * to end.
16th row *P4, C3F, P1, K1, P1, C3B, P4, rep from * to end.
18th row *P5, C3F, P1, C3B, P5, rep from * to end.
20th row As 2nd.
22nd row *P5, C3B, P1, C3F, P5, rep from * to end.
24th row *P4, C3B, P3, C3F, P4, rep from * to end.
26th row *P4, K2, P2, (K1, yfwd to make one st, K1, yfwd, K1) all into next st, turn and P5, turn and K5, turn and P2 tog, P1, P2 tog, turn and sl 1, K2 tog, psso – called B1 –, P2, K2, P4, rep from * to end.
28th row *P4, C3F, P3, C3B, P4, rep from * to end.
30th row As 18th.
These 30 rows form the pattern.

Shoulder bag
Size
30.5cm (*12in*) wide by 30.5cm (*12in*) deep

Tension
24 sts and 32 rows to 10cm (*3.9in*) over st st worked on No.8 needles

Materials
4 × 50grm balls of any Double Knitting
One pair No.8 needles

Bag
Using No.8 needles cast on 85 sts. Work in Aran diamond and bobble cable patt. Rep 30 patt rows 6 times in all, then first 20 rows once more. Cast off.

To make up
Fold work in half with RS facing. Join side seams and turn RS out. Turn in 1.5cm (*½in*) hem round top edge and sl st down. Make plait approx 152.5cm (*60in*) long, leaving tassels at both ends. Sew plait to side seams above tassels, leaving rest of plait free for strap.

Aran patterns

Aran panels

The variety and complexity of Aran stitches which may be formed give such scope for textured patterns that it is sometimes difficult to know where to begin a design and how best to combine these stitches to produce the most effective fabric. If each stitch is run on into the next, all definition will be lost and none of the stitches will show to their best advantage. Because these stitches nearly always have a raised texture, their beauty is enhanced if they are worked against a purled background. Similarly, if each panel of stitches is enclosed with a rope of twisted stitches and alternated with panels of either purl or moss stitches, each separate Aran panel stands out without detracting in any way from the next panel. The poncho design given here uses these techniques to full effect. It is made from two simple sections and the size can easily be adjusted by amending the number of stitches in each purl panel.

Poncho
Size
Approx 89cm (*35in*) square, excluding fringe

Tension
18 sts and 24 rows to 10cm (*3.9in*) over st st worked on No.7 needles

Materials
17 × 50grm balls Mahony Blarney Bainin wool
One pair No.7 needles
One pair No.8 needles
Set of 4 No.9 needles pointed at both ends
One No.7 circular Twin-Pin
One No.8 circular Twin-Pin
One cable needle

Poncho first section
Using No.8 circular Twin-Pin cast on 146 sts. K4 rows g st.
Next row (inc row) K3, pick up loop lying between needles and P tbl – called M1 –, K2, M1, *(K2, M1) twice, (K2, K into front and back of next st – called Kfb –) twice, K3, (M1, K2) twice, *, **(M1, K2) twice, (P1, M1, P1, P into front and back of next st – called Pfb –, P1, M1, P1, K2) twice, M1, K2, M1, **, ***K2, Pfb, K2, Kfb, K3, Pfb, K1, Pfb, K2, Kfb, K3, Pfb, K2, ***, rep from ** to **, then from *** to ***, then from ** to ** again, then rep from * to * once more, M1, K2, M1, K3. 204 sts.
Change to No.7 circular Twin-Pin. Commence patt.
1st row K2, P1, K1 tbl, P2, K1 tbl, *P2, sl next st on to cable needle and hold at front of work, P1, then K1 tbl from cable needle – called T2L –, P1, T2L, P9, sl next st on to cable needle and hold at back of work, K1 tbl, then P1 from cable needle – called T2R –, P1, T2R, P2, *, K1 tbl, P2, K1 tbl, **(P2, K8) twice, P2, K1 tbl, P2, K1 tbl, P2, K2, P3, into next st (K1, (yfwd, K1) twice, turn, P these 5 sts, turn, K5, turn, P5, turn, sl 2nd, 3rd and 4th sts over first st, then K first and last st tog tbl – called MB –) P3, sl next 3 sts on to cable needle and hold at back of work, K2, sl P st from cable needle onto left hand needle and hold cable needle at front of work, P1 from left hand needle, then K2 from cable needle – called Cr5 –, P3, MB, P3, K2, P2, K1 tbl, P2, K1 tbl, **, rep from ** to ** once more, (P2, K8) twice, P2, K1 tbl, P2, K1 tbl, rep from * to * once more, K1 tbl, P2, K1 tbl, P1, K2.
2nd row K3, *P1 tbl, K2, P1 tbl, K3, P1 tbl, K2, P1 tbl, K9, P1 tbl, K2, P1 tbl, K3, *, P1 tbl, K2, P1 tbl, **(K2, P8) twice, K2, P1 tbl, K2, P1 tbl, K2, (P2, K7, P2, K1) twice, K1, P1 tbl, K2, P1 tbl, **, rep from ** to ** once more, (K2, P8) twice, K2, rep from * to * once more, P1 tbl, K2, P1 tbl, K3.
3rd row K2, P1, *K1 tbl, P2, K1 tbl, P3, T2L, P1, T2L, P7, T2R, P1, T2R, P3, *, K1 tbl, P2, K1 tbl, **(P2, sl next 2 sts on to cable needle and hold at back of work, K2, then K2 from cable needle – called C4B –, sl next 2 sts on to cable needle and hold at front of work, K2, then K2 from cable needle – called C4F –) twice, P2, K1 tbl, P2, K1 tbl, P2, (sl next 2 sts on to cable needle and hold at front of work, P1, then K2 from cable needle – called C3L –, P5, sl next st on to cable needle and hold at back of work, K2, then P1 from cable needle – called C3R –, P1) twice, P1, K1 tbl, P2, K1 tbl, **, rep from ** to ** once more, (P2, C4B, C4F) twice, P2, rep from * to * once more, K1 tbl, P2, K1 tbl, P1, K2.
4th row K3, P1 tbl, K2, *P1 tbl, K4, P1 tbl, K2, P1 tbl, K7, P1 tbl, K2, P1 tbl, K4, *, P1 tbl, K2, P1 tbl, **(K2, P8) twice, K2, P1 tbl, K2, P1 tbl, (K3, P2, K5, P2) twice, K3, P1 tbl, K2, P1 tbl, **, rep from ** to ** once more, (K2, P8) twice, K2, P1 tbl, K2, rep from * to * once more, P1 tbl, K2, P1 tbl, K3.
5th row K2, P1, K1 tbl, *P2, K1 tbl, P4, T2L, P1, T2L, P5, T2R, P1, T2R, P4, *, K1 tbl, P2, K1 tbl, **(P2, K8) twice, P2, K1 tbl, P2, K1 tbl, (P3, C3L, P3, C3R) twice, P3, K1 tbl, P2, K1 tbl, **, rep from ** to ** once more, (P2, K8) twice, P2, K1 tbl, rep from * to * once more, K1 tbl, P2, K1 tbl, P1, K2.
6th row K3, P1 tbl, *K2, P1 tbl, (K5, P1 tbl, K2, P1 tbl) twice, K5, *, P1 tbl, K2, P1 tbl, **(K2, P8) twice, K2, P1 tbl, K2, P1 tbl, K4, P2, K3, P2, K5, P2, K3, P2, K4, P1 tbl, K2, P1 tbl, **, rep from ** to ** once more, (K2, P8) twice, K2, P1 tbl, rep from * to * once more, P1 tbl, K2, P1 tbl, K3.

T2L, P1, T2L, P5, *, K1 tbl, P2, K1 tbl, **(P2, K8) twice, P2, K1 tbl, P2, K1 tbl, P5, Cr5, P3, MB, P3, Cr5, P5, K1 tbl, P2, K1 tbl,**, rep from ** to ** once more, (P2, K8) twice, P2, K1 tbl, rep from * to * once more, K1 tbl, P2, K1 tbl, P1, K2.

10th row K3, P1 tbl, *K2, P1 tbl, (K5, P1 tbl, K2, P1 tbl) twice, K5, *, P1 tbl, K2, P1 tbl, **(K2, P8) twice, K2, P1 tbl, K2, P1 tbl, K5, P2, K1, P2, K7, P2, K1, P2, K5, P1 tbl, K2, P1 tbl, **, rep from ** to ** once more, (K2, P8) twice, K2, P1 tbl, rep from * to * once more, P1 tbl, K2, P1 tbl, K3.

11th row K2, P1, K1 tbl, *P2, K1 tbl, P4, T2R, P1, T2R, P5, T2L, P1, T2L, P4, *, K1 tbl, P2, K1 tbl, **(P2, C4F, C4B) twice, P2, K1 tbl, P2, K1 tbl, P4, C3R, P1, C3L, P5, C3R, P1, C3L, P4, K1 tbl, P2, K1 tbl, **, rep from ** to ** once more, (P2, C4F, C4B) twice, P2, K1 tbl, rep from * to * once more, K1 tbl, P2, K1 tbl, P1, K2.

12th row K3, P1 tbl, *K2, P1 tbl, K4, P1 tbl, K2, P1 tbl, K7, P1 tbl, K2, P1 tbl, K4, *, P1 tbl, K2, P1 tbl, **(K2, P8) twice, K2, P1 tbl, K2, P1 tbl, K4, P2, K3, P2, K5, P2, K3, P2, K4, P1 tbl, K2, P1 tbl, **, rep from ** to ** once more, (K2, P8) twice, K2, P1 tbl, rep from * to * once more, P1 tbl, K2, P1 tbl, K3.

13th row K2, P1, K1 tbl, *P2, K1 tbl, P3, T2R, P1, T2R, P7, T2L, P1, T2L, P3, *, K1 tbl, P2, K1 tbl, **(P2, K8) twice, P2, K1 tbl, P2, K1 tbl, (P3, C3R, P3, C3L) twice, P3, K1 tbl, P2, K1 tbl, **, rep from ** to ** once more, (P2, K8) twice, P2, K1 tbl, rep from * to * once more, K1 tbl, P2, K1 tbl, P1, K2.

14th row K3, P1 tbl, *K2, P1 tbl, K3, P1 tbl, K2, P1 tbl, K9, P1 tbl, K2, P1 tbl, K3, *, P1 tbl, K2, P1 tbl, **(K2, P8) twice, K2, P1 tbl, K2, P1 tbl, (K3, P2, K5, P2) twice, K3, P1 tbl, K2, P1 tbl,**, rep from ** to ** once more, (K2, P8) twice, K2, P1 tbl, rep from * to * once more, P1 tbl, K2, P1 tbl, K3.

15th row K2, P1, K1 tbl, *P2, K1 tbl, P2, T2R, P1, T2R, P9, T2L, P1, T2L, P2, *, K1 tbl, P2, K1 tbl, **(P2, C4F, C4B) twice, P2, K1 tbl, P2, K1 tbl, P2, (C3R, P5, C3L, P1) twice, P1, K1 tbl, P2, K1 tbl, **, rep from ** to ** once more, (P2, C4F, C4B) twice, P2, K1 tbl, rep from * to * once more, K1 tbl, P2, K1 tbl, P1, K2.

16th row K3, P1 tbl, *K2, P1 tbl, (K2, P1 tbl) twice, K11, (P1 tbl, K2) twice, *, P1 tbl, K2, P1 tbl, **(K2, P8) twice, K2, P1 tbl, K2, P1 tbl, K2, (P2, K7, P2, K1) twice, K1, P1 tbl, K2, P1 tbl, **, rep from ** to ** once more, (K2, P8) twice, K2, P1 tbl, rep from * to * once more, P1 tbl, K2, P1 tbl, K3.

These 16 rows form patt. Cont in patt until 8th row of 6th patt has been completed.

Shape neck

Next row Patt 93 sts, *(K2 tog, K1) twice, K2 tog, P2, (K2 tog, K1) twice, K2 tog, *, (P1, K2 tog) twice, **P5, K2 tog, P1, K2 tog, (P1, P2 tog) twice, (P1, K2 tog) twice, P5, **, (K2 tog tbl, P1) twice, rep from * to * once more, (P1, K2 tog) twice, P2, P2 tog, (P1, K2 tog) twice, P3, (K2 tog tbl, P1) twice, P2 tog, P2, K2 tog tbl, P1, K2 tog tbl, K2. 172 sts.

Next row Cast off 79 sts, patt to end. 93 sts.

7th row K2, P1, K1 tbl, *P2, K1 tbl, P5, T2L, P1, T2L, P3, T2R, P1, T2R, P5, *, K1 tbl, P2, K1 tbl, **(P2, C4B, C4F) twice, P2, K1 tbl, P2, K1 tbl, P4, C3L, P1, C3R, P5, C3L, P1, C3R, P4, K1 tbl, P2, K1 tbl, **, rep from ** to ** once more, (P2, C4B, C4F) twice, P2, K1 tbl, rep from * to * once more, K1 tbl, P2, K1 tbl, P1, K2.

8th row K3, P1 tbl, *K2, P1 tbl, K6, P1 tbl, K2, P1 tbl, K3, P1 tbl, K2, P1 tbl, K6, *, P1 tbl, K2, P1 tbl, **(K2, P8) twice, K2, P1 tbl, K2, P1 tbl, K5, P2, K1 P2, K7, P2, K1, P2 K5, P1 tbl, K2, P1 tbl, **, rep from ** to ** once more, (K2, P8) twice, K2, P1 tbl, rep from * to * once more, P1 tbl, K2, P1 tbl, K3.

9th row K2, P1, K1 tbl, *P2, K1 tbl, P5, T2R, P1, T2R, P3,

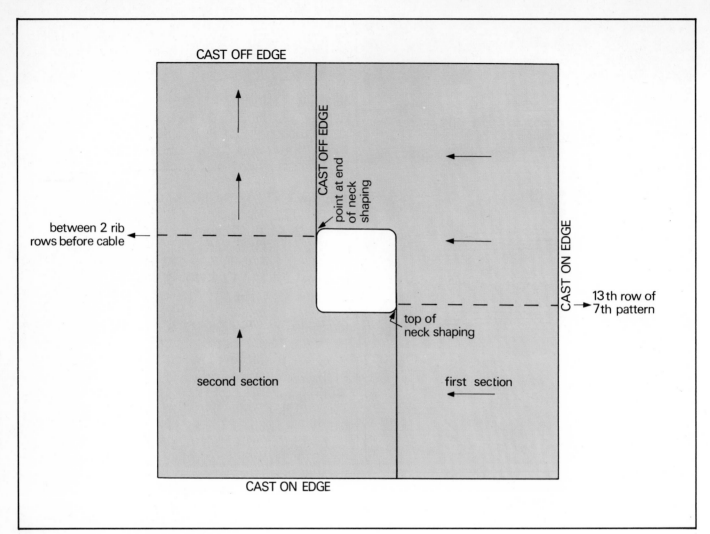

CAST OFF EDGE

CAST OFF EDGE

point at end of neck shaping

between 2 rib rows before cable

top of neck shaping

CAST ON EDGE

13th row of 7th pattern

second section

first section

CAST ON EDGE

Next row Patt to last 2 sts, P2 tog.
Keeping patt correct, cont dec one st at beg of next and every foll alt row 5 times in all. Work 8 rows without shaping. Inc one st at end of next and every alt row 6 times in all. 93 sts.
Next row K2, K2 tog, P1, K2 tog, P2, P2 tog, (P1, K2 tog tbl) twice, P3, (K2 tog, P1) twice, P2 tog, P2, (K2 tog tbl, P1) twice, rep from * to * of 1st shaping row, (P1, K2 tog) twice, rep from ** to ** of 1st shaping row, patt to end. 69 sts.
Cast off loosely.

Second section

Using No.8 needles cast on 83 sts. K 4 rows g st.
Next row (inc row) K3, M1, K2, M1, rep from * to * of inc row in first section, then from ** to ** in same row, then from *** to *** in same row, then from ** to ** again, omitting M1 at end of Row. 116 sts.
Change to No.7 needles. Commence patt.
1st row K1, P1, K1 tbl, (P2, K8) twice, P2, K1 tbl, P2, K1 tbl, P2, K2, P3, MB, P3, Cr5, P3, MB, P3, K2, P2, K1 tbl, P2, K1 tbl, (P2, K8) twice, P2, K1 tbl, P2, K1 tbl, P2, T2L, P1, T2L, P9, T2R, P1, T2R, P2, K1 tbl, P2, K1 tbl, P1, K2.
2nd row K3, P1 tbl, K2, P1 tbl, patt as now set to last 3 sts, P1 tbl, K2.
Cont in patt as now set until 8th row of 6th patt has been completed.

Shape neck

1st row K1, P1, K1 tbl, P2, (K2 tog, K1) twice, K2 tog, P2, (K2 tog, K1) twice, K2 tog, patt to end.
2nd row Patt 93 sts and leave these sts on a holder, cast off 12 sts, patt to end. 5 sts.
Dec one st at neck edge on foll 3 alt rows. Cast off. With RS of work facing, rejoin yarn to rem sts at neck edge, cont in patt dec one st at neck edge on foll 3 alt rows. 90 sts. Cont without shaping until 13th patt rep has been completed. Change to No.8 needles.
Next row K2, (K2 tog, K2, K2 tog, K1) 12 times, K2 tog, K2. 65 sts.
K 3 rows g st. Cast off.

To make up

Join both sections as shown in diagram, noting positions of top of neck shaping on second section and point at end of neck shaping on first section. Press seams on wrong side under a damp cloth with a warm iron.
Neckband Using set of 4 No.9 needles, K up 104 sts all round neck edge. Work 5 rounds K1, P1 rib. Cast off in rib, working K2 tog at each corner.
Fringe Cut yarn into lengths of 25.5cm (*10in*). Using 3 strands folded in half, draw centre of threads through edge of poncho and knot. Rep at 1.5cm (½*in*) intervals all round outer edge.

Aran shaping

Aran shaping

Where each Aran panel is combined with alternate panels of purl or moss stitches, it is simple to make provision for any shaping (see overleaf).

Because Aran stitches are rather complex, it is not advisable to try and combine them with any increasing or decreasing and most designs take this into account. The number of stitches required, say, for a raglan armhole and sleeve top shaping are carefully calculated to ensure that the correct number of stitches are decreased in a plain panel, without interfering with the Aran panels.

The variety of Aran designs available is sometimes restricted by this problem of shaping. This can be overcome, however, by the skilful use of shaping in each alternate plain panel and by the careful choice of a basic stitch, such as garter stitch or ribbing, to complete the shaped sections. The camisole top shown here perfectly illustrates these techniques.

Camisole top
Sizes
To fit 81.5[86.5:91.5]cm (*32[34:36]in*) bust
Length to shoulder, 47[49:51]cm (*18[19¼:20]in*)
The figures in brackets [] refer to the 86.5 (*34*) and 91.5cm (*36in*) sizes respectively

Tension

32 sts and 40 rows to 10cm (3.9*in*) over rev st st worked on No.11 needles

Materials

4 × 50grm balls Mahony's Blarney Killowen 4 ply wool
One pair No.11 needles
One No. 11 circular Twin-Pin
One No.12 circular Twin-Pin
7 buttons

Camisole fronts and back

Using No.12 circular Twin-Pin cast on 237[253:269] sts and work in one piece, beg at lower edge.
1st row K1, *P1, K1, rep from * to end.
2nd row P1, *K1, P1, rep from * to end.
Rep last 2 rows 3 times more, then 1st row once more.
Next row P to end.
Next row P to end to form hemline.
Base row Cast on 7 sts for right front band, turn, K8, *P2, K15, P2, K8[10:12], P2, K3, P1, K2, P1, K8, P2, K8[10:12], rep from * 3 times more, P2, K15, P2, K1, turn and cast on 7 sts for left front band. 251[267:283] sts. Change to No.11 circular Twin-Pin. Commence patt.
1st row (RS) K7, P1, *K 2nd st on left hand needle, then first st – called T2 –, P7, K1, P7, T2, P8[10:12], T2, P7, K 2nd st on left hand needle, then P first st – called C2R–, P1, C2R, P3, T2, P8[10:12], T2, P2, K2, P7, K2, P2, T2, P8[10:12], T2, P7, C2R, P1, C2R, P3, T2, P8[10:12], rep from * once more, T2, P7, K1, P7, T2, P1, K7.
2nd row K8, *P2, K7, P1, K7, P2, K8[10:12], P2, K4, P1, K2, P1, K7, P2, K8[10:12], P2, K2, P3, K5, P3, K2, P2, K8[10:12], P2, K4, P1, K2, P1, K7, P2, K8[10:12], rep from * once more, P2, K7, P1, K7, P2, K8.
3rd row K7, P1, *T2, P6, K1, P1, K1, P6, T2, P8[10:12], T2, P6, C2R, P1, C2R, P4, T2, P8[10:12], T2, (P3, K3) twice, P3, T2, P8[10:12], T2, P6, C2R, P1, C2R, P4, T2, P8[10:12], rep from * once more, T2, P6, K1, P1, K1, P6, T2, P1, K7.
4th row K8, *P2, K6, P1, K1, P1, K6, P2, K8[10:12], P2, K5, P1, K2, P1, K6, P2, K8[10:12], P2, K4, P3, K1, P3, K4, P2, K8[10:12], P2, K5, P1, K2, P1, K6, P2, K8[10:12], rep from * once more, P2, K6, P1, K1, P1, K6, P2, K8.
5th row (buttonhole row) K2, K2 tog, (yrn) twice, sl 1, K1, psso, K1, P1, *T2, P5, (K1, P1) twice, K1, P5, T2, P8[10:12], T2, P5, C2R, P1, C2R, P5, T2, P8[10:12], T2, P5, K5, P5, T2, P8[10:12], T2, P5, C2R, P1, C2R, P5, T2, P8[10:12], rep from * once more, T2, P5, (K1, P1) twice, K1, P5, T2, P1, K7.
6th row K8, *P2, K5, (P1, K1) twice, P1, K5, P2, K8[10:12], P2, K6, P1, K2, P1, K5, P2, K8[10:12], P2, K6, P3, K6, P2, K8[10:12], P2, K6, P1, K2, P1, K5, P2, K8[10:12], rep from * once more, P2, K5, (P1, K1) twice, P1, K5, P2, K3, drop one loop of double loop to make long st and work K1, P1 into same st, K3.
Work 5 more buttonholes in same way with 18[20:22] rows between each buttonhole.
7th row K7, P1, *T2, P4, (K1, P1) 3 times, K1, P4, T2, P8[10:12], T2, P4, C2R, P1, C2R, P6, T2, P8[10:12], T2, P5, K5, P5, T2, P8[10:12], T2, P4, C2R, P1, C2R, P6, T2,

P8[10:12], rep from * once more, T2, P4, (K1, P1) 3 times, K1, P4, T2, P1, K7.
8th row K8, *P2, K4, (P1, K1) 3 times, P1, K4, P2, K8[10:12], P2, K7, P1, K2, P1, K4, P2, K8[10:12], P2, K4, P3, K1, P3, K4, P2, K8[10:12], P2, K7, P1, K2, P1, K4, P2, K8[10:12], rep from * once more, P2, K4, (P1, K1) 3 times, P1, K4, P2, K8.
9th row K7, P1, *T2, P3, (K1, P1) 4 times, K1, P3, T2, P8[10:12], T2, P3, C2R, P1, C2R, P7, T2, P8[10:12], T2, (P3, K3) twice, P3, T2, P8[10:12], T2, P3, C2R, P1, C2R, P7, T2, P8[10:12], rep from * once more, T2, P3, (K1, P1) 4 times, K1, P3, T2, P1, K7.
10th row K8, *P2, K3, (P1, K1) 4 times, P1, K3, P2, K8[10:12], P2, K8, P1, K2, P1, K3, P2, K8[10:12], P2, K2, P3, K5, P3, K2, P2, K8[10:12], P2, K8, P1, K2, P1, K3, P2, K8[10:12], rep from * once more, P2, K3, (P1, K1) 4 times, P1, K3, P2, K8.
11th row K7, P1, *T2, P2, (K1, P1) 5 times, K1, P2, T2, P8[10:12], T2, P3, K1, P2, K1, P8, T2, P8[10:12], T2, P2, K2, P7, K2, P2, T2, P8[10:12], T2, P3, K1, P2, K1, P8, T2, P8[10:12], rep from * once more, T2, P2, (K1, P1) 5 times, K1, P2, T2, P1, K7.
12th row K8, *P2, K2, (P1, K1) 5 times, P1, K2, P2, K8[10:12], P2, K8, P1, K2, P1, K3, P2, K8[10:12], P2, K15, P2, K8[10:12], P2, K8, P1, K2, P1, K3, P2, K8[10:12], rep from * once more, P2, K2, (P1, K1) 5 times, P1, K2, P2, K8.
13th row K7, P1, *T2, P3, (K1, P1) 4 times, K1, P3, T2, P8[10:12], T2, P3, P 2nd st on left hand needle, then K first st – called C2L –, P1, C2L, P7, T2, P8[10:12], T2, P6, K3, P6, T2, P8[10:12], T2, P3, C2L, P1, C2L, P7, T2, P8[10:12], rep from * once more, T2, P3, (K1, P1) 4 times, K1, P3, T2, P1, K7.

Shape waist

14th row K8, *P2, K3, (P1, K1) 4 times, P1, K3, P2, sl 1, K1, psso, K4[6:8], K2 tog, P2, K7, P1, K2, P1, K4, P2, sl 1, K1, psso, K4[6:8], K2 tog, P2, K5, P5, K5, P2, sl 1, K1, psso, K4[6:8], K2 tog, P2, K7, P1, K2, P1, K4, P2, sl 1, K1, psso, K4[6:8], K2 tog, rep from * once more, P2, K3, (P1, K1) 4 times, P1, K3, P2, K8. 235[251:267] sts.
15th row K7, P1, *T2, P4, (K1, P1) 3 times, K1, P4, T2, P6[8:10], T2, P4, C2L, P1, C2L, P6, T2, P6[8:10], T2, P4, K3, P1, K3, P4, T2, P6[8:10], T2, P4, C2L, P1, C2L, P6, T2, P6[8:10], rep from * once more, T2, P4, (K1, P1) 3 times, K1, P4, T2, P1, K7.
16th row K8, *P2, K4, (P1, K1) 3 times, P1, K4, P2, K6[8:10], P2, K6, P1, K2, P1, K5, P2, K6[8:10], P2, (K3, P3) twice, K3, P2, K6[8:10], P2, K6, P1, K2, P1, K5, P2, K6[8:10], rep from * once more, P2, K4, (P1, K1) 3 times, P1, K4, P2, K8.
17th row K7, P1, *T2, P5, (K1, P1) twice, K1, P5, T2, P6[8:10], T2, P5, C2L, P1, C2L, P5, T2, P6[8:10], T2, P2, K3, P5, K3, P2, T2, P6[8:10], T2, P5, C2L, P1, C2L, P5, T2, P6[8:10], rep from * once more, T2, P5, (K1, P1) twice, K1, P5, T2, P1, K7.
18th row K8, *P2, K5, (P1, K1) twice, P1, K5, P2, K6[8:10], P2, K5, P1, K2, P1, K6, P2, K6[8:10], P2, K2, P2, K7, P2, K2, P2, K6[8:10], P2, K5, P1, K2, P1, K6, P2, K6[8:10], rep from * once more, P2, K5, (P1, K1) twice, P1, K5, P2, K8.

19th row K7, P1, *T2, P6, K1, P1, K1, P6, T2, P6[8:10], T2, P6, C2L, P1, C2L, P4, T2, P6[8:10], T2, P2, K3, P5, K3, P2, T2, P6[8:10], T2, P6, C2L, P1, C2L, P4, T2, P6[8:10], rep from * once more, T2, P6, K1, P1, K1, P6, T2, P1, K7.

20th row K8, *P2, K6, P1, K1, P1, K6, P2, sl 1, K1, psso, K2[4:6], K2 tog, P2, K4, P1, K2, P1, K7, P2, sl 1, K1, psso, K2[4:6], K2 tog, P2, (K3, P3) twice, K3, P2, sl 1, K1, psso, K2[4:6], K2 tog, P2, K4, P1, K2, P1, K7, P2, sl 1, K1, psso, K2[4:6], K2 tog, rep from * once more, P2, K6, P1, K1, P1, K6, P2, K8. 219[235:251] sts.

21st row K7, P1, *T2, P7, K1, P7, T2, P4[6:8], T2, P7, C2L, P1, C2L, P3, T2, P4[6:8], T2, P4, K3, P1, K3, P4, T2, P4[6:8], T2, P7, C2L, P1, C2L, P3, T2, P4[6:8], rep from * once more, T2, P7, K1, P7, T2, P1, K7.

22nd row K8, *P2, K7, P1, K7, P2, K4[6:8], P2, K3, P1, K2, P1, K8, P2, K4[6:8], P2, K5, P5, K5, P2, K4[6:8], P2, K3, P1, K2, P1, K8, P2, K4[6:8], rep from * once more, P2, K7, P1, K7, P2, K8.

23rd row K7, P1, *T2, P15, T2, P4[6:8], T2, P8, K1, P2, K1, P3, T2, P4[6:8], T2, P6, K3, P6, T2, P4[6:8], T2, P8, K1, P2, K1, P3, T2, P4[6:8], rep from * once more, T2, P15, T2, P1, K7.

24th row K8, *P2, K15, P2, K4[6:8], P2, K3, P1, K2, P1, K8, P2, K4[6:8], P2, K15, P2, K4[6:8], P2, K3, P1, K2, P1, K8, P2, K4[6:8], rep from * once more, P2, K15, P2, K8.

These 24 rows set patt for Aran panels with rev st st between each one. Cont in patt as now set, dec 2 sts as before within each rev st st panel on foll alt row.

203[219:235] sts. Cont in patt until work measures 11.5[12:12.5]cm (4½[4¾:5]in) from hemline, ending with a RS row.

Next row K8, *P2, patt 15, P2, pick up loop lying between needles and K tbl – called M1 –, K2[4:6], M1, rep from * 7 times more, P2, patt 15, P2, K8.

Cont in patt, inc 2 sts as before within each rev st st panel on foll 20th row twice more. 251[267:283] sts. Cont in patt without shaping until work measures 28[29:30.5]cm (11[11½:12]in) from hemline, ending with a WS row.

Shape yoke
Next row K8, *K2 tog, K6, K2 tog, K7, K2 tog, K8[10:12], rep from * 7 times more, K2 tog, K6, K2 tog, K7, K2 tog, K8. 224[240:256] sts.

Beg with a K row, cont in g st until work measures 30.5[31.5:33]cm (12[12½:13]in) from hemline, ending with a WS row.

Divide for armholes
Change to No.11 needles.

Next row K55[58:61], turn and leave rem sts on holder. Complete right front first.

Shape armhole
Cast off at beg of next and every foll alt row 2 sts 3 times and one st 3[4:5] times, *at the same time* work 7th buttonhole 18[20:22] rows above previous buttonhole. K 2 rows, ending at front edge.

Shape neck
Cast off at beg of next and every foll alt row 23[24:25] sts once, 4 sts once, 2 sts 3 times and one st 3 times. 10[11:12] sts. Cont without shaping until work measures 47[49:51]cm (18[19¼:20]in) from hemline. Cast off.

With RS of work facing, rejoin yarn to back sts, cast off first 8[10:12] sts, K until there are 98[104:110] sts on right hand needle, turn and leave rem sts on holder for left front. Complete back first.

Shape armholes
Cast off 2 sts at beg of next 5 rows.

Shape back neck
Next row Cast off 2, K until there are 26[28:30] sts on right hand needle, cast off 34[36:38] sts for neck, K to end.

Dec one st at armhole edge on every alt row 3[4:5] times in all, *at the same time* cast off at neck edge on every alt row 4 sts once, 2 sts 3 times and one st 3 times. 10[11:12] sts. Cont without shaping until work measures 47[49:51]cm (18[19¼:20]in) from hemline. Cast off.

With WS of work facing, rejoin yarn to rem back sts and complete as given for first side, reversing shaping. With RS of work facing, rejoin yarn to rem left front sts, cast off 8[10:12] sts, K to end. 55[58:61] sts. Complete to match right front, reversing shaping and omitting buttonhole.

To make up
Press under a damp cloth with a warm iron. Join shoulder seams. Turn hem to WS at lower edge and sl st down. Press seams. Sew on buttons.

LACE STITCHES
Simple lace

Knitted lace stitches do not need to be complicated in order to produce openwork fabrics. Some of the most effective traditional patterns require only a few stitches and as little as two rows to form the pattern repeat.

The principle used for almost all lace stitches is that of decreasing one or more stitches at a given point in a row and compensating for these decreased stitches, either in the same row or a following row, by working more than once into a stitch or making one or more stitches by taking the yarn over or round the right hand needle the required number of times, as referred to earlier. Use a 4 ply yarn and No.10 needles to practice these simple lace stitches.

Laburnum stitch
Cast on a number of stitches divisible by 5 + 2.
1st row P2, *K3, P2, rep from * to end.
2nd row K2, *P3, K2, rep from * to end.
3rd row P2, *keeping yarn at front of work, sl 1, ybk, K2 tog, psso, bring yarn over top of needle from back to front then round needle again, P2, rep from * to end.
4th row K2, *P into the back of the first made st then into the front of the second made st, P1, K2, rep from * to end.
These 4 rows form the pattern.

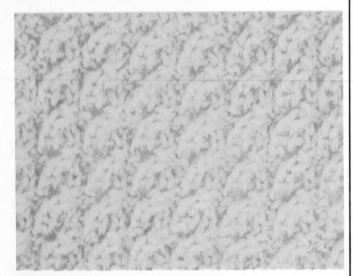

Indian pillar stitch
Cast on a number of stitches divisible by 4 + 3.
1st row (RS) P to end.
2nd row K2, *insert needle P-wise into the next 3 sts as if to P3 tog but instead work (P1, K1, P1) into these 3 sts, K1, rep from * to last st, K1. These 2 rows form the pattern.

Indian pillar stitch

Faggoting rib
Cast on a number of stitches divisible by 5 + 1.
1st row P1, *K2, yfwd, sl 1, K1, psso, P1, rep from * to end.
2nd row K1, *P2, yrn, P2 tog, K1, rep from * to end.
These 2 rows form the pattern.

Lace rib
Cast on a number of stitches divisible by 5 + 2.
1st row P2, *K1, yfwd, sl 1, K1, psso, P2, rep from * to end.
2nd row K2, *P3, K2, rep from * to end.
3rd row P2, *K2 tog, yfwd, K1, P2, rep from * to end.
4th row As 2nd.
These 4 rows form the pattern.

Eyelet cable rib

Cast on a number of stitches divisible by 5 + 2.

1st row P2, *K3, P2, rep from * to end.
2nd row K2, *P3, K2, rep from * to end.
3rd row P2, *sl 1, K2, psso the K2, P2, rep from * to end.
4th row K2, *P1, yrn, P1, K2, rep from * to end.
These 4 rows form the pattern.

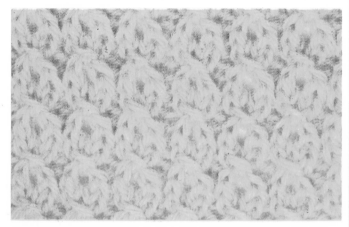

Cat's eye pattern

Cast on a number of stitches divisible by 4.

1st row K4, *yfwd over and round the needle again to make 2 sts, K4, rep from * to end.
2nd row P2, *P2 tog, P the first made st and K the second made st, P2 tog, rep from * to last 2 sts, P2.
3rd row K2, yfwd, *K4, yfwd over and round the needle again, rep from * to last 6 sts, K4, yfwd, K2.
4th row P3, *(P2 tog) twice, P the first made st and K the second made st, rep from * to last 7 sts, (P2 tog) twice, P3.
These 4 rows form the pattern.

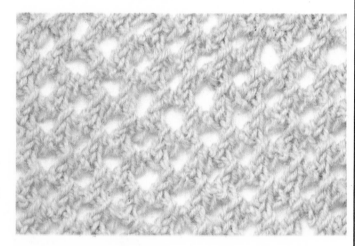

Open star stitch

Cast on a number of stitches divisible by 3.

1st row K2, *yfwd, K3 then pass the first of these 3 sts over the other 2 and off the right hand needle, rep from * to last st, K1.
2nd row P to end.
3rd row K1, *K3 then pass the first of these 3 sts over the other 2, yfwd, rep from * to last 2 sts, K2.
4th row P to end.
These 4 rows form the pattern.

Open star stitch

Hyacinth stitch

Cast on a number of stitches divisible by 6 + 3.

1st, 3rd and 5th rows P to end.
2nd row K1, *(K1, P1, K1, P1, K1) all into next st, K5 tog, rep from * to last 2 sts, (K1, P1, K1, P1, K1) into next st, K1.
4th row K1, *K5 tog, (K1, P1, K1, P1, K1) all into next st, rep from * to last 6 sts, K5 tog, K1.
6th row K to end winding yarn 3 times round right hand needle for each st.
7th row P to end dropping the extra loops.
The 2nd to 7th rows form the pattern.

Diagonal openwork stitch

Cast on a number of stitches divisible by 2 + 1.

1st row K1, *yfwd, K2 tog, rep from * to end.
2nd row P to end.
3rd row K2, *yfwd, K2 tog, rep from * to last st, K1.
4th row P to end.
These 4 rows form the pattern.

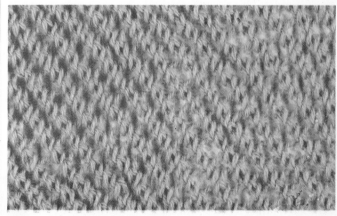

More simple lace

This chapter gives more simple lace patterns which are easy to work and produce most effective fabrics. Use a 3 or 4 ply yarn and No.11 or No.10 needles to practise these stitches.

Lace diamond pattern
Cast on a number of stitches divisible by 6 + 1.
1st row P1, *K5, P1, rep from * to end.
2nd row K1, *P5, K1, rep from * to end.
3rd row P1, *yon, sl 1, K1, psso, K1, K2 tog, yrn, P1, rep from * to end.
4th row K1, *K into back of next st – called K1B –, P3, K1B, K1, rep from * to end.
5th row P2, *yon, sl 1, K2, psso the 2 sts, yrn, P3, rep from * to last 5 sts, yon, sl 1, K2, psso the 2 sts, yrn, P2.
6th row K2, *K1B, P2, K1B, K3, rep from * to last 6 sts, K1B, P2, K1B, K2.
7th row P2, *K2 tog, yfwd, sl 1, K1, psso, P3, rep from * to last 6 sts, K2 tog, yfwd, sl 1, K1, psso, P2.
8th row K1, *P2 tog tbl, yrn, P1, yrn, P2 tog, K1, rep from * to end.
These 8 rows form the pattern.

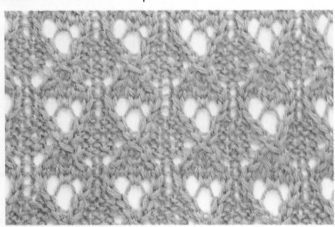

Embossed leaf pattern
Cast on a number of stitches divisible by 7.
1st row P to end.
2nd row K to end.
3rd row P3, *yon, K1, yrn, P6, rep from * to last 4 sts, yon, K1, yrn, P3.
4th row K3, *P3, K6, rep from * to last 6 sts, P3, K3.
5th row P3, *K1, (yfwd, K1) twice, P6, rep from * to last 6 sts, K1, (yfwd, K1) twice, P3.
6th row K3, *P5, K6, rep from * to last 8 sts, P5, K3.
7th row P3, *K2, yfwd, K1, yfwd, K2, P6, rep from * to last 8 sts, K2, yfwd, K1, yfwd, K2, P3.
8th row K3, *P7, K6, rep from * to last 10 sts, P7, K3.
9th row P3, *K3, yfwd, K1, yfwd, K3, P6, rep from * to last 10 sts, K3, yfwd, K1, yfwd, K3, P3.
10th row K3, *P9, K6, rep from * to last 12 sts, P9, K3.

11th row P3, *sl 1, K1, psso, K5, K2 tog, P6, rep from * to last 12 sts, sl 1, K1, psso, K5, K2 tog, P3.
12th row As 8th.
13th row P3, *sl 1, K1, psso, K3, K2 tog, P6, rep from * to last 10 sts, sl 1, K1, psso, K3, K2 tog, P3.
14th row As 6th.
15th row P3, *sl 1, K1, psso, K1, K2 tog, P6, rep from * to last 8 sts, sl 1, K1, psso, K1, K2 tog, P3.
16th row As 4th.
17th row P3, *sl 1, K2 tog, psso, P6, rep from * to last 6 sts, sl 1, K2 tog, psso, P3.
18th row As 2nd.
19th row As 1st.
20th row As 2nd.
These 20 rows form the pattern.

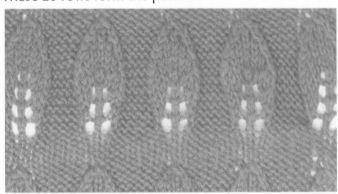

Snowdrop lace pattern
Cast on a number of stitches divisible by 8 + 3.
1st row K1, K2 tog, yfwd, *K5, yfwd, sl 1, K2 tog, psso, yfwd, rep from * to last 8 sts, K5, yfwd, sl 1, K1, psso, K1.
2nd and every alt row P to end.
3rd row As 1st.
5th row K3, *yfwd, sl 1, K1, psso, K1, K2 tog, yfwd, K3, rep from * to end.
7th row K1, K2 tog, yfwd, *K1, yfwd, sl 1, K2 tog, psso, yfwd, rep from * to last 4 sts, K1, yfwd, sl 1, K1, psso, K1.
8th row As 2nd.
These 8 rows form the pattern.

Falling leaf pattern

Cast on a number of stitches divisible by 10 + 1.

1st row K1, *yfwd, K3, sl 1, K2 tog, psso, K3, yfwd, K1, rep from * to end.

2nd and every alt row P to end.

3rd row K1, *K1, yfwd, K2, sl 1, K2 tog, psso, K2, yfwd, K2, rep from * to end.

5th row K1, *K2, yfwd, K1, sl 1, K2 tog, psso, K1, yfwd, K3, rep from * to end.

7th row K1, *K3, yfwd, sl 1, K2 tog, psso, yfwd, K4, rep from * to end.

9th row K2 tog, *K3, yfwd, K1, yfwd, K3, sl 1, K2 tog, psso, rep from * to last 9 sts, K3, yfwd, K1, yfwd, K3, sl 1, K1, psso.

11th row K2 tog, *K2, yfwd, K3, yfwd, K2, sl 1, K2 tog, psso, rep from * to last 9 sts, K2, yfwd, K3, yfwd, K2, sl 1, K1, psso.

13th row K2 tog, *K1, yfwd, K5, yfwd, K1, sl 1, K2 tog, psso, rep from * to last 9 sts, K1, yfwd, K5, yfwd, K1, sl 1, K1, psso.

15th row K2 tog, *yfwd, K7, yfwd, sl 1, K2 tog, psso, rep from * to last 9 sts, yfwd, K7, yfwd, sl 1, K1, psso.

16th row As 2nd.

These 16 rows form the pattern.

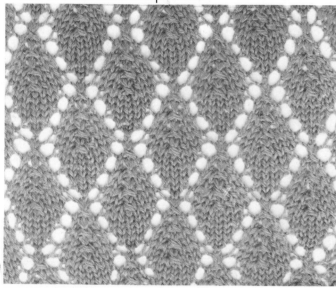

Cat's paw pattern

Cast on a number of stitches divisible by 12 + 1.

1st row K5, *yfwd, sl 1, K2 tog, psso, yfwd, K9, rep from * to last 8 sts, yfwd, sl 1, K2 tog, psso, yfwd, K5.

2nd and every alt row P to end.

3rd row K3, *K2 tog, yfwd, K3, yfwd, sl 1, K1, psso, K5, rep from * to last 10 sts, K2 tog, yfwd, K3, yfwd, sl 1, K1, psso, K3.

5th row As 1st.

7th row K to end.

9th row K2 tog, *yfwd, K9, yfwd, sl 1, K2 tog, psso, rep from * to last 11 sts, yfwd, K9, yfwd, sl 1, K1, psso.

11th row K2, *yfwd, sl 1, K1, psso, K5, K2 tog, yfwd, K3, rep from * to last 11 sts, yfwd, sl 1, K1, psso, K5, K2 tog, yfwd, K2.

13th row As 9th.

15th row As 7th.

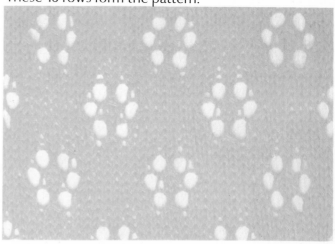

16th row As 2nd.
These 16 rows form the pattern.

Gothic Pattern

Cast on a number of stitches divisible by 10 + 1.

1st row K1, *yfwd, sl 1, K1, psso, K5, K2 tog, yfwd, K1, rep from * to end.

2nd and every alt row P to end.

3rd row K2, *yfwd, sl 1, K1, psso, K3, K2 tog, yfwd, K3, rep from * to last 9 sts, yfwd, sl 1, K1, psso, K3, K2 tog, yfwd, K2.

5th row K3, *yfwd, sl 1, K1, psso, K1, K2 tog, yfwd, K5, rep from * to last 8 sts, yfwd, sl 1, K1, psso, K1, K2 tog, yfwd, K3.

7th row K4, *yfwd, sl 1, K2 tog, psso, yfwd, K7, rep from * to last 7 sts, yfwd, sl 1, K2 tog, psso, yfwd, K4.

9th row K1, *yfwd, sl 1, K1, psso, K2 tog, yfwd, K1, rep from * to end.

10th row As 2nd.

11th-18th rows Rep the 9th and 10th rows 4 times more.

19th row K2, *yfwd, sl 1, K1, psso, K3, K2 tog, yfwd, K3, rep from * to last 9 sts, yfwd, sl 1, K1, psso, K3, K2 tog, yfwd, K2.

21st row K3, *yfwd, sl 1, K1, psso, K1, K2 tog, yfwd, K5, rep from * to last 8 sts, yfwd, sl 1, K1, psso, K1, K2 tog, yfwd, K3.

23rd row K4, *yfwd, sl 1, K2 tog, psso, yfwd, K7, rep from * to last 7 sts, yfwd, sl 1, K2 tog, psso, yfwd, K4.

24th row As 2nd.

These 24 rows form the pattern.

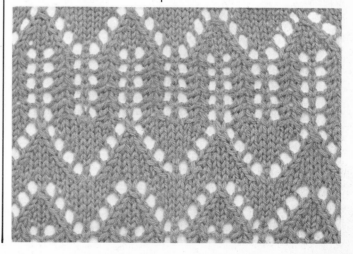

Traditional lace patterns

The history of lace stitches spans several centuries; many of the stitches, like those described in this chapter, have traditional names which are both beautiful and descriptive.

Shell and shower

Cast on a number of stitches divisible by 12 + 3.

1st row K2, *yfwd, K4, sl 1, K2 tog, psso, K4, yfwd, K1, rep from * to last st, K1.

2nd and every alt row P to end.

3rd row K3, *yfwd, K3, sl 1, K2 tog, psso, K3, yfwd, K3, rep from * to end.

5th row K1, K2 tog, *yfwd, K1, yfwd, K2, sl 1, K2 tog, psso, K2, yfwd, K1, yfwd, sl 1, K2 tog, psso, rep from * to last 12 sts, yfwd, K1, yfwd, K2, sl 1, K2 tog, psso, K2, yfwd, K1, yfwd, sl 1, K1, psso, K1.

7th row K1, *yfwd, sl 1, K1, psso, K2, yfwd, K1, sl 1, K2 tog, psso, K1, yfwd, K3, rep from * to last 2 sts, yfwd, K2 tog.

9th row K2, *yfwd, sl 1, K2 tog, psso, yfwd, K1, rep from * to last st, K1.

10th row As 2nd

These 10 rows form the pattern.

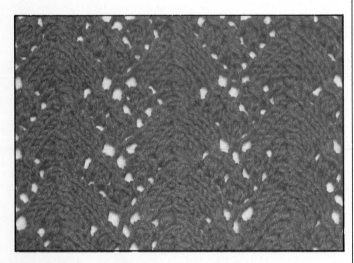

Ogee lace

Cast on a number of stitches divisible by 24 + 1.

1st row *K2, yfwd, K2 tog, K1, K2 tog, K3, yfwd, sl 1, K1, psso, yrn, P1, yon, K2, yfwd, sl 1, K1, psso, K1, sl 1, K1, psso, K1, sl 1, K1, psso, yfwd, K1, rep from * to last st, K1.

2nd row P1, *P7, yrn, P2 tog, P5, yrn, P2 tog, P8, rep from * to end.

3rd row *K1, yfwd, K2 tog, K1, K2 tog, K3, yfwd, sl 1, K1, psso, K1, yfwd, K1, yfwd, K3, yfwd, sl 1, K1, psso, K1, sl 1, K1, psso, K1, sl 1, K1, psso, yfwd, rep from * to last st, K1.

4th row P1, *P6, yrn, P2 tog, P7, yrn, P2 tog, P7, rep from * to end.

5th row *K3, K2 tog, K3, yfwd, sl 1, K1, psso, K1, yfwd, K3, yfwd, K3, yfwd, sl 1, K1, psso, K1, sl 1, K1, psso, K2, rep from * to last st, K1.

6th row P1, *P5, yrn, P2 tog, P9, yrn, P2 tog, P6, rep from * to end.

7th row *K2, K2 tog, K3, yfwd, sl 1, K1, psso, K3, yfwd, K1, yfwd, K5, yfwd, sl 1, K1, psso, K1, sl 1, K1, psso, K1, rep from * to last st, K1.

8th row P1, *P4, yrn, P2 tog, P11, yrn, P2 tog, P5, rep from * to end.

9th row *K1, K2 tog, K3, yfwd, sl 1, K1, psso, K3, yfwd, K3, yfwd, K5, yfwd, sl 1, K1, psso, K1, sl 1, K1, psso, rep from * to last st, K1.

10th row P1, *P3, yrn, P2 tog, P13, yrn, P2 tog, P4, rep from * to end.

11th row Sl 1, K1, psso, *K3, yfwd, sl 1, K1, psso, K1, sl 1, K1, psso, yfwd, K2, yfwd, K1, yfwd, K2, yfwd, K2 tog, K3, yfwd, sl 1, K1, psso, K1, sl 1, K2 tog, psso, rep from * to last 23 sts, K3, yfwd, sl 1, K1, psso, K1, sl 1, K1, psso, yfwd, K2, yfwd, K1, yfwd, K2, yfwd, K2 tog, K3, yfwd, sl 1, K1, psso, K1, sl 1, K1, psso.

12th row P1, *P2, yrn, P2 tog, P15, yrn, P2 tog, P3, rep from * to end.

13th row Sl 1, K1, psso, *K2, yfwd, sl 1, K1, psso, K5, yfwd, K3, yfwd, K7, yfwd, sl 1, K1, psso, sl 1, K2 tog, psso, rep from * to last 23 sts, K2, yfwd, sl 1, K1, psso, K5, yfwd, K3, yfwd, K7, yfwd, sl 1, K1, psso, sl 1, K1, psso.

14th row K1, *P1, yrn, P2 tog, P17, yrn, P2 tog, P1, K1, rep from * to end.

15th row *P1, yon, K2, yfwd, sl 1, K1, psso, K1, sl 1, K1, psso, K1, sl 1, K1, psso, yfwd, K3, yfwd, K2 tog, K1, K2 tog, K3, yfwd, sl 1, K1, psso, yrn, rep from * to last st, P1.

16th row As 12th.

17th row *K1, yfwd, K3, yfwd, sl 1, K1, psso, K1, sl 1, K1, psso, K1, sl 1, K1, psso, yfwd, K1, yfwd, K2 tog, K1, K2 tog, K3, yfwd, sl 1, K1, psso, K1, yfwd, rep from * to last st, K1.

18th row As 10th.

19th row *K2, yfwd, K3, yfwd, sl 1, K1, psso, K1, sl 1, K1, psso, K5, K2 tog, K3, yfwd, sl 1, K1, psso, K1, yfwd, K1, rep from * to last st, K1.

20th row As 8th.

21st row *K1, yfwd, K5, yfwd, sl 1, K1, psso, K1, sl 1, K1, psso, K3, K2 tog, K3, yfwd, sl 1, K1, psso, K1, yfwd, rep from * to last st, K1.

22nd row As 6th.

23rd row *K2, yfwd, K5, yfwd, sl 1, K1, psso, K1, sl 1, K1, psso, K1, K2 tog, K3, yfwd, sl 1, K1, psso, K3, yfwd, K1, rep from * to last st, K1.

24th row As 4th.
25th row *K1, yfwd, K2, yfwd, K2 tog, K3, yfwd, sl 1, K1, psso, K1, sl 1, K2 tog, psso, K3, yfwd, sl 1, K1, psso, K1, sl 1, K1, psso, yfwd, K2, yfwd, rep from * to last st, K1.
26th row As 2nd.
27th row *K2, yfwd, K7, yfwd, sl 1, K1, psso, sl 1, K2 tog, psso, K2, yfwd, sl 1, K1, psso, K5, yfwd, K1, rep from * to last st, K1.
28th row P1, *P8, yrn, P2 tog, P1, K1, P1, yrn, P2 tog, P9, rep from * to end.
These 28 rows form the pattern.

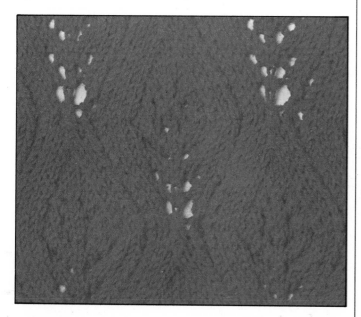

Spanish lace

Cast on a number of stitches divisible by 34 + 4.
1st row K2, *K3, K2 tog, K4, yrn, P2, (K2, yfwd, sl 1, K1, psso) 3 times, P2, yon, K4, sl 1, K1, psso, K3, rep from * to last 2 sts, K2.
2nd row P4, *P2 tog tbl, P4, yrn, P1, K2, (P2, yrn, P2 tog) 3 times, K2, P1, yrn, P4, P2 tog, P4, rep from * to end.
3rd row K3, *K2 tog, K4, yfwd, K2, P2, (K2, yfwd, sl 1, K1, psso) 3 times, P2, K2, yfwd, K4, sl 1, K1, psso, K2, rep from * to last st, K1.
4th row P2, *P2 tog tbl, P4, yrn, P3, K2, (P2, yrn, P2 tog) 3 times, K2, P3, yrn, P4, P2 tog, rep from * to last 2 sts, P2.
Rep the 1st to 4th rows twice more.
13th row *(K2, yfwd, sl 1, K1, psso) twice, P2, yon, K4, sl 1, K1, psso, K6, K2 tog, K4, yrn, P2, K2, yfwd, sl 1, K1, psso, rep from * to last 4 sts, K2, yfwd, sl 1, K1, psso.
14th row *(P2, yrn, P2 tog) twice, K2, P1, yrn, P4, P2 tog, P4, P2 tog tbl, P4, yrn, P1, K2, P2, yrn, P2 tog, rep from * to last 4 sts, P2, yrn, P2 tog.
15th row *(K2, yfwd, sl 1, K1, psso) twice, P2, K2, yfwd, K4, sl 1, K1, psso, K2, K2 tog, K4, yfwd, K2, P2, K2, yfwd, sl 1, K1, psso, rep from * to last 4 sts, K2, yfwd, sl 1, K1, psso.
16th row *(P2, yrn, P2 tog) twice, K2, P3, yrn, P4, P2 tog, P2 tog tbl, P4, yrn, P3, K2, P2, yrn, P2 tog, rep from * to last 4 sts, P2, yrn, P2 tog.

Rep the 13th to 16th rows twice more.
These 24 rows form the pattern.

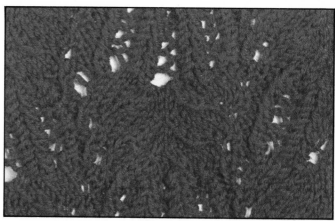

Candlelight lace

Cast on a number of stitches divisible by 12 + 1.
1st row K1, *yfwd, sl 1, K1, psso, K7, K2 tog, yfwd, K1, rep from * to end.
2nd and every alt row P to end.
3rd row K1, *yfwd, K1, sl 1, K1, psso, K5, K2 tog, K1, yfwd, K1, rep from * to end.
5th row K1, * yfwd, K2, sl 1, K1, psso, K3, K2 tog, K2, yfwd, K1, rep from * to end.
7th row K1, *yfwd, K3, sl 1, K1, psso, K1, K2 tog, K3, yfwd, K1, rep from * to end.
9th row K1, *yfwd, K4, sl 1, K2 tog, psso, K4, yfwd, K1, rep from * to end.
11th row *K4, K2 tog, yfwd, K1, yfwd, sl 1, K1, psso, K3, rep from * to last st, K1.
13th row *K3, K2 tog, K1, (yfwd, K1) twice, sl 1, K1, psso, K2, rep from * to last st, K1.
15th row *K2, K2 tog, K2, yfwd, K1, yfwd, K2, sl 1, K1, psso, K1, rep from * to last st, K1.
17th row *K1, K2 tog, K3, yfwd, K1, yfwd, K3, sl 1, K1, psso, rep from * to last st, K1.
19th row K2 tog, *K4, yfwd, K1, yfwd, K4, sl 1, K2 tog, psso, rep from * to last 11 sts, K4, yfwd, K1, yfwd, K4, sl 1, K1, psso.
20th row As 2nd.
These 20 rows form the pattern.

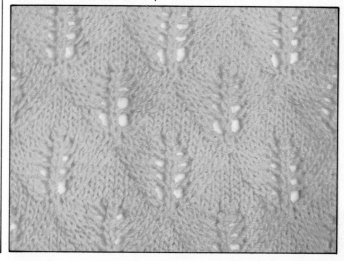

Larger lace patterns

The traditional lace stitches described here vary in complexity but each of them can be used to form a fabric of delicate beauty.

Wheatear pattern
Cast on a number of stitches divisible by 11.
1st row (RS) *K1, (K1, yfwd to make a st, K1, yfwd, K1) all into same st, turn and K5, turn and P5, turn and K1, sl 1, K2 tog, psso, K1, turn and P3 tog – called B1 –, K2, yfwd, K1, yfwd, K4, K2 tog, rep from * to end, noting that one extra st is inc in each rep on this and every RS row.
2nd, 4th, 6th, 8th and 10th rows *P2 tog, P10, rep from * to end.
3rd row *K5, yfwd, K1, yfwd, K3, K2 tog, rep from * to end.
5th row *K6, yfwd, K1, yfwd, K2, K2 tog, rep from * to end.
7th row *K7, (yfwd, K1) twice, K2 tog, rep from * to end.
9th row *K8, yfwd, K1, yfwd, K2 tog, rep from * to end.
11th row *Sl 1, K1, psso, K4, yfwd, K1, yfwd, K2, B1, K1, rep from * to end.
12th, 14th, 16th and 18th rows *P10, P2 tog tbl, rep from * to end.
13th row *Sl 1, K1, psso, K3, yfwd, K1, yfwd, K5, rep from * to end.
15th row *Sl 1, K1, psso, K2, yfwd, K1, yfwd, K6, rep from * to end.
17th row *Sl 1, K1, psso, (K1, yfwd) twice, K7, rep from * to end.
19th row *Sl 1, K1, psso, yfwd, K1, yfwd, K8, rep from * to end.
20th row As 12th.
These 20 rows form the pattern.

Fountain pattern
Cast on a number of stitches divisible by 16 plus 1.
1st row (WS) P to end.
2nd row Sl 1, K1, psso, *yfwd, K2, K2 tog, yfwd, K1, yfwd, sl 1, K2 tog, psso, yfwd, K1, yfwd, sl 1, K1, psso, K2, yfwd, sl 1, K2 tog, psso, rep from * ending last rep K2 tog instead of sl 1, K2 tog, psso.
3rd and every alt row P to end.
4th row Sl 1, K1, psso, *K3, yfwd, K2 tog, yfwd, K3, yfwd, sl 1, K1, psso, yfwd, K3, sl 1, K2 tog, psso, rep from * ending last rep as 2nd row.
6th row Sl 1, K1, psso, *(K2, yfwd) twice, K2 tog, K1, sl 1, K1, psso, (yfwd, K2) twice, sl 1, K2 tog, psso, rep from * ending last rep as 2nd row.
8th row Sl 1, K1, psso, *K1, yfwd, K3, yfwd, K2 tog, K1, sl 1, K1, psso, yfwd, K3, yfwd, K1, sl 1, K2 tog, psso, rep from * ending last rep as 2nd row.
These 8 rows form the pattern.

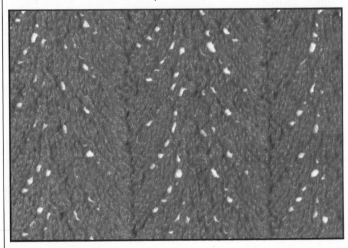

Oriel pattern
Cast on a number of stitches divisible by 12 plus 1.
1st row (RS) P1, *sl 1, K1, psso, K3, yrn, P1, yon, K3, K2 tog, P1, rep from * to end.
2nd row K1, *P5, K1, rep from * to end.
Rep 1st and 2nd rows twice more.
7th row P1, *yon, K3, K2 tog, P1, sl 1, K1, psso, K3, yrn, P1, rep from * to end.
8th row As 2nd.
9th row P2, *yon, K2, K2 tog, P1, sl 1, K1, psso, K2, yrn, P3, rep from * ending last rep P2 instead of P3.
10th row K2, *P4, K1, P4, K3, rep from * ending last rep K2 instead of K3.
11th row P3, *yon, K1, K2 tog, P1, sl 1, K1, psso, K1, yrn, P5, rep from * ending last rep P3 instead of P5.
12th row K3, *P3, K1, P3, K5, rep from * ending last rep K3 instead of K5.
13th row P4, *yon, K2 tog, P1, sl 1, K1, psso, yrn, P7, rep

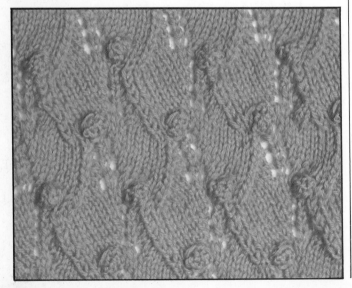

from * ending last rep P4 instead of P7.
14th row K4, *P2, K1, P2, K7, rep from * ending last rep K4 instead of K7.
15th row As 7th.
16th row As 2nd.
Rep 15th and 16th rows twice more.
21st row As 1st.
22nd row As 2nd.
23rd row P1, *sl 1, K1, psso, K2, yrn, P3, yon, K2, K2 tog, P1, rep from * to end.
24th row K1, *P4, K3, P4, K1, rep from * to end.
25th row P1, *sl 1, K1, psso, K1, yrn, P5, yon, K1, K2 tog, P1, rep from * to end.
26th row K1, *P3, K5, P3, K1, rep from * to end.
27th row P1, *sl 1, K1, psso, yrn, P7, yon, K2 tog, P1, rep from * to end.
28th row K1, *P2, K7, P2, K1, rep from * to end.
These 28 rows form the pattern.

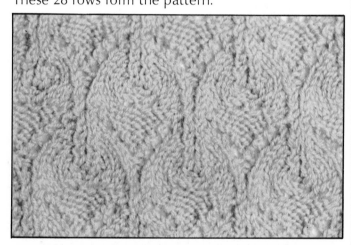

Bell pattern

Cast on a number of stitches divisible by 18 plus 1, noting that the number of stitches do not remain the same on every row but will revert to the original number on the 12th, 14th, 26th and 28th rows.
1st row (RS) K1, *(P2, K1) twice, yfwd, K2 tog, yfwd, K1, yfwd, sl 1, K1, psso, yfwd, (K1, P2) twice, K1, rep from * to end.
2nd row *(P1, K2) twice, P9, K2, P1, K2, rep from * to last st, P1.
3rd row K1, *(P2, K1) twice, yfwd, K2 tog, yfwd, K3, yfwd, sl 1, K1, psso, yfwd, (K1, P2) twice, K1, rep from * to end.
4th row *(P1, K2) twice, P11, K2, P1, K2, rep from * to last st, P1.
5th row K1, *(P2 tog, K1) twice, yfwd, K2 tog, yfwd, sl 1, K1, psso, K1, K2 tog, yfwd, sl 1, K1, psso, yfwd, (K1, P2 tog) twice, K1, rep from * to end.
6th row *(P1, K1) twice, P11, K1, P1, K1, rep from * to last st, P1.
7th row K1, *(P1, K1) twice, yfwd, K2 tog, yfwd, K1 tbl, yfwd, sl 1, K2 tog, psso, yfwd, K1, tbl, yfwd, sl 1, K1, psso, yfwd, (K1, P1) twice, K1, rep from * to end.
8th row *(P1, K1) twice, P13, K1, P1, K1, rep from * to last st, P1.
9th row K1, *(K2 tog) twice, yfwd, K2 tog, yfwd, K3,

yfwd, K1, yfwd, K3, yfwd, sl 1, K1, psso, yfwd, (sl 1, K1, psso) twice, K1, rep from * to end.
10th, 12th and 14th rows P to end.
11th row K1, *(K2 tog, yfwd) twice, sl 1, K1, psso, K1, K2 tog, yfwd, K1, yfwd, sl 1, K1, psso, K1, K2 tog, (yfwd, sl 1, K1, psso) twice, K1, rep from * to end.
13th row K2 tog, *yfwd, K2 tog, yfwd, K1 tbl, yfwd, sl 1, K2 tog, psso, yfwd, K3, yfwd, sl 1, K2 tog, psso, yfwd, K1 tbl, yfwd, sl 1, K1, psso, yfwd, sl 1, K2 tog, psso, rep from * ending last rep sl 1, K1, psso, instead of sl 1, K2 tog, psso.
15th row K1, *yfwd, sl 1, K1, psso, yfwd, (K1, P2) 4 times, K1, yfwd, K2 tog, yfwd, K1, rep from * to end.
16th row P5, *(K2, P1) 3 times, K2, P9, rep from * ending last rep P5 instead of P9.
17th row K2, *yfwd, sl 1, K1, psso, yfwd, (K1, P2) 4 times, K1, yfwd, K2 tog, yfwd, K3, rep from * ending last rep K2 instead of K3.
18th row P6, *(K2, P1) 3 times, K2, P11, rep from * ending last rep P6 instead of P11.
19th row K1, *K2 tog, yfwd, sl 1, K1, psso, yfwd, (K1, P2 tog) 4 times, K1, yfwd, K2 tog, yfwd, sl 1, K1, psso, K1, rep from * to end.
20th row P6, *(K1, P1) 3 times, K1, P11, rep from * ending last rep P6 instead of P11.
21st row K2 tog, *yfwd, K1 tbl, yfwd, sl 1, K1, psso, yfwd, (K1, P1) 4 times, K1, yfwd, K2 tog, yfwd, K1 tbl, yfwd, sl 1, K2 tog, psso, rep from * ending last rep sl 1, K1, psso, instead of sl 1, K2 tog, psso.
22nd row P7, *(K1, P1) 3 times, K1, P13, rep from * ending last rep P7 instead of P13.
23rd row K1, *yfwd, K3, yfwd, sl 1, K1, psso, yfwd, (sl 1, K1, psso) twice, K1, (K2 tog) twice, yfwd, K2 tog, yfwd, K3, yfwd, K1, rep from * to end.
24th and 26th rows P to end.
25th row K1, *yfwd, sl 1, K1, psso, K1, K2 tog, (yfwd, sl 1, K1, psso) twice, K1, (K2 tog, yfwd) twice, sl 1, K1, psso, K1, K2 tog, yfwd, K1, rep from * to end.
27th row K2, *yfwd, sl 1, K2 tog, psso, yfwd, K1 tbl, yfwd, sl 1, K1, psso, yfwd, sl 1, K2 tog, psso, yfwd, K2 tog, yfwd, K1 tbl, yfwd, sl 1, K2 tog, psso, yfwd, K3, rep from * ending last rep K2 instead of K3.
28th row P to end.
These 28 rows form the pattern.

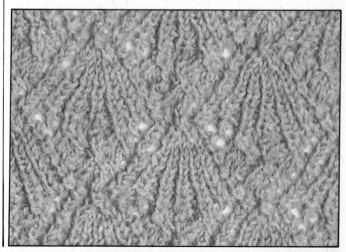

PATTERN SHAPES AND PICTURES

Patterned shapes and pictures can be achieved in knitting by means of different textures and stitches, using a single, overall colour. This technique can be incorporated into any plain, basic shape most effectively, either as a repeating border such as the fir trees and tulip stitches shown here, or as a single motif, such as the house pattern, centrally placed on the front of a jersey.

Before beginning to knit, work out the position for the border or motif, making sure that you have the correct multiples of stitches for the border repeat or that a motif is centrally placed.

Fir tree border

This pattern requires multiples of 12 stitches plus 1 and is worked against a reversed stocking stitch background.

1st row (RS) K1, *P1, K1, rep from * to end.
2nd row P1, *K1, P1, rep from * to end.
3rd row P6, *K1, P11, rep from * to last 7 sts, K1, P6.
4th row K6, *P1, K11, rep from * to last 7 sts, P1, K6.
Rep last 2 rows 3 times more.
11th row P2, *K1, P3, rep from * to last 3 sts, K1, P2.
12th row K2, *P1, K3, rep from * to last 3 sts, P1, K2.
13th row P2, *K2, P2, K1, P2, K2, P3, rep from * to last 11 sts, K2, P2, K1, P2, K2, P2.
14th row K2, *P2, K2, P1, K2, P2, K3, rep from * to last 11 sts, P2, K2, P1, K2, P2, K2.
15th row P2, *K3, P3, rep from * to last 5 sts, K3, P2.
16th row K2, *P3, K3, rep from * to last 5 sts, P3, K2.
17th row P2, *K4, P1, K4, P3, rep from * to last 11 sts, K4, P1, K4, P2.
18th row K2, *P4, K1, P4, K3, rep from * to last 11 sts, P4, K1, P4, K2.
19th row P3, *K7, P5, rep from * to last 10 sts, K7, P3.
20th row K3, *P7, K5, rep from * to last 10 sts, P7, K3.
21st row P4, *K5, P7, rep from * to last 9 sts, K5, P4.
22nd row K4, *P5, K7, rep from * to last 9 sts, P5, K4.
23rd row P5, *K3, P9, rep from * to last 8 sts, K3, P5.
24th row K5, *P3, K9, rep from * to last 8 sts, P3, K5.
25th row P6, *K1, P11, rep from * to last 7 sts, K1, P6.
26th row K6, *P1, K11, rep from * to last 7 sts, P1, K6.
These 26 rows complete the border pattern.

Tulip bed border

This pattern requires multiples of 20 stitches plus 1 and is worked against a stocking stitch background.
1st row (RS) K5, *K2 tog, yfwd, K1, yfwd, K2 tog, P1, sl 1, K1, psso, yfwd, K1, yfwd, sl 1, K1, psso, K9, rep from * ending last rep K5 instead of K9.

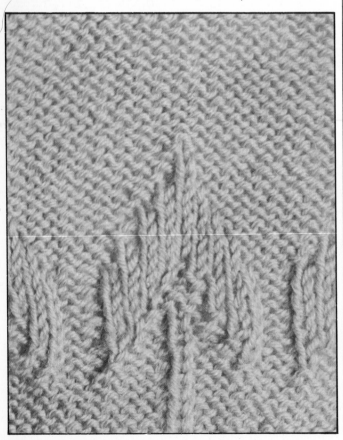

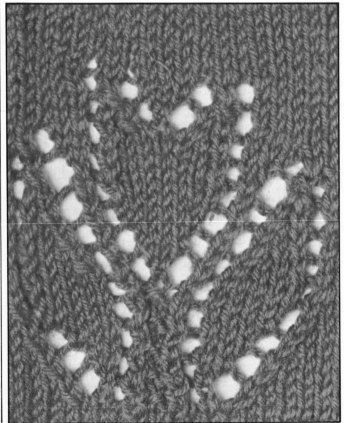

2nd and every alt row P to end.
3rd row K4, *K2 tog, yfwd, K2, yfwd, K2 tog, P1, sl 1, K1, psso, yfwd, K2, yfwd, sl 1, K1, psso, K7, rep from * ending last rep K4.
5th row K3, *K2 tog, yfwd, K3, yfwd, K2 tog, P1, sl 1, K1, psso, yfwd, K3, yfwd, sl 1, K1, psso, K5, rep from * ending last rep K3.
7th row K2, *K2 tog, yfwd, K4, yfwd, K2 tog, P1, sl 1, K1, psso, yfwd, K4, yfwd, sl 1, K1, psso, K3, rep from * ending last rep K2.
9th row K1, *K2 tog, yfwd, K5, yfwd, K2 tog, P1, sl 1, K1, psso, yfwd, K5, yfwd, sl 1, K1, psso, K1, rep from * to end.
11th row K2, *yfwd, K2 tog, K2, (K2 tog, yfwd) twice, K1, (yfwd, sl 1, K1, psso) twice, K2, sl 1, K1, psso, yfwd, K3, rep from * ending last rep K2.
13th row K2, *yfwd, K2 tog, K1, (K2 tog, yfwd) twice, K3, (yfwd, sl 1, K1, psso) twice, K1, sl 1, K1, psso, yfwd, K3, rep from * ending last rep K2.
15th row K2, *yfwd, (K2 tog) twice, yfwd, K2 tog, yfwd, K5, yfwd, sl 1, K1, psso, yfwd, (sl 1, K1, psso) twice, yfwd, K3, rep from * ending last rep K2.
17th row K2, *yfwd, sl 2, K1, p2sso, yfwd, K2 tog, yfwd, K7, yfwd, sl 1, K1, psso, yfwd, sl 2, K1, p2sso, yfwd, K3, rep from * ending last rep K2.
19th row K2, *K2 tog, yfwd, K2, yfwd, K2 tog, K5, sl 1, K1, psso, yfwd, K2, yfwd, sl 1, K1, psso, K3, rep from * ending last rep K2.
21st row K6, *yfwd, K2 tog, K5, sl 1, K1, psso, yfwd, K11, rep from * ending last rep K6.
23rd row K6, *yfwd, (K2 tog) twice, yfwd, K1, yfwd, (sl 1, K1, psso) twice, K11, rep from * ending last rep K6.
25th row K6, *yfwd, sl 2, K1, p2sso, yfwd, K3, yfwd, sl 2, K1, p2sso, yfwd, K11, rep from * ending last rep K6.
26th row As 2nd.
These 26 rows complete the border pattern.

House motif
This pattern is worked over 28 stitches in all against a reversed stocking stitch background.
1st row (RS) P2, K7, K into front of 2nd st on left hand needle then into front of first st – called T2R –, P6, K into back of 2nd st on left hand needle then into front of first st – called T2L –, K7, P2.
2nd row K2, P9, K6, P9, K2.
Rep 1st and 2nd rows once more.
5th row P2, K2, (K2, yfwd, K2 tog for window), K1, T2R, P6, T2L, K1, (K2, yfwd, K2 tog), K2, P2.
6th row K2, P2, (P2, yrn, P2 tog), P3, K6, P3, (P2, yrn, P2 tog), P2, K2.
Rep 5th and 6th rows twice more.
11th row P2, K2, (K2, yfwd, K2 tog), K1, T2R, P1, (P1, K1, P1) all into next st, turn and K3, turn and P3 then lift 2nd and 3rd sts over first st to form door knob, P4, T2L, K1, (K2, yfwd, K2 tog), K2, P2.
12th row As 6th.
Rep 5th and 6th rows twice more.
17th row As 1st.

18th row As 2nd.
19th row P2, K8, T2R, P4, T2L, K8, P2.
20th row K2, P10, K4, P10, K2.
21st row P2, K9, T2R, P2, T2L, K9, P2.
22nd row K2, P11, K2, P11, K2.
23rd row P2, K10, T2R, T2L, K10, P2.
24th row K2, P24, K2.
25th row P2, K24, P2.
26th row As 24th.
27th row P2, K2, (K2, yfwd, K2 tog for window), K4, (K2, yfwd, K2 tog), K4, (K2, yfwd, K2 tog), K2, P2.
28th row K2, P2, (P2, yrn, P2 tog), P4, (P2, yrn, P2 tog), P4, (P2, yrn, P2 tog), P2, K2.
Rep 27th and 28th rows twice more, then 25th and 26th rows twice more.
37th row K to end.
38th row K to end.
39th row P1, K26, P1.
40th row K to end.
41st row P2, K24, P2.
42nd row K to end.
43rd row P3, K22, P3.
44th row K to end.
45th row P4, K20, P4.
46th row K to end.
47th row P5, K18, P5.
48th row K to end.
49th row P10, (K1, P1) twice, K1, P13.
50th row K13, (P1, K1) twice, P1, K10.
Rep 49th and 50th rows 3 times more.
These 56 rows complete motif.

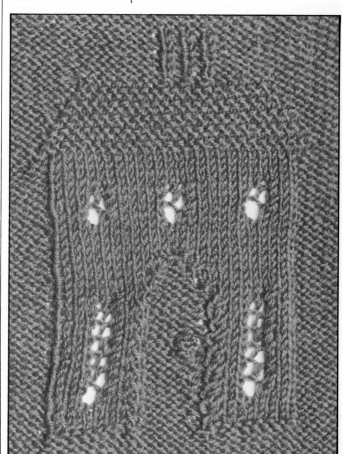

A simple patterned jersey

This chapter shows a simple jersey shape which incorporates the house motif given in the previous chapter on patterned shapes and motifs.

Jersey
Sizes
To fit 86 [91:96]cm (34[36:38]in) bust

Length to shoulder, 58.5[59:59.5]cm (23[23¼:23½]in)
Sleeve seam, 18cm (7in)
The figures in brackets [] refer to the 91 (36) and 96cm (38in) sizes respectively

Tension
28 sts and 36 rows to 10cm (3.9in) over st st worked on

No.10 needles

Materials
12[13:14] × 25grm balls Sirdar Superwash Wool 4 ply
One pair No.10 needles
One pair No.11 needles

Back
Using No.11 needles cast on 120[124:128]sts. Work 5cm (2in) K1, P1 rib. Change to No.10 needles. Beg with a P row work 4 rows reversed st st.
Next row P2, (patt 28 sts as given for 1st row of house motif, P16 [18:20] sts) twice, patt 28 sts as given for 1st row of house motif, P2.
Next row K2, (patt 28 sts as given for 2nd row of house motif, K16 [18:20] sts) twice, patt 28 sts as given for 2nd row of house motif, K2.
Cont in patt as now set until 56 patt rows have been completed. Beg with a P row work 4 rows reversed st st.
Next row P24 [25:26] sts, patt 28 sts as given for 1st row of house motif, P16 [18:20] sts, patt 28 sts as given for 1st row of house motif, P24 [25:26].
Next row K24 [25:26] sts, patt 28 sts as given for 2nd row of house motif, K16 [18:20] sts, patt 28 sts as given for 2nd row of house motif, K24 [25:26].
Cont in patt as now set until second 56 patt rows have been completed. Beg with a P row work 4 rows reversed st st.
Next row P46 [48:50] sts, patt 28 sts as given for 1st row of house motif, P46 [48:50].
Next row K46 [48:50] sts, patt 28 sts as given for 2nd row of house motif, K46 [48:50].
Cont in patt as now set until work measures 40.5cm (16in) from beg, ending with a K row.
Shape armholes
Keeping patt correct until third 56 patt rows have been completed, then cont in reversed st st across all sts, cast off at beg of next and every row 5 sts twice and 2 sts 4 times. Dec one st at each end of next and foll 5 alt rows. 90[94:98]sts. Cont without shaping until armholes measure 18[18.5:19]cm (7[7¼:7½]in) from beg, ending with a K row.
Shape shoulders
Cast off at beg of next and every row 7 sts 4 times and 11[12:13] sts twice. Leave rem 40[42:44] sts on holder for centre back neck.

Front
Work as given for back until armhole shaping is completed and third 56 patt rows have been worked. Cont without shaping in reversed st st until armholes measure 12.5[13:14]cm (5[5¼:5½]in) from beg, ending with a K row.
Shape neck
Next row P35[36:37] sts, cast off 20[22:24] sts, P to end. Complete this side first. K 1 row. Cast off at beg of next and every alt row 2 sts 3 times, then dec one st at neck edge on every alt row 4 times. 25[26:27] sts.

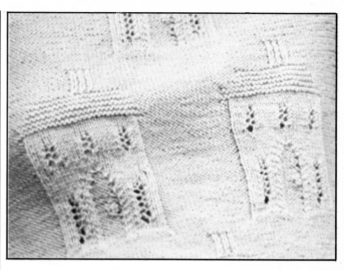

Cont without shaping until armhole measures same as back to shoulder, ending at armhole edge.
Shape shoulder
Cast off at beg of next and every alt row 7 sts twice and 11[12:13] sts once.
With WS of work facing, rejoin yarn to rem sts and complete to match first side, reversing shaping.

Sleeves
Using No.11 needles cast on 76[78:80] sts. Work 2.5cm (1in) K1, P1 rib. Change to No.10 needles. Beg with a P row work 4 rows reversed st st.
Next row P2, patt 28 sts as given for 1st row of house motif, P16[18:20] sts, patt 28 sts as given for 1st row of house motif, P2.
Next row K2, patt 28 sts as given for 2nd row of house motif, K16[18:20] sts, patt 28 sts as given for 2nd row of house motif, K2.
Cont in patt as now set, inc one st at each end of next and every foll 6th row until there are 86[90:94] sts, working extra sts into reversed st st, until 56 patt rows have been completed. Cont in reversed st st across all sts.
Shape top
Cast off 5 sts at beg of next 2 rows. Dec one st at each end of next and foll 10[11:12] alt rows; ending with a K row. Cast off at beg of next and every row 2 sts 6 times, 3 sts 6 times and 4 sts 4 times. Cast off rem 8[10:12] sts.

Neckband
Join right shoulder seam. Using No.11 needles and with RS of work facing, K up 20[21:22] sts down left front neck, K up 20[22:24] sts across front neck, K up 20[21:22] sts up right front neck and K across 40[42:44] back neck sts on holder. 100[106:112] sts. Work 5cm (2in) K1, P1 rib. Cast off in rib.

To make up
Press as directed on ball band. Join rem shoulder and neckband seam. Set in sleeves. Join side and sleeve seams. Fold neckband in half to WS and sl st down. Press seams.

SHETLAND LACE

Of all the traditional knitting techniques which have flourished in Britain, such as Aran and Fair Isle patterns, typical Shetland Isle lace stitches are among the most beautiful.

The finest examples come from Unst, the most northerly of all the Shetland Islands, where a few skilled knitters have carried on the tradition for many generations.

The stitches are few in number, only ten being truly native, and were inspired by examples of fine Spanish lace brought to the Shetland Isles as part of an exhibition in the early nineteenth century. Each stitch has been adapted to represent the natural beauty of the islands and carry such evocative names as 'Ears o'Grain', 'Print o'the Wave' and 'Fir Cones'.

Even today, the yarn used for the superb examples of this craft is hand spun to a single ply of such delicate fineness that few knitters would be able to work with it. However, a 2 ply yarn worked on No.12 needles can produce a reasonable facsimile of this most beautiful and rewarding method of knitting.

Casting on and off for lace knitting

Thick, harsh lines caused by casting on and off, or seaming, must be avoided or they will immediately detract from the delicate appearance of the lace.

Use the 2 needle method of casting on but instead of inserting the right hand needle between the last

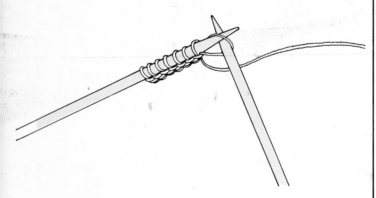

2 stitches on the left hand needle, insert it from front to back into the last stitch on the left hand needle and then draw a loop through to form the next stitch, transferring this to the left hand needle. This forms a loose, open edge.

Casting off should be worked in the usual way, using a needle 2 times larger to work the casting off than the size used for the main fabric.

Where the fabric has to be joined, it is best to use a spare length of yarn for casting on which can later be

withdrawn, to allow the first and last rows to be grafted together for an invisible join.

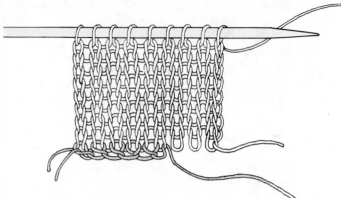

Crown of Glory pattern

This stitch is also known by the descriptive name of Cat's paw. Cast on a number of stitches divisible by 14 plus 5.

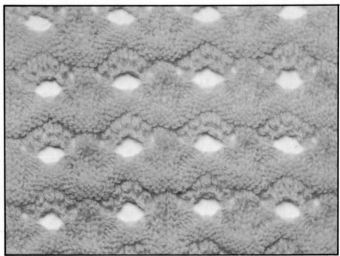

1st row (RS) K3, *sl 1, K1, psso, K9, K2 tog, K1, rep from * to last 2 sts, K2.

2nd row P2, *P1, P2 tog, P7, P2 tog tbl, rep from * to last 3 sts, P3.

3rd row K3, *sl 1, K1, psso, K2, yrn 3 times, K3, K2 tog, K1, rep from * to last 2 sts, K2.

4th row P2, *P1, P2 tog, P2, (K1, P1, K1, P1, K1) all into yrn 3 times making 5 sts, P1, P2 tog tbl, rep from * to last 3 sts, P3.

5th row K3, *sl 1, K1, psso, K6, K2 tog, K1, rep from * to last 2 sts, K2.

6th row P2, *P1, P2 tog, P6, rep from * ending last rep P3.

7th row K3, *K1, (yfwd, K1) 6 times, K1, rep from * to last 2 sts, K2.

8th row P to end.

9th and 10th rows K to end.

11th row P to end.

12th row K to end.
These 12 rows form the pattern.

Razor shell pattern

This stitch takes its name from the shells on the beach. It can be worked over multiples of 4, 6, 8, 10 or 12 stitches. For the sample shown here, cast on a number of stitches divisible by 6 plus 1.

1st row (WS) P to end.
2nd row K1, *yfwd, K1, sl 1, K2 tog, psso, K1, yfwd, K1, rep from * to end.
These 2 rows form the pattern.

Horseshoe print pattern

Derived from the imprint of horseshoes on wet sand, this sample requires a number of stitches divisible by 10 plus 1.

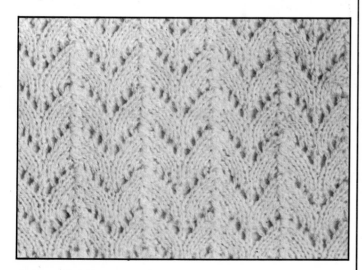

1st row (WS) P to end.
2nd row K1, *yfwd, K3, sl 1, K2 tog, psso, K3, yfwd, K1, rep from * to end.
3rd row As 1st.
4th row P1, *K1, yfwd, K2, sl 1, K2 tog, psso, K2, yfwd, K1, P1, rep from * to end.
5th row K1, *P9, K1, rep from * to end.
6th row P1, *K2, yfwd, K1, sl 1, K2 tog, psso, K1, yfwd, K2, P1, rep from * to end.

7th row As 5th.
8th row P1, *K3, yfwd, sl 1, K2 tog, psso, yfwd, K3, P1, rep from * to end.
These 8 rows form the pattern.

Fern pattern

This stitch is often used as a shawl border, as the shape of the lace motif allows for easy corner shaping. The size of the lace motif can vary but the working method remains the same. For the sample shown here, cast on a number of stitches divisible by 15.

1st row (RS) *K7, yfwd, sl 1 K-wise, K1, psso, K6, rep from * to end.
2nd row P to end.
3rd row *K5, K2 tog, yfwd, K1, yfwd, sl 1 K-wise, K1, psso, K5, rep from * to end.
4th row P to end.
5th row *K4, K2 tog, yfwd, K3, yfwd, sl 1 K-wise, K1, psso, K4, rep from * to end.
6th row P to end.
7th row *K4, yfwd, sl 1 K-wise, K1, psso, yfwd, sl 1, K2 tog, psso yfwd, K2 tog, yfwd, K4, and rep from * to end.
8th row P to end.
9th row *K2, K2 tog, yfwd, K1, yfwd, sl 1 K-wise, K1, psso, K1, K2 tog, yfwd, K1, yfwd, sl 1 K-wise, K1, psso, K2, rep from * to end.
10th row P to end.
11th row *K2, (yfwd, sl 1 K-wise, K1, psso) twice, K3, (K2 tog, yfwd) twice, K2, rep from * to end.
12th row *P3, (yrn, P2 tog) twice, P1, (P2 tog tbl, yrn) twice, P3, rep from * to end.
13th row *K4, yfwd, sl 1 K-wise, K1, psso, yfwd, sl 1, K2 tog, psso, yfwd, K2 tog, yfwd, K4, and rep from * to end.
14th row *P5, yrn, P2 tog, P1, P2 tog tbl, yrn, P5, rep from * to end.
15th row *K6, yfwd, sl 1, K2 tog, psso, yfwd, K6, rep from * to end.
16th row P to end.
These 16 rows form the pattern.

A Shetland lace shawl

The gossamer Shetland lace shawl shown here is a superb example of what is known as a 'wedding ring' shawl. It is so fine that it can easily be pulled through a wedding ring, hence its name, and it can be likened to a spider's web, having no beginning and no ending. This shawl is reproduced by kind permission of Highland Home Industries of Edinburgh, who still use a few highly skilled Shetland Islanders to make these garments in their own homes. Traditionally this would be made as a christening shawl but it could also be used as a beautiful winter wedding veil. As can be imagined, these shawls are in great demand but take so long to knit that they are literally worth their weight in gold. The yarn used has been homespun and is so fine that two strands together have been used to knit this shawl. It has been spun from the fine, soft wool which grows around the sheep's neck.

The needles used to knit this shawl are still called by their traditional name of 'wires' and, in all probability, the pattern has been passed from one generation to another by word of mouth and the instructions will never have been written down.

Once a shawl of this delicacy has been completed, it will be washed and then 'dressed', or stretched into shape. To dress the shawl in the traditional manner special wooden frames, as large as a bed, are needed. The shawl would be laced to this frame with lacing through every point along the edges of the border and left to dry naturally. In this way, the shawl is kept taut and square and each point, or scallop of the border is stretched out to its correct shape.

In this Chapter we give another two traditional lace stitches, to inspire you to experiment with this most beautiful craft.

Fir cone pattern

As its name implies, this pattern represents the cones of fir trees and the number of times the pattern rows are repeated can be varied. For the sample shown here cast on a number of stitches divisible by 10 plus 1.

1st row (RS) K1, *yfwd, K3, sl 1, K2 tog, psso, K3, yfwd, K1, rep from * to end.

2nd row P to end.

Rep these 2 rows 3 times more.

9th row K2 tog, *K3, yfwd, K1, yfwd, K3, sl 1, K2 tog, psso, rep from * to last 9 sts, K3, yfwd, K1, yfwd, K3, sl 1, K1, psso.

10th row P to end.

Rep 9th and 10th rows 3 times more.

These 16 rows form the pattern.

Print o' the wave pattern

This beautiful, undulating pattern is a reminder that the sea is a constant part of life in the islands. To work this sample, cast on a number of stitches divisible by 22 plus 3 *very* loosely.

1st row (RS) K4, *K2 tog, K3, (yfwd, K2 tog) twice, yfwd, K13, rep from * to end, ending last rep with K12 instead of K13.

2nd and every alt row P to end.

3rd row K3, *K2 tog, K3, yfwd, K1, yfwd, (sl 1, K1, psso, yfwd) twice, K3, sl 1, K1, psso, K7, rep from * to end.

5th row K2, *K2 tog, (K3, yfwd) twice, (sl 1, K1, psso, yfwd) twice, K3, sl 1, K1, psso, K5, rep from * to last st, K1.

7th row K1, *K2 tog, K3, yfwd, K5, yfwd, (sl 1, K1, psso, yfwd) twice, K3, sl 1, K1, psso, K3, rep from * to last 2 sts, K2.

9th row *K12, yfwd, (sl 1, K1, psso, yfwd) twice, K3, sl 1, K1, psso, K1, rep from * to last 3 sts, K3.

11th row *K7, K2 tog, K3, (yfwd, K2 tog) twice, yfwd, K1, yfwd, K3, sl 1, K1, psso, rep from * to last 3 sts, K3.

13th row K6, *K2 tog, K3, (yfwd, K2 tog) twice, (yfwd, K3) twice, sl 1, K1, psso, K5, rep from * to end, ending last rep with K2 instead of K5.

15th row K5, *K2 tog, K3, (yfwd, K2 tog) twice, yfwd, K5, yfwd, K3, sl 1, K1, psso, K3, rep from * to end, ending last rep with K1 instead of K3.

16th row As 2nd.

These 16 rows form the pattern.

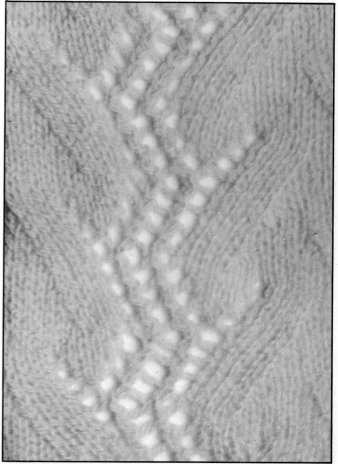

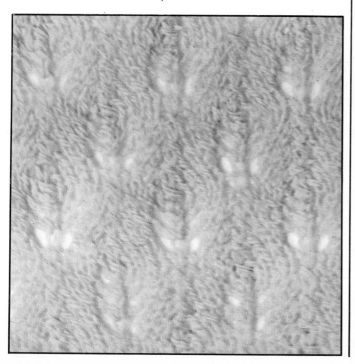

PICOT KNITTING

Picot knitting is an unusual technique which imitates Irish crochet, working with a pair of knitting needles instead of a crochet hook. It looks its best when it is worked in a very fine cotton, such as No.20, and on No.13 or 14 needles.

It has many applications and can be used as edgings, insertions, motifs or as an all-over background fabric. The dainty baby bonnet shown here is an example of how the various methods can be combined to form a garment.

To make a picot point

Make a slip loop in the usual way and place this on the left hand needle, *cast on 2 stitches, making 3 in all. Knit and cast off 2 of these 3 stitches, leaving one stitch on the needle. This forms one picot point. Transfer the remaining stitch to the left hand needle and repeat from * until the required length of picot points is completed. Fasten off.

The size of these picot points may be varied by casting on and off 3 stitches, 4 stitches or as many as required. This strip forms the basis of picot work and can be used to join medallions together, as flower centres, or as a simple edging.

It can also be used to form a dainty cast off edge on a garment, as follows:

Casting off row Insert the needle through the first st of the row to be cast off, *cast on 2 sts, knit and cast off 2 sts, knit the next st of the row, knit and cast off one st, transfer the rem st to the left hand needle, rep from * to end of row.
Fasten off.

Picot point crown

This method is worked across a number of stitches to give the width of edging required. Once this first section has been completed, it forms the basis for what is termed a 'lacis', or openwork fabric, and is referred to as a 'strip' and not a row. To continue working strips to build up a lacis, the last stitch is not fastened off.

Cast on a number of stitches divisible by 5 plus one.
1st row K to end.
2nd row Insert needle into the first st, *cast on 2 sts, cast off 2 sts, transfer rem st to left hand needle, *, rep from * to * 3 times more, (4 picot points formed), knit and cast off next 5 sts, transfer rem st to left hand needle, rep from * to end.
This completes first strip.
Next strip *Transfer rem st to left hand needle, make 4 picot points as given in 2nd row of first strip, join to centre of next picot crown in first strip by picking up and knitting a st between the 2 centre picot points, cast off one st, rep from * to end of strip.
Cont in this way until lacis is required depth. Fasten off.

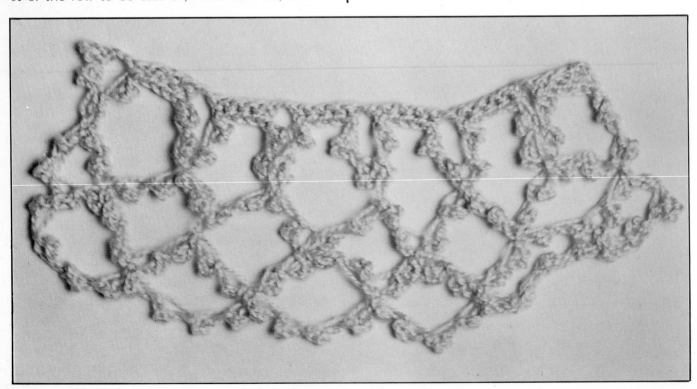

Picot point medallion

This simple motif can be used separately or to form the centre of a flower. Each separate motif can be stitched from the top of one point to the corresponding point of the next motif to form a daisy edging and a number of rows can be joined in the same way to form delicate shawls or interesting table linen, such as place mats and coasters.

However you wish to use these medallions, you can make as many picot points as you like, varying the size of each picot point as already explained. The example shown here has 6 picot points, using 3 stitches instead of 2 for each point.

Make a slip loop and place on left hand needle, *cast on 3 sts, making 4 in all, cast off 3 of these sts, transfer rem st to left hand needle, rep from * 5 times more.

To join into a circle, insert needle into the first loop and draw up a st, cast off one st. Fasten off.

To continue making a flower motif, do not fasten off but transfer remaining stitch to left hand needle, ready to commence the first petal.

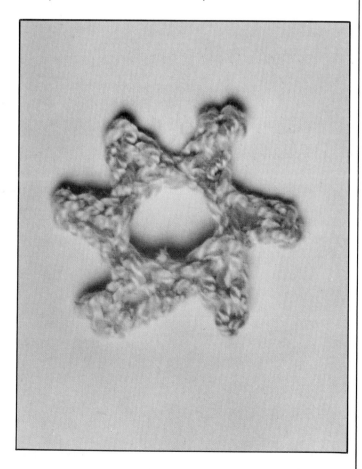

Picot point flower

Make a medallion as given above. Cast on one st, making 2 stitches on left hand needle.

1st row K1, K into front then into back of next st – called M1. 3 sts.
2nd and 4th rows K to end.
3rd row K2, M1.
5th row K3, M1. 5 sts.
K 4 rows g st.

10th row Cast off one st, K to end. 4 sts.
11th row K to end.
Rep last 2 rows twice more.
16th row Cast off one st, pick up and knit a loop between next 2 picot points, cast off one st, transfer rem st to left hand needle.
Cont in this way making 6 petals in all, or as required, joining last petal to same place as first petal, as given for picot point medallion.

Picot flower and lacis motif

Make a picot point flower and fasten off. Rejoin yarn to centre of any petal tip.

1st round *Make 4 picot points casting on and off 2 sts for each point, K up one st at tip of next petal, cast off one st, transfer rem st to left hand needle, rep from * all round flower.

2nd round Make 4 picot points and join between 2nd and 3rd picots of 1st round, make another 4 picot points and miss 2 picot points of 1st round, join between next 2 picot points of 1st round, cont in this way to end of round, joining last stitch to same place as first stitch. Fasten off.

3rd round Rejoin yarn between 2nd and 3rd of any picot points, *make 4 picot points and join between 2nd and 3rd of next 4 picot points, rep from * to end of round, joining as before. 12 loops. Fasten off.

4th round Rejoin yarn between 2nd and 3rd of any picot points, *make 3 picot points and join into same place to form a picot crest, make 4 picot points and join between 2nd and 3rd of next 4 picot points, rep from * to end of round, joining as before. Fasten off. Make as many more motifs as required, joining picot crests of each motif where they touch, to form a row.

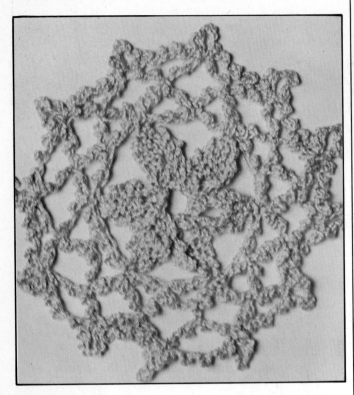

Baby bonnet
Size
To fit 0 to 3 months

Tension
32 sts and 60 rows to 10cm (*3.9in*) over g st worked on No.13 needles

Materials
1 × 25grm ball of Sunbeam St. Ives 3 ply
One pair No.13 needles
0.90 metre (*1yd*) ribbon for ties

Bonnet
Make one flower and lacis motif, omitting 4th round, to form centre of crown.
Make 11 picot point medallions and join into a row, joining the centre picots each side, leaving 2 free at top and bottom. Sew round edge of centre motif, joining 2 free points of each medallion to the centre 2 picots of each loop and leaving one loop free for bottom edge of bonnet.
Make a strip of 42 picots, mark the last picot with contrast thread and turn.
Next row Make 4 picots, join between 3rd and 4th picots after marker, *make 4 picots, miss 4 picots, join between 4th and 5th picots, rep from * to last 3 picots, make 4 picots, join to end of strip after last picot. Fasten off and turn.

Next row Rejoin yarn between 2nd and 3rd picots of first loop, *make 4 picots, join between 2nd and 3rd picots of next loop, rep from * to end. Do not fasten off but turn.
Next row Make 4 picots, join between 2nd and 3rd picots of first loop, *make 4 picots, join between 2nd and 3rd picots of next loop, rep from * to end, make 4 picots, join to beg of previous row where yarn was rejoined.
Rep last 2 rows once more. Fasten off.
Join the cast on edge of this strip to the centre piece, joining the first 2 picots to the 2 picots of first medallion, *miss 2 picots, join next 2 picots to 2 points of next medallion, rep from * to end.

To make up
Pin out and press under a damp cloth with a warm iron. Sew ribbon to each corner to tie at front.

FILET KNITTING

The word 'filet' means 'net', and this type of square mesh fabric can be produced in both knitting and crochet. Just as with crochet, patterns can be introduced into the mesh background, consisting of solid parts of the pattern, which are referred to as 'blocks', and open parts of the pattern which are called 'spaces'. The stitch used to produce filet lace fabric is garter stitch throughout, so it is a very simple method to work.

This fabric looks best when it is worked in a fine cotton on small size needles, to give a lace effect. It has many uses but is better used for insertions and edgings, rather than as an all-over fabric.

To knit filet lace
Working a block These comprise solid sections of garter stitch and each block consists of three knitted stitches in width and four rows in depth. Whether working an insertion or an edging, a number of extra stitches are required at the beginning and end of the rows and these are knitted throughout in the usual way.

Working a space These are the open sections of a design and each space is worked over three stitches. The third stitch of each space is knitted in the usual way and is either used as an edge stitch, or as a bridging stitch between spaces or between spaces and blocks. Each space is worked over two rows in depth:–

After completing a block of three knitted stitches or the edge stitches, as the case may be, bring the yarn forward between the needles, take it over the right hand needle and to the front again – called y2rn.

Over the next three stitches, slip the first stitch knitwise, then slip the 2nd stitch knitwise, using the point of the left hand needle lift the first stitch over the 2nd stitch and off the right hand needle.

Slip the 3rd stitch knitwise, using the point of the left hand needle lift the 2nd stitch over the 3rd stitch and off the right hand needle, return the 3rd stitch to the left hand needle and knit this in the usual way.

This working method is referred to as a space. There are now three loops on the right hand needle again, composed of the yarn twice round the needle and one knitted stitch. On the following row the first yarn round the needle is knitted and the 2nd yarn round the needle is purled, then the 3rd stitch is knitted, to complete the space.

Working basic filet net
This is worked entirely in spaces, plus one edge stitch at the beginning of the row. The 3rd stitch of each space forms the bridging stitch between each space.

Working blocks and spaces
As each block requires four rows to complete it and a space only requires two rows, the pattern rows must be worked twice to give the necessary square shape to each block.

When a block changes to a space in a pattern, treat the three stitches of the block as a space, or when changing a space to a block, work the three stitches of the space as a block.

Filet lace insertion
This simple pattern can be used in many ways, either as centre front panels on a fabric or knitted blouse, as

an insertion on a dainty petticoat or on household linens.

It is worked over a total of five squares, each consisting of three stitches, plus three edge stitches at the beginning of the rows and two edge stitches at the end of the rows. Only two stitches are required to balance the end of the rows, as the last stitch of the last space is taken into this edge. The chart given here does not show the edge stitches.

Cast on a total of 20 stitches to work the insertion.

1st row (RS) K3 edge sts, work 2 spaces, K3 sts for a block, work 2 spaces, K2 edge sts.

2nd and every alt row K to end, purling the 2nd yarn round needle of every space.

Rep 1st and 2nd rows once more to complete the centre block.

5th row K3 edge sts, work 1 space, (K3 sts for a block, work 1 space) twice, K2 edge sts.

6th row As 2nd.

Rep 5th and 6th rows once more to complete the

blocks, then rep them twice more to complete another block.

13th row As 1st.

Chart for lace insertion

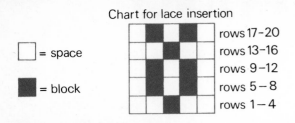

□ = space

■ = block

| | | | | | rows 17-20 |
| rows 13-16 |
| rows 9-12 |
| rows 5-8 |
| rows 1-4 |

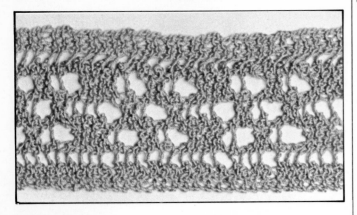

14th row As 2nd.

Rep 13th and 14th rows once more to complete the centre block.

17th row As 5th.

18th row As 6th.

Rep 17th and 18th rows once more to complete the blocks.

These 20 rows form the pattern and are repeated for the required length of the insertion.

Filet lace edging

This pattern has a serrated edge along one side and

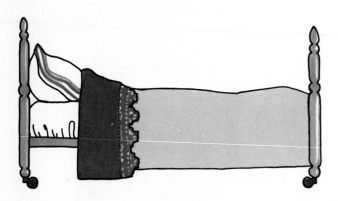

forms an ideal trimming for all types of household linens. The serrated edge is formed by casting on additional stitches two rows before they are taken into the pattern.

This pattern consists of three squares at the beginning, each comprising three stitches, plus one edge stitch at the beginning of the row only, the last edge stitch being formed by the last stitch of the last space. The chart given here does not show the edge stitch.

Cast on a total of 10 stitches to begin the edging.

1st row (RS) K1 edge st, work 1 space, K3 sts for a block, work 1 space.

2nd and every alt row K to end, purling the 2nd yarn round needle of every space.

3rd row As 1st, then turn and cast on 6 sts to form 2 extra spaces on the 5th row.

5th row K1 edge st, work 1 space, K3 sts for a block, work 3 spaces.

7th row As 5th, then turn and cast on 3 sts to form 1 extra space on the 9th row.

9th row K1 edge st, work 1 space, K3 sts for a block,

Chart for lace edging

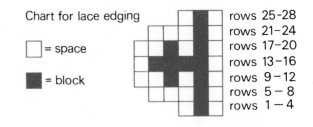

□ = space

■ = block

| | | | | | | rows 25-28 |
| rows 21-24 |
| rows 17-20 |
| rows 13-16 |
| rows 9-12 |
| rows 5-8 |
| rows 1-4 |

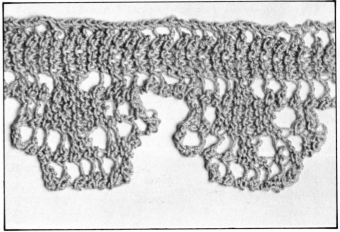

work 1 space, K3 sts for a block, work 2 spaces.

10th row As 2nd.

Rep 9th and 10th rows once more to complete blocks.

13th row K1 edge st, work 1 space, K12 sts to form 4 blocks, work 1 space.

14th row As 2nd.

Rep 13th and 14th rows once more to complete blocks.

17th row As 9th.

18th row As 2nd.

19th row As 17th.

20th row Cast off 3 sts to reduce one space, then work as 2nd row to end.

21st row As 5th.

22nd row As 2nd.

23rd row As 21st.

24th row Cast off 6 sts to reduce 2 spaces, then work as 2nd row to end.

25th row As 1st.

26th row As 2nd.

Rep 25th and 26th rows once more to complete block. These 28 rows form the pattern and are repeated for the required length of the edging.